YEAR OF THE RAT

2020, As It Happened, Around the World

By Jorah Kai

Copyright Page

© 2023 Jorah Kai. All rights reserved.

Year of the Rat is a work of creative nonfiction. At times, satire and surrealism are used to underscore the absurdity of real-world events. Where events are presented as factual, they reflect the author's direct observations. Where they are untrue, they are used to provoke thought, critique society, or provide levity during dark times.

All contributors to *Year of the Rat* gave express permission for their words to be included. Their entries were written specifically for this collection—with the exception of the contribution by Jean-Claude Van Damme, which is a faithful transcription of his keynote speech delivered publicly at the COVID-19 Response & Recover Conference, where he headlined alongside Jorah Kai. The photo used is the official image from the event's public website. This usage falls under the Fair Use doctrine of U.S. copyright law (17 U.S. Code § 107), which allows for the reproduction of publicly delivered material in limited, contextual use for purposes such as documentation, commentary, and nonfictional reporting.

Additionally, a brief quotation by actor Sylvester Stallone, originally stated in a televised interview, appears in this work. It is used here under the same Fair Use provisions, solely for literary, transformative, and satirical purposes. No endorsement or affiliation by Mr. Stallone is implied or intended.

Many of these entries were originally published online as part of *The Invisible War* project and appeared in *Kai's Diary*, a pandemic slice-of-life column (2020–2023) for iChongqing, part of the Chongqing Daily News Group. The initial collection was featured on the front page of CTV News Canada in 2020, where it remains. The column, which received recognition from the Chongqing Journalists Association and was syndicated internationally in both

English and Chinese, has been revised and reframed here as a cohesive, original volume—edited for longevity and posterity.

Names, characters, places, and incidents are based on true stories, though some have been altered to protect the innocent or to serve the narrative. If celebrities appear in dreams offering the author life advice, they are most likely fictional, satirical, or metaphorical interpretations, and no claim is made that they literally astral-projected to participate in this memoir.

No part of this book may be reproduced, stored in a retrieval system, or transmitted in any form or by any means—electronic, mechanical, photocopying, recording, or otherwise—without prior written permission from the copyright holder, except for brief quotations used in reviews or critical articles, as permitted by law.

To request permissions, contact the publisher: books@morepublishing.co

Paperback: ISBN 978-1-959604-09-9
Hardcover ISBN 978-1-959604-13-6
eBook: ISBN 978-1-959604-00-6
First paperback edition published February 2023

Credits

Written by Jorah Kai
Cover Design: Jorah Kai
Cover Illustrations and Design: Wang Kai
Edited by Catherine Chen and Jorah Kai

Disclaimer

Year of the Rat is a literary, transmedia exploration of the pandemic era, blending global commentary, personal reflections, and guest diary contributions from over thirty cities worldwide.

Special Thanks

The author, Jorah Kai, would like to extend heartfelt thanks to CTV News Canada and iChongqing for giving him the opportunity to tell his story through *Kai's Diary*. Their early support and exposure helped spark a snowball effect, leading to contributions from dozens of authors across the globe and the creation of three books. This collaboration has been a testament to the power of collective storytelling during dark times.

THE LIGHTHOUSE AND THE YEAR OF THE METAL RAT

From January 25 to mid-March 2020, China operated at its highest emergency level. Wuhan, a city of 11 million, and the surrounding Hubei province—home to over 50 million people—were placed under lockdown on January 23 and 24 in an effort to contain the COVID-19 epidemic. Although containment did not ultimately succeed, the spread was significantly slowed, buying the world precious time to prepare and allowing scientists to study the virus.

During this time in Chongqing, public gatherings were banned, shops closed, and nonessential travel discouraged. Citizens were urged to self-quarantine in their homes to reduce the spread. As the Spring Festival began, virtually no one in China was working—a serendipitous coincidence. The government extended the holiday, and for nearly two months, one in five humans on Earth sheltered in place. Factories stood idle. Roads emptied. The skies went quiet. Those who ventured out for work or essential shopping wore masks, and outings were limited—typically, one person per household, twice a week.

Meanwhile, in much of the world, including Europe and the Americas, COVID-19 spread unchecked. As China closed its borders, barring reentry to both Chinese citizens and foreigners alike, global fear intensified. The future remained uncertain, and the road ahead seemed impossible to navigate. Yet, amid the chaos, China's experience offered a glimmer of hope—a lighthouse in the storm, a model for a different path.

As of March 25, Chongqing lowered its alert level, and even Wuhan began to ease restrictions, though many were reluctant to give up their masks, a small yet comforting form of protection. Shops reopened, and streets began to fill once more.

But as China adapted, the rest of the world faced deeper fractures. In *Year of the Rat*, the sequel to the international bestseller *The*

Invisible War (Kai's Diary), Jorah Kai documents the global pandemic experience, starting with the world's largest "Zero COVID bubble" and expanding to the worldwide struggle against the virus. Across thirty-three cities in sixteen countries, the pandemic tore through every corner of the globe, exposing deep divisions in public opinion and policy.

Some wore masks and practiced social distancing to protect the vulnerable. Others, however, rejected these measures as tyranny, protesting loudly against restrictions, often with disruptive demonstrations of "personal freedom." Fake news and algorithmic echo chambers created "alternative facts," while unhinged conspiracies overshadowed serious, existential challenges. In this divided world, survival became a shared struggle—a collective testimony of humanity in crisis.

MEET *the* CAST

In order of appearance

Jorah Kai
Writer, Teacher
Chongqing, China

Lulu Knowles
Teacher, Hooper
Vung Tau, Vietnam

Rhett Morita
Actor, Director,
Toronto, Canada

Dara Mac
Musician, Kai's Mom
Prince Edward Island,
Canada

Kait Marcelle
Burlesque Philosopher
San Diego, USA

Sarah Rollinson
Writer, Mom
Jeddah, Saudi Arabia

MEET *the* CAST

In order of appearance

Alessia Martino
Food Critic, Educator
Turin, Italy

DJ Josette
DJ, Teacher – Buenos Aires, Argentina

MC Zulu
Activist, Veteran, MC
Chicago, USA

Lisa
Photographer,
Reformed Antimasker
Antigonish, Canada

Cadence
Burlesque Mom,
Activist
Hamilton, Canada

Ken 2
Travel Philosopher
Tokyo, Japan

MEET *the* CAST

In order of appearance

Corrie Lee Lemoncat
Model Mycologist
Ottawa, Canada

Sasha
Advocate, Mom

Anonymous Nurse,
New York City, USA

Bruce Deliverants
Event Promoter
Diehard, Australia

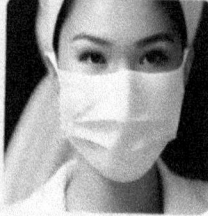

Cindy
CSR - Cagayan De
Oro, Philippines

Harriote Lampe
Chef, Mask Masker
Montreal, Canada

MEET *the* CAST

In order of appearance

Camilo Sons of Leonard
Twente, Netherlands

Kevin
Nurse
New York City, USA

JCVD
Actor, Martial Artist
Los Angeles, USA

Dr. Mike
Doctor, Musician
Cape Breton Island
Canada

Dammien Alexander
Rock Star
Antigua, Guatemala

Nunich
Comedian, DJ, Mom
Los Angeles, USA

MEET *the* CAST

In order of appearance

Aliker p'Ocitti
Author, Teacher
Kampala, Uganda

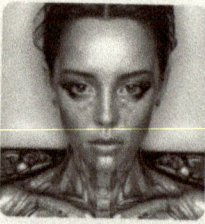

Skye Lazure,
Bollywood Actress
Melbourne, Australia

Aliya Ishtar
Poet, Healer
London, UK

Stephen Williams
Nurse
Philadelphia, USA

Aaron G
Activist
Washington, USA

Masia One
Rapper, Producer
Singapore

MEET *the* CAST

In order of appearance

Charmika Monet
Stoic Philosopher
Tokyo, Japan

Alina
Student
Kazan, Russia

Cook
Dj, Internet Troll
Ottawa, Canada

Chris Sky
Prominent Antimasker
for 'Freedom'
Toronto, Canada

Rebecca Lippiatt
Photographer,
Scientist, Mom
Edmonton, Canada

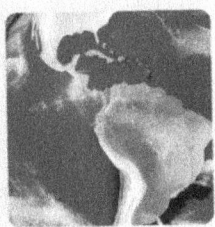

You
All around the world

Acknowledgments

This book is dedicated to the countless frontline healthcare workers
who gave all they had—and then gave even more.

Thank you to the friends around the world who opened your hearts and shared your lives during a time of global uncertainty. Whether for therapy, for posterity, or for art, your words matter. Thank you, doubly, for allowing me to publish them. This collection is something we can all look back on—an echo of a moment, preserved in time.

Epigraph

"If you do not change direction, you may end up where you are heading."
—**Lao Tzu**

2737 BCE–2012 CE – Babylon & Burning Man – "Hammurabi's Laws, Tea Time, and the God Phone"

Part I: The First Cup

The story of tea began in China. Legends tell that in 2737 BCE, the Chinese emperor Shen Nung was sitting beneath a tree while his servant boiled drinking water. Some leaves from the tree blew into the pot. Shen Nung, a renowned herbalist, decided to try the accidental infusion.

From ancient capitals like Chang'an (modern-day Xi'an) and Luoyang, the Silk Road bifurcated through the five Central Asian countries (the Stans) and continued through Afghanistan, Iran, Iraq, and Turkey—then into Greece and Italy, and across the Mediterranean, or southward through Israel into Africa.

Chinese civilization depended on irrigated farming and long-distance trade. Its people exchanged goods with the Mesopotamians, the Indus Valley people, and the Swahili along Africa's eastern coast.

Merchants carried silk to Europe, where it adorned royalty and the elite. Other prized commodities included jade, porcelain, spices, and tea. In return, horses, glassware, textiles, and other goods made the journey eastward.

Three thousand years before a goat herder named Kaldi allegedly discovered the magic of coffee beans in the Ethiopian highlands—or perhaps earlier, in the Port of Mokha, Yemen—it was tea that got the world out of bed.

Part II: Hammurabi's Tea Code

"An aye ... for an aye," said Hammurabi, sixth king of the Amorite First Dynasty of Babylon.

"What?" asked his barista, before quickly lowering his gaze. "I mean—what, Your Majesty?"

Hammurabi, known as a hard worker and a micro-manager of construction projects, was also an insufferable mumbler before his first cup of green tea. Fidgeting with his slender hands, he said nothing.

"Pardon me, Your Grace. Did you say you wanted spices in your morning cup?" Apsu's right eye twitched. His relationship with the king—who was, effectively, the ruler of the known world—was precarious. And yet Hammurabi, curiously, tolerated Apsu's irreverence—as long as the tea was perfect. Still, the mumbling worried him. Tea sommeliers had been jailed—or worse—for less.

The king shot dagger eyes at Apsu, his long, lean frame curling up like a cobra. Then, just as suddenly, the tension melted from his face. He could smell the fragrant steep as Apsu approached with his favorite three-faced goat mug—a birthday gift from Pharaoh Nebnun the Usurper.

Thinking of Nebnun's terrible fate after just two years on the throne, and how his successor, Sehetepibre, had offered no birthday gifts at all, Hammurabi's face darkened. His eyes became stormy pools of malice.

Apsu noticed and paled. He stumbled slightly but managed to steady the tea without spilling—almost. A few droplets of scalding liquid splashed on Hammurabi's exposed toes.

"My... apologies, Your Grace," Apsu said, offering the mug.

Hammurabi smiled, suddenly amused. "Step forward, Apsu."

Wincing, Apsu obeyed.

The king tilted the cup and let a thin stream of hot tea drizzle onto Apsu's foot. Apsu howled and hopped back in pain.

"An aye for an aye," Hammurabi repeated, grinning like a child with a new toy.

Apsu, still smarting, said nothing. The king sighed.

"I'm working on a code," he said. "A form of efficient—brutal, perhaps—justice, to strengthen the rule of law in Babylon."

"Excellent, Your Grace," Apsu said, stroking his beard. "A way to punish your servants more efficiently?"

Taken aback, Hammurabi shook his head. He sipped the floral tea. "No. It's meant for all classes—from slave to noble. Even royalty shall not be above the law. All must answer equally for their mistakes."

"So," Apsu ventured, "if you spilled tea on my foot, I could do the same to yours?"

"Perhaps I'd pay you a fine. Or pay your master. But yes—I'd still be accountable. As it stands, I am not."

Apsu frowned. "But how will you convince the gentry to endure punishment willingly, when they currently stand immune?"

"Because it is fair. Because it is just. And because, by my royal word, I command it."

Apsu lowered his gaze, unconvinced. The king studied him.

"Speak freely, Apsu. Why are you not impressed?"

"Because," said Apsu, "they will call it arbitrary. They will never punish themselves willingly. Nothing on earth could make them. Unless... unless it were the will of the gods."

Hammurabi's eyes lit up. His grin widened.

"Well then," he said, "it is good news to present. For I heard them in a dream. The laws were given to me by Shamash—the god of justice himself."

"Truly?" Apsu leaned in, intrigued. "And what else did Shamash say?"

Hammurabi drained the last of his tea and clapped his hands.

"Summon the finest stone carvers in Babylon. We will write the Code of Hammurabi in stone, and the people will rejoice—for it is the word of the gods."

And so it was done. The laws were carved into stone tablets and erected across the city. For the first time, a ruler governed all of Mesopotamia without revolt. Hammurabi reformed the calendar, managed vast public works, and continued to honor the traditions of Sumer, Akkad, and the lands he conquered. His name meant "the kinsman is a healer." But his justice was merciless.

Nearly 4,000 years later, Hammurabi is still remembered for his 282 laws—what he believed were fair consequences for breaking the social contract. And when pushed, he had a divine alibi:

God told him to do it.

Part III: The Dust and the Desert

I once saw a phone booth to God at Burning Man. I didn't touch it. I wasn't in the right headspace for that kind of contact.

Someone I loved had just died—suddenly, tragically—while I was on a four-month tour across North America with the Root Sellers. I was numb, grieving, and sleepwalking through the end of the tour as we made our way from Vancouver to Seattle, Portland, San Francisco, and finally, into the heart of the Black Rock Desert.

The Black Rock Playa spans roughly 200 square miles, the ghost of ancient Lake Lahontan. Each year, Black Rock City—a temporary, wildly creative, dust-covered utopia—rises from this harsh landscape. It rests on the ancestral lands of the Northern Paiute people, whose descendants today include the Pyramid Lake Paiute Tribe.

The playa is silt, alkali, and lava beds—a moonscape in Nevada's Black Rock–High Rock Canyon Conservation Area. It's brutal. It eats your flesh and burns your lungs. Dust storms can sweep in and blind you. Without goggles or a mask, you'll suffer—maybe worse. It takes grit, madness, or both to survive there.

My brother Galen and I were driving north from California when the van broke down. We poured glowing green radiator fluid across the cracked highway and baked under the sun for hours.

Eventually, a tow truck arrived, but it had space for only two. I sent Galen and his girlfriend ahead. I'd been terrible company, and the silence was welcome.

Later, I hitchhiked from the back of a dead goat—the animal that represents my Chinese zodiac sign. Eventually, a cube van rolled by. Inside were two Canadians hauling expired cakes to the festival. Freegans. Heroes.

I'd left my supplies—tent, food, water—with Galen. All I had was one liter of water, a tutu (for Tutu Tuesday), and the clothes on my back. That night, I rolled into Black Rock City for the first time. The moon was fat and red. The revelers were wild. Mutant vehicles roared across the dust. Monsters danced. Steam-powered beasts howled.

It felt like stumbling into an ancient myth—some oasis of madness and meaning in a dangerous land. A bazaar of the bizarre. I feasted on bananas, martinis, bacon-wrapped scallops, and stranger delights. As they say on the playa: **The playa provides.**

Part IV: Tutu Tuesday and the God Phone

Eventually, I found the God Phone. But I didn't pick it up. I wasn't ready.
If no one answered, I'd feel abandoned. If it was a prank, I'd feel mocked. And if it was *actually* God?
I wasn't ready for that kind of realness.
Fiction is the art of lying to tell the truth.
Creative nonfiction is a dance—a twisting, turning rhythm of **truthiness** designed to create meaning.
So I'll be honest with you:
I'm going to lie to you now. But only once. And only to make a point.
Eventually, I did pick up the God Phone. I asked,
"Some people say that if we were meant to wear masks, we'd have been born with them. Does that make sense?"
The voice on the other end didn't hesitate.
"Were you born with clothes? No. But you cast aside innocence and left the garden. You wear clothes to protect yourself. And when the storm comes, you wear a mask for the same reason. To survive. To honor me, honor yourself. Don't be a dumbass."
Anyway, that's what God said.

March 19, 2020 – Chongqing, China – "My Apocalypse – The In-Between"

Part I: Waking in the Light

Day 56. I wake up at 11:11 a.m. again. I must have slept for six hours. I feel human again.

I make some coffee, tidy up, and get right back to work. Shaolin will come home today or tomorrow, and I want to have my manuscript polished by then.

She calls to wish me a good day. She's getting baby Ethan ready to go downtown to Jiefangbei to enjoy the beautiful, sunny spring day. The sun is shining. It's 20 degrees outside.

I heat up some carrots and rice she left for me and have a nice, light lunch.

Outside, Ethan meets another boy, and they play for a while. He takes his first ride on a scooter with a bit of help. Soon he won't need it; one day, he'll be big, strong, smart, and capable. With a name like "Xiang Ethan," which sounds like "looks like a doctor," I know he's going to change the world. A grandfather always knows.

It's delightful to work with friends to polish my document. My beta readers hover around the manuscript like bees among my flowers, pollinating this, spreading that. We work hard—flowers and bees—to make honey.

My doggos bark, *rap rap rap*, until I give up on eating and dump the carrots and rice into their dish. When they finish licking their chops, they bask on a cushion by the window as the golden sun reminds them of joy outside these four walls.

Soon, I'll take them out to enjoy the fresh air. I can already picture it—old Ben Ben finding his running legs again, tail wagging, and Hachoo doing laps around him as only the young can.

My friend Andrea takes the bus over. He's always been brave during this time and makes me feel too careful in my tower on campus, scrying and shouting at the world. I suit up to meet him at the gate, experimenting with my headset mic between two masks, the speaker strapped to my belt to amplify my muffled voice. He thinks I'm nuts—but in a good way. He gives me eye drops and vitamin D pills. My eyes have been fried lately, and I'm excited to go home and drop them in my eye holes.

We walk in the sunshine, and the lady baker snaps photos as we pass her bakery.

I return home, teach Lil' Kim for an hour, then take the pups outside. At first, they're tentative, taking everything in. The smells inform them of all they've missed. Ben Ben stands on his back paws to sniff a tree before lifting a leg.

We have our Twitter; they have their pitter-patter.

I shout, "Come on!" and they bolt toward me, tails wagging, chasing, barking, playing. Except for my gas mask, it feels completely normal.

Part II: Science, Solitude, and the State of the World

Today, there are 220,000 documented cases of COVID-19, with 8,980 deaths and 85,769 recoveries. Around the world, the virus is in different stages—burning hot in some places, quietly booming in others. Wherever it touches, it disturbs the very fabric of society—transforming things that ideas and men could not.

Barely three months old, COVID-19 has already brought about some form of socialism by necessity. America and many other countries are experimenting with healthcare for all, a reduction in pollution, remote work, and a kind of universal basic income—elements of a new paradigm that 2020 has thrust upon us.

In Chongqing, where we've held it back, we must stay watchful. Entry now requires a negative nucleic acid PCR test. Tourists must self-isolate for fourteen days. One day, we hope for a vaccine. Until then, we stand vigilant—a beacon for the world.

I never heard back from the remote island of Ireland, but it seems Chongqing will keep me here another year. *Plus ça change, plus c'est la même chose*—the more things change, the more they stay the same.

Part III: Dancing, Distance, and the God Between

I make a tuna fish sandwich with garlic and a hint of peanut butter while my Bluetooth speaker pumps cyberpunk synthwave—trance beats and industrial riffs.
I flip my knives into the air, catch them by the hilt, spin, wave my arms to the rhythm as I chop salad greens.
If I can't dance, it's not my apocalypse.
Jay has been hurting since returning to America. His family barricaded themselves in a remote village and refused to join him. He's become increasingly critical and cynical, full of zealous fervor. I couldn't think of anything more Christlike than reaching out during a crisis to send a stranger masks to protect his family and becoming wartime buddies. But when I wouldn't pray to Jesus—having already found Jeffy Spaghetti—he blocked me.
I hope he finds his family again.
A new Chinese study reports that those with blood type A may be more vulnerable to infection, while those with type O—who have both anti-A and anti-B antibodies—may have some protection. Another revelation: the SARS-CoV-2 spike protein binds to human cells 10 to 20 times more aggressively than that of its cousin SARS. This explains the rapid spread. These unique spike proteins will likely be the key to developing a vaccine.
I take the dogs out again. They sniff everything, a little tentative at first, but soon they're running and playing while I soak up the brilliant sun. It creeps across the sky like a guilty husband stumbling home from the bar—tipsy, but warm and full of belly laughter.
After a good hour, I return home, wash up, change clothes, and relax.

Shaolin calls again. She's getting baby Ethan ready for a walk downtown in the sunshine. It's 20 degrees. Spring is here.

Her father's garden is full of yellow blossoms from blooming paw-paw trees. Bees buzz around the flowers, pollinating and making honey.

A cat meows nearby, and down below, the city hums. Life finds a way.

March 26, 2020 – Chongqing, China – "The Lighthouse"
Part I: Brilliance in the Storm

Day 63. Everyone can be a lighthouse in the storm. We are all luminescent beings of incredible potential, capable of cutting through darkness and fog with our brilliance.

A lighthouse.

Some are more like trees—calm in crisis, standing tall. A tree soaks up pollution, replenishes oxygen, and gives us clean air. But in a storm, you'd want to be a gnarly old tree with thick skin and deep roots. The others—the tender, the brittle—risk getting pulled up and scattered like leaves across Kansas. It doesn't have to be that way.

It's been eight days since my last entry. Eight is a lucky number in China. An auspicious time to return to the page.

My rebel alliance—a motley crew of teachers, engineers, rappers, pillow fighters, doctors, musicians, circus performers, biomed techs, and throat singers—has pulled off something wild. We took a 60-day blog and turned it into a novel in just a few days, barely sleeping. It's been typeset and triple-checked and handed off to the publisher for imminent digital release. I hope it helps—to educate, to inspire, to help people navigate self-isolation with dignity, maybe even with joy. I've found it can be fun, this quiet apocalypse. But the global numbers are skyrocketing. Exponential growth is doing what it does best—picking up speed. The sickening moments are still ahead. I want to run and hide, but I won't. If my words—my silly metaphors and stubborn hope—help even one person find shelter until the flood recedes, then it will have been worth it.

We're not out of the woods. The numbers will surge even as we shelter in place. The worst of it is already baked into the dough. The lag time is real. We won't see the results of our efforts for two weeks. It will be the longest, darkest stretch of night.

But we will be lost together. And even in a community of social distance, we will find strength—and maybe build something better than what we had before.

Part II: The Invisible Race

A week ago, on March 18, there were 175,000 global cases. Today, there are 531,600.

The United States has surged to the top of the charts, gaining 17,057 cases in a single day. They now stand at 85,268 cases and 1,293 deaths. China is still second, with 81,235 cases and 3,287 deaths—but their borders are now closed. Even foreigners with valid VISAs, residences, and apartments full of rotting cheese can't return.

If I leave, I can't come back. I understand why. Nearly 600 "backflow" cases slipped through the mandatory self-quarantine. China said enough was enough.

Italy is in third, racing to overtake China with 80,589 cases and 10,361 deaths. But signs of slowing in Lombardy suggest their curve is bending. They may run out of gas before America does.

Friends ask me why I keep pushing mask usage when TV doctors say they don't help. I'm tired of saying it, but I won't stop. We must all act like we're infected. Studies show 30 to 50 percent of cases are asymptomatic. That means many of us are walking plague factories, unintentionally endangering the vulnerable.

So I ask two questions—because when people don't listen to answers, you must give them better questions:

What must a virus need to spread?
A virus needs hosts. It needs opportunity.

It travels on breath, coughs, sneezes—droplets. It floats, sinks, clings to surfaces. If we self-isolate, the virus has nowhere to go. If we go out, we wear masks and goggles. We protect our entry points—mouth, nose, eyes. Even a poorly sealed mask blocks billions of particles and buys your body time. Time is everything.

Gloves help. Not touching your mask helps. Not touching your face helps. Not feeding your baby with contaminated hands helps.

Being outside is like space travel now. If you don't suit up, you're gonna have a bad time.

Part III: Grief, Growth, and #2020vision

Spain is struggling—57,786 cases, 4,365 deaths. I watch a video of a Spanish doctor weeping, begging the world to listen. They didn't respect the plague. Now, ventilators are being reassigned in battlefield triage. Older patients are given painkillers to die comfortably, while younger ones get the machines. Some stay on them for three weeks or more. The moment the curve overwhelms the system, everything gets uglier.

Germany, Iran, France, Switzerland, the U.K., South Korea—each has a place in the COVID charts. Canada is 14th with 4,043 cases. I remember when we had just one. Then 100. Then 1,000. Now it's a flood. What April brings depends on us.

Some people lash out. I'm called crazy on Facebook. Told I'm sick. Blocked for trying to help. That's grief, I remind myself. The five stages, live on every timeline. Denial. Anger. Bargaining. Panic.

We—the quick adapters—must be kind. And we must be firm. Teach people the rules of this new game. Leave them questions so they can find the truth themselves.

What if you were on a spaceship and lost atmosphere? Would you grab your pressure suit or drift out, eyeballs frozen? The rules changed overnight. The air is poison. Learn the rules. Or suffer.

Trump wants crowded churches for Easter while the virus burns through the country. The empire has no clothes. It's hanging from a skyscraper by its toes, hallucinating. Cuomo asks for 30,000 ventilators. Pence sends 2,000. It's absurd.

Meanwhile, my grandmother is being told not to wear a mask by well-meaning fools. At least Mom talks sense into her. An eagle flies overhead. A good omen.

Prince Charles tests positive. The Queen retreats. Johnson videoconferences from quarantine. The Canada Emergency Response Benefit kicks in—$2,000/month for affected workers. One hundred billion in relief. The beginning of something like universal basic income.

There's hope. Iceland is testing everyone. Infection rates in the general population are just 0.1%. They'll isolate, contain, and burn it out.

Shaolin teaches her mom how to make an egg cake. We drink coffee and make pancakes. I buzz with caffeine, vibrating with purpose. Life's little rituals persist.

Part IV: Through the Fog

We walk to Ren Ren Le. No temperature check for the first time in two months. Things are loosening. At home, they still beep us. We're not febrile.
Chongqing is standing strong. It's been 27 days since a local case. Our fatality rate is 1.04%; our recovery rate is 99%. Two imported cases were caught and quarantined before they could spread. Our protocols hold.
Factories are reopening. Clubs on 9th Street are packed again. But I'm not going just yet. Caution is my compass.
March 24 saw hail the size of fists fall from the sky—coronavirus-shaped chunks of ice. The weather is as weird as everything else.
I teach a class. Hire a translator for *The Invisible War*. We start planning editions in Italian, Spanish, French. Momentum builds.
Shaolin and I walk to Starbucks. It's 29 degrees. T-shirts and masks. She orders her caramel macchiato. I get a cold brew espresso tonic with lime. We sit in the amphitheater, where we sat sixty days ago before everything changed. Somehow, we made it through the storm. It feels like a dream.
She listens to me read. She likes it. I find typos and make a note to fix them.
Trump helps market the book by ranting about "invisible enemies" on TV. Two girls run by without masks. Shaolin masks up. I turn my face and hold my breath. We still trust, but we stay cautious.
People wear masks like fashion now. Blue dresses, pink scarves, black prints. I want one with my face on it. In 2020, even PPE became personal.
We eat fajitas. No cheese, but they're still wonderful. I think of the cheese rotting in apartments across China and wish I could save it with my belly.

Studies show a third to half of infections are asymptomatic. The key is universal masking. You cover the mouths of the healthy, and the virus dies off.

Chongqing's protocols work. If your city doesn't protect you, protect yourself. If you can't come to us, make your own haven.

Don't let anyone near you without a mask. Stay two meters from the masked, four or five from the unmasked. Get what you need. Then go home.

Things will get better. But first, they'll get darker. The COVID-IOTS will get sick. That's inevitable.

A retired ER doc in my family says Canada will contain this after two weeks of stay-home orders, followed by nationwide testing and contact tracing. I believe him.

Another hailstorm shakes our building. Biblical rain lashes the windows. The earth groans in her hospital bed. Maybe we were the virus. Maybe she's trying to heal.

A friend reposts my Chongqing update with the comment, *"I hope this means it's almost over."* For cities with strong protocols, maybe it is. For the rest, it could linger for years.

That's why you look for the lighthouse.

Last night, I couldn't write. The border closure hit too hard. But after some sleep, I've returned. Here's my post.

I teach IELTS at 8 a.m. Apocalypse or not, the grind continues.

Shaolin coughs. I bring her a hot bandage and boil water for honey tea. I snap when I can't find her sweater. My nerves are frayed. Yoda would not be pleased. I will now be forced to lift rocks with my mind in penance.

But still—Chongqing stands on the hill, our light burning strong. Other lighthouses will rise. And in their glow, others will find safety.

In the chaos and darkness of this storm, we can all be lighthouses.

March 27, 2020 – Chongqing, China – "The Edge of the Universe"

Day 64
Somewhere at the edge of the universe—
I'm not sure if it's the beginning or the end,
but it's certainly not the mushy center—
three witches scrub, hang, and fold the laundry of the dead.
They mend bullet holes, wash out blood, sweat, and dirt,
then fold with care and pack away the last worn clothes
of those who cross back to the source.
I visited them for tea. They were morose and swamped.
They asked me to tell you: please stay home.
Things are going well in China—or at least in the slice of China I see from Chongqing. But there are bumps in the road as schools re-open. A Senior 3 program in Guizhou, one of the first to resume on March 16, reported 209 students falling ill by March 24. Symptoms included fever, diarrhea, and body aches. Nearly all were sent to hospital. By March 28, 196 had recovered; ten remained under care. The other three were not mentioned in official reports. Though it hasn't been confirmed as a COVID outbreak—"food poisoning," some say—tensions are high. I'm grateful to still be teaching my classes online.
Meanwhile, in the West, nurses in some parts of America are told to make their own masks or wear bandanas. How are Canada and the U.S. still not mobilizing factories to mass-produce PPE? This is wartime, yet we're relying on the compassion of home sewists and hobbyists with 3D printers. One doctor, 68, is dying in New York. His son wrote about him—healthy just weeks ago, now gravely ill after performing high-risk intubations with a mask that didn't fit tightly. His final words: COVID-19 can be very, very bad.

These exhausted professionals are paying the price because others went on spring break, or laughed it off as just the flu. Because some young and healthy people didn't take it seriously.

Please stay home. Let them rest.

Remember, this virus travels through "healthy-seeming" carriers. SARS was easier to contain because symptoms were visible. COVID-19 hides. It spreads silently, often through people who never get sick themselves. That's why we all must act as if we're infected—stay home, wear masks. If you don't have a mask, wear a bandana. Jay Ould once said, "Bandanas are for fools." Well, maybe this is the time for fools to save the world.

Our Ayi came today. The security guard was hesitant to let her in. Even when I came down to vouch for her, he wasn't having it. Eventually, he reviewed her government-issued medical clearance and relented. Inside, she wore her own mask; we gave her blue gloves. Shaolin and I donned our masks, too. I worked like that for an hour or two, and when she left, the house sparkled. My slippers didn't squeak, and I could breathe easier.

I hear cinemas in Shanghai reopened recently—only to be shuttered again. Tensions are rising. Foreigners in China are seeing signs banning them from businesses, or warning them away entirely. My friend Joe says he's seen rumors that doctors have stopped mass testing in order to present an illusion of control, so they can later blame foreigners for reimporting the virus. We must resist the urge to blame. We are all human.

I spent the day editing. I drank coffee, nibbled snacks, ate rice and garlic-fried green beans with Shaolin. We worked on layout and proofreading, and for all the pressure, the tasks felt oddly soothing. I'm relieved I slept 6–7 hours last night. I'll try to keep it up.

We took a walk. Taught a class. It went well. Shaolin helped me edit. I created a beta-reader audiobook for a few friends to catch problems before print. Wartime measures.

Mom is well—safe, careful. The Island followed Uncle Vic's advice, and cases remain limited. Isolation works. My dad, in Ottawa, is in a tougher spot. He writes:
Kai, I think all over the world, people are getting exhausted.
That's what Uncle Vic was so mad about. The stupidity and arrogance of the spreaders is killing the lives of medical people.
Thanks for all your nagging. At least I've been comfortable for two weeks, not freaking out.
I haven't gone out in 26 days, except once to pick up green beans from Ming's front door.
I tell him: imagine you hadn't listened to me—then you'd be mad at both of us.
He laughs. "Today," he says, "I'm sorry, Uncle Albert, but I haven't done a bloody thing all day."
I tell him that's fine—but don't burn through your pantry. If he pokes his head out in two months and has no food, that's bad too.
I suggest canned goods and dry staples from Costco, left to cool in the garage. He agrees. He's even Googling solar phone chargers now. Progress.
Trump is sending 10,000 troops to the Canadian border. Why? Does he think we're going to sneak over to pay American health care prices?
One of Shaolin's friends sends an update from the States:
It's terrible here, like China six weeks ago.
I've had to let 75% of my employees go.
Restaurants are shut. Nonessential businesses will close tomorrow.
I'm importing PPE for the state, so my company stays open.
Every day more people get sick. Thousands are dying.
Everyone is scared.
Shaolin tells me 10,000 Spanish doctors are sick. We have 597,000 official cases now—likely twice, or ten times that number still baking quietly. Italy has passed China in cases. The top three: America,

Italy, China. If Italy's quarantine efforts are finally taking effect, we'll see that spread. But only if we take it seriously.

The air is poison.

The floor is lava.

You are an astronaut.

Now go.

April 1, 2020 – Chongqing, China – "Better Late Than Never"

Part I: Lemon Soufflés and Revel Alliances
Day 69. Grandmothers across Greece keep watch from balconies, assisting police in maintaining order as quarantines spread across Europe.
We make a lemon soufflé. It's surprisingly light and fluffy, and with practice, it might be as good as the one we had at Cézembre in Paris.
In a one-day firestorm of fundraising, the Wu-Tang Clan donates thousands and helps raise $170,000 for the Ottawa Food Bank. Praise be, RZA. What can't you do? Alibaba sends Canada 500,000 test kits and one million masks. Mercedes F1 engineers develop a breathing aid for COVID patients in under 100 hours. A Canadian tech startup has designed a respirator using ubiquitous parts and could produce a million units—if Trudeau releases federal emergency funding.
Finally, we have good news. Better late than never.
Trudeau federalizes local PPE production. Toys 'R' Us is donating monitors to help elderly patients communicate. Wartime footing has truly begun, as the global caseload surpasses one million.
Trudeau's benefits packages are taking shape. Companies rehiring laid-off workers will receive a 75% wage subsidy. "$750 on a $1,000 paycheck, funded by taxes? Mr. Moneybags Trudeau, are you really gonna do that?" Just watch him.

Part II: The Sit-Down Duck
I take a picture in my top hat and cyber shades, holding a ridiculous amount of toilet paper, and post it online. Maybe I'll get invited to The Island.

As I juggle cover designs, outreach, and domestic tensions with Shaolin, our housekeeper arrives. I hand her gloves. I'm in the middle of making hummus—too dry, then too wet. Disaster artistry.

Then it hits me: I'm eating in the open, around someone who's been outside, in others' homes. Civilians make these mistakes. I'm a sitting duck. So I retreat, mask up, and return to warrior mode. People are watching. I must set an example.

The Revel Alliance? It began as a joke, then a post, then a group with 400+ members overnight. A green zone online, where high-AQ folks can drop their masks and talk science, share sourdough tips, and swap baking victories. Like that lemon soufflé. It made Shaolin smile. We can't always be happy, but we can try to stay in the light.

Part III: Social Distance and Social Fabric

My first friend tests positive—she's in Africa. Movement is banned. Malls are shut. Four meters between shoppers. Five-person maximum gatherings. Curfew at 7 p.m. Government food rations. This is very real.

Back west, people try for two meters but without masks? It's not enough. MIT says a sneeze can travel ten meters in half a second, filling an entire bus with viral particles. Or a fart. Just wear a mask. Dylan, in L.A., was heckled for wearing PPE. Dangerous misinformation is putting lives at risk. The CDC, in a bid to preserve hospital resources, gave guidance so bad it borders on malpractice. But now? They're reconsidering. "CDC considers reversing itself on masks." Reads to me like: "CDC considers waking up drunk at the wheel."

Still, we persist. The Revel Alliance is growing stronger. I remind myself to be kind, to be patient. Most people weren't locked down for 70 days and given 2020 vision early. And now even the doubters are quiet.

Part IV: Sewing Circles and Soft Power

Shaolin makes baozi—pillowy, perfect. We've learned so much during this special time.

I'm invited to speak at union conferences. They want 2,000 copies of my book. But will it be too late by then? Will the war be won or lost?

We're sewing masks from HEPA air filters. My mom signs up for volunteer therapy work with frontliners. The Revel Alliance launches its crisis team.

Finger-pointing abounds. China, Italy, Spain, the U.S.—all accused of downplaying numbers. But if your intel can tap Merkel's phone, why can't you assess real data? Watch what countries *do*, not what they *say*.

Meanwhile, urns pile up outside Wuhan funeral homes. The official death toll of 3,200 looks awfully low.

Part V: The Curve and the Cutting Edge

Boris Johnson is sick. Charles too. The Queen is not amused. Germany's finance minister kills himself in despair. A Syrian friend claims old people who cough twice are shot. Camillo hopes it's a rumor.

The WHO says COVID isn't airborne. MIT says otherwise. Hospitals find viral particles in their HVAC systems. The truth? It hangs in the air, waits in silence.

The solutions are simple. Shut the borders. Quarantine. Mask up. Talk less. Breathe smart. A low viral load means a fighting chance. Even cotton masks matter.

My Beijing editor scolds me: "Your edits are too slow! People are dying!" Then she delays the proof by ten days. Enter Chen Xi, our calm and capable mediator.

Dash drops lyrics so good I weep during a Zoom call with Beijing's biggest printer. The dam breaks. I am human again.

Part VI: Humor, Spaghetti Monsters, and the Masked Dance

I discover a painting of the Flying Spaghetti Monster battling the COVID meatball. I order it on a T-shirt. Along with my book cover. And Devon's pandemic mindset diagram. Fashion-forward PPE.

Canada institutes million-dollar fines for quarantine-breakers. I imagine pandemic bounty hunters rounding up five defiant old snowbirds for a 20% cut. It has cinematic potential.

Hospitals silence whistleblowing doctors. Trump delays ventilator aid. Cuomo begs. Brooklyn ERs buckle. Cuomo's rising. America's falling.

Hanley, Yukon's top doc, says: "This is a war. We need to act like it." Old vaccines are being tested. Las Vegas houses the homeless in parking lot grids while hotels sit empty. Lennon said, "Reality leaves a lot to the imagination."

In one branch of the metaverse, President Sanders saved 900,000 lives. In this one, we still have time.

Part VII: From Mask Hacks to Bloodletting

Shaolin replaces our wood chopsticks with steel ones. She says the others were moldy. I think she's prepping me for battle.

Benben thanks us for chicken soup by peeing on the floor. We mop, triage-style, and move on.

Shaolin asks me to clean the dog poop off the balcony. As I slosh the soapy water, I stab my palm with the broom's metal rim. Blood gushes. Stigmata. I disinfect and bandage. Then lunch. Then a mask. Always the mask.

The pain has cracked me open. Thanks to Dash, I feel again. I'm soft but clear, and I lead with purpose. No screaming. Just clarity.

Part VIII: The First Dancer

Justin Bieber's mom is on the phone. "Tell your boy we need his help."

I've spent so long trying not to crush the dream that I forgot to document it. Better late than never.

For those outside Asia, I know it's hard to be the first one in your town to wear a mask. It's like being the first one to dance at a party. People stare. Call you weird. But then someone joins. Then another. And another. Soon, there's a dance floor.

And the real weirdos? They're the ones stuck watching from the walls.

So dance. Be first. Be brave. Be better. It's not too late.

Not yet.

April 4, 2020 – Vung Tau, Vietnam – "Wear a Mask, Take a Hula Hoop" (Lulu)

It's been seven weeks and six days since they took my job away.

My friend Kep and I first talked about the viral outbreak in China during the Tet Holiday. The first rumors of infections in Hanoi reached us in late January, just as we were heading to a crowded park in the front beach area of my city—Vung Tau, Vietnam. It's a popular seaside getaway town in the south of the country with a population of about 500,000, just two hours from Saigon.

After a few quiet days of Tet, Vung Tau was flooded with Saigoneers eager to escape the sweaty sauna of the big city for the cleaner air and coastal breeze of our seaside paradise. The park was decorated with Year of the Rat paraphernalia, and people swarmed around to pose with Mickey Mouse and what were quite obviously Alvin and the Chipmunks knock-offs.

Kep and I dressed up to get our own photos with the celebrity rat impersonators and b-list rodents. But the thought of a contagious virus so close to home made me nervous. I obliged my friend and took dozens of photos of her, but declined to be in any myself. No one wants to look back at pictures of me nauseous with anxiety next to a poorly crafted Theodore statue.

Within days, my expat friends began suggesting we stock up on masks and hand sanitizer in preparation for returning to classrooms filled with kids who'd just finished traveling all over the country. By now, it was early February, and there were 14 confirmed cases in Vietnam, all in the north.

I geared up for a long weekend of work and went to school.

The office was a disorganized mess. There was plenty of talk about the virus and how it spread—we all knew what should be done—but our school's administration wasn't prepared. Children came to class without masks, some of them visibly sick. I tried to teach through a mask while my TAs encouraged students to remove theirs so they could be heard more clearly.

I spent half my classes that weekend arguing with my boss, the TAs, and other teachers about how we could keep students and staff safe. I was one of only two foreign teachers who wore a mask in every class. The administrators would arrive forty minutes into the session to check temperatures and hand out masks to the children. There were questions. Everyone was confused. The students were unfazed. The weekend somehow ended without incident.

On Monday, schools and language centers began to close. Ours was shut for a week, with promised updates to follow.

Every Tuesday afterward, the expat teachers would debate whether we'd be called in again. Eventually, the updates stopped coming. The discussions faded. It became an indefinite vacation.

Vietnam's current numbers are a reflection of those early actions, among other smart and timely government responses.

Some language centers quickly shifted classes online. Others struggled to convince parents it was a good idea. But overall, shutting down schools—those beautiful, chaotic viral amplifiers—was the right move.

If you do have to go out, wear a mask. And take a hula hoop to keep people at a safe distance.

It's dangerous to go alone! Take this!

April 5, 2020 – Chongqing, China – "Finding Kai-ndness"

Day 73

Hello, my name is Kai, and I'm an addict. I'm addicted to trying to save the world—and it's destroying my life.

On the weekend, just like in the old days, Mat Trouble is on point, spinning a four-hour set on TroubleMaker Radio. It's already Saturday morning for me, but I bust some moves. Not everyone is ready to join me yet, but someone has to start the dance.

We argue and fight late into the night. Shaolin cries into a couch cushion, ready to give up on me. Obsessed and defiant, I'm burning out like a dying star, self-immolating for the chance to change the world.

I try, patiently, to bridge the distance—but it's a vast chasm, chipped away by moments over two long months. The pressure has escalated: the stress of the book deal, the media tour, the crushing Chinese editor, and other extenuating factors. All around us, couples are losing their cool. We did well to make it to Day 70.

We go shopping after some strong coffee, and it's almost normal. They don't even take our temperatures anymore. But everyone still wears masks. When everyone has a mask, I realize I probably don't need my goggles anymore—and that's a comfort. I shove them in my pocket.

I record a short video for a union conference in Toronto. We want to train their workers on how to be AsCans—Astronaut Candidates—and how to survive in this new world of cosmic horror.

The floor is lava. The air is poison. But here's how to make a space suit. Apocalypse bunny, looking for love: Y/N/M?

Love in the time of COVID,
Where even a breakup

YEAR OF THE RAT

Is some next-level laser
Splitting your space station in twine.
Being a children's TV show host by day, a 24-hour obsessed journalist by night, and a revolutionary leader for protective fashion—it's exhausting. My marriage is hanging on by a thread. We're hemorrhaging students, and Shaolin can't pretend to be okay with it anymore.
I play hockey with my dad, and my New Jersey Devils slay his All-Stars 4–1. I play like the devil is on my tail. Every breath is full of defiant life, but I'm tough, I'm fierce, and I'm not patient. I'm unkind. Un-Kai-nd.
In two days, I start a media tour for the book. I'm not sure my marriage will survive unless I unplug for the next 24 hours and recoup. Adam, an old friend, is wonderful enough to help with the new blog site. Turns out, after eight hours of sleep, I can wake up and solve some of my most immediate problems. Still, I'm grateful to have him on board for the bigger ones. This rollout matters. It's our front-facing effort to rebuild a better society. You know, no biggie.
Reports are coming in from strong voices around the world. I held my hill for 70 days, but now it's time to rest and recharge—and make space for others to rise and speak their truth. My role is changing. It's scary but exciting. I resist, not ready to let go of the front line. But Shaolin pushes me. I'm learning to listen, despite myself.
The Revel Alliance is thriving. I love you. We've got excellent new mods and admins now.
I whip eggs with those sleek, steel chopsticks. It takes time, it takes focus, it takes dedication to get them to bubble up. It's not easy, but it gets done. Wax on, wax off. Shaolin knows.
I make a promise—not her angry demand, but a halfway meeting—to only save people during business hours for a while. To unplug for the weekend. To make a nice dinner. I chop potatoes and

green onions, garlic and ginger, and I savor the aroma of new hope rising in the pan.

See you soon. Stay safe.

April 5, 2020 – Toronto, Canada – "Be Like Water" (Rhett Morita)

Fluid. Adaptable. Able to change from gas to liquid to solid—and back again.

For most of us North Americans, life has been flipped on its head in a month or less.

The inconceivable (à la Wallace Shawn from The Princess Bride) "new normal" has arrived, with no escape—regardless of social, religious, governmental, economic, or educational status. From celebrities to cardinals, presidents to PhDs, factory workers to factory owners, every single human being on this blue planet is in this together. Whether you're 8 or 88, Black, white, red, brown, or yellow. World-class athletes, weekend warriors, toddlers taking their first steps—we are all human. We breathe, feel, drink, eat, and think. Yes, we've got those... other functions, too.

But now, we're more aware of our sameness—our shared vulnerability—regardless of your follower count, the size of your stock portfolio, your freezer, or your fists.

This is a new time, where AQ—Adaptability Quotient—may be the most important skill of all. Yes, even more important than your TikTok game.

We're being forced into new ways of living in a heightened state of awareness of this invisible assassin. I call it the Ninja Virus—silent, fast, unseen. And deadly.

I've been reflecting. I was already on high alert by the end of January, thanks to a 23-year-old tip from The Coming Plague by Laurie Garrett. SARS didn't set off my alarms—not even when I was in the thick of it in Toronto. But this time, I felt it.

I started wearing a mask in early March. By the 7th, I was basically in self-isolation. I told my agent on the 9th I was stepping back from auditions—those rooms were impossible to control. I was already wiping down everything, carrying Lysol wipes and Purell. People gave me looks.

Funny thing—earlier this week, my agent told me someone from the audition I skipped on the 9th tested positive for COVID-19.

That's when I knew I was right to trust my instincts.

Did I need the money? Desperately. I've barely worked this year, and after four callbacks, I was close to a breakthrough. But sometimes you have to choose health over hope. And two weeks later, the entire industry shut down.

Now, I venture out maybe once a week for groceries, sometimes twice. Always in full gear. I wear an N99 mask, usually under a fabric face shield, and sometimes a bandana on top—for style, sure, but also an added layer. I only use each setup once, then seal it in a garbage bag for washing 3–4 days later.

The first few times, I felt claustrophobic—aware of my breath, the warmth and moisture kicking back against my face with every exhale. It made me anxious at first. But now? After maybe seven trips out, it feels normal. Comforting, even.

When I'm not wearing a mask, I feel exposed—like a hockey player skating without a cup.

(Which, yes, I've done once. Never again.)

So here I am: a month ago, no mask. Now? I feel naked without one.

I know not to get cocky or reckless. I'm not invulnerable. But this new normal feels natural now—just like the rising number of masked shoppers I see. A month ago, maybe 1%. Yesterday? 60–65%.

We are changing, and we must remain fluid. Anticipate what's needed—not just react to outdated news cycles and stats. This is a time to be proactive, self-responsible. If you can be ahead of the curve, you're not early. You're on time.

YEAR OF THE RAT

Be like water.
—Rhett "The Jett" Morita

April 6, 2020 – Prince Edward Island, Canada – "Doing More with Less" (Dara Mac)

Day 17. I woke up much earlier than usual today and saw that my son, Kai, had tried to call from China. I reached out on WeChat, and he shared the lyrics to a song his friend Dash had written about the "Invisible War," the title of Kai's forthcoming book about his experience of COVID-19 in Chongqing. It was a moving, emotional way to wake up, bleary-eyed and trying to make sense of the unfolding global pandemic. It brought back warm memories of a more sociable time—when I made dinner for Kai, Dash, and Galen after a Root Sellers gig in Charlottetown. They crashed at my house that night. It's been years now, and I'm still hoping a summer visit with Kai might be possible.

I climbed down the ladder from the loft of my tiny home to feed the cats and make coffee in the Bodum. Italian Roast Just Us beans, roasted in Nova Scotia—still the best-tasting coffee around. There's no running water in the house, but I've lived this way for years. Thankfully, Kai gave our family the early warning about the Coronavirus, which gave each of us a chance to prepare and stock up on essentials. I had also been closely following his 60-day self-isolation in China, all while wrestling with my own mixed feelings about socializing here on PEI.

Until a few weeks ago, our government still had a wait-and-see attitude about the 97 cruise ships scheduled to dock at the Charlottetown Harbour between April and October—even after the Japan cruise ship fiasco made clear how easily the virus spreads on board. The first case on PEI was announced March 14: a woman in her 50s working for the Department of Veterans Affairs had returned from a Caribbean cruise. She was asymptomatic and hadn't been self-isolating. The next week, everything accelerated.

Kai shared a letter written by his Uncle Vic, a retired ER doctor, with strong recommendations on flattening the curve. I forwarded it to my MP, who replied within minutes to say he had sent it to PEI's Chief Medical Health Officer, who passed it to the Premier. That day, during the province's news conference, strict new guidelines were announced. PEI closed all non-essential businesses, restricted traffic on the Confederation Bridge, and issued fines for violating social distancing. We were urged to stay home unless absolutely essential. On PEI, "essential" also includes liquor stores—not surprising, given our high rates of addiction.

Most of my career as a social worker and clinical therapist has been in the field of mental health and addiction. This is year two of my retirement from front-line work. In my final years at PEI Health, the mantra became "Do More With Less." That meant one person doing two, sometimes three, full-time jobs. In such an intense, unpredictable, and emotionally exhausting environment, burnout wasn't a question of *if*, but *when*.

Eventually, I was pushed over the edge. I spent four months in my tiny home, shades drawn, barely speaking to anyone. So this stay-at-home order doesn't feel entirely foreign to me.

These days, the Confederation Bridge restrictions bring more comfort than anxiety. Our CMHO and Premier have made it clear: PEI is small and densely populated. If community transmission begins, we'll be a cruise ship petrie dish. I haven't been to Charlottetown—to a grocery store, a gym, or laundromat—in three weeks. I don't plan to go any time soon.

Problem-solving and survival strategies are the theme now. Learning how to make do. It's taken my focus away from drumming, which I now consider my full-time job. I've been taking online lessons for over a year, and though my in-person teacher and I are taking a break, my passion remains strong. I recently read about the therapeutic value of drumming—and I can attest, it's real.

My favorite foods are gone now—yogurt, raw cashews, dried fruit, rice cakes. This is week three, and today I ate my last frozen Montreal bagel. It reminded me of my youth, standing in line at Fairmount Bagel, burning our hands through the brown paper bag because they were too hot to wait. Storm chips? Gone on day one.

Now I'm sprouting seed mixes, making bean soup, growing microgreens. I've already added some to today's soup. I've started seedlings for my outdoor garden, once the three feet of snow melts. I buy eggs, cheese, honey, and GF mixes from neighbors and local producers—e-transfer and contactless pickup only. These are things I've *wanted* to do for years, and now I *am* doing them.

My new challenge is simple: how long can I go without shopping, without driving, without spending money?

"Doing more with less" is now my personal motto.

And it finally feels like mine.

April 7, 2020 – San Diego, USA – "Breakneck Speeds" (Kait Marcelle)

Some things happen so quickly, you barely notice them—even when they're right in front of your face. In my area, barriers suddenly appeared between workers and the public at what few "essential" stores remain open. It feels like two very different weeks collapsed into just one.

On Monday, people snickered at me for wearing a mask in public. By Thursday evening, requests were pouring in to make more masks, and by Friday, the county issued a mandate: everyone must wear a mask in public at all times. It was as if the collective consciousness snapped into a new reality overnight.

Most places are closed. Essential services—auto repair, supermarkets, pet supply, construction, shipping, phone services, liquor stores, takeout restaurants—continue to operate, but the rest of life has slowed or vanished.

I feel like I'm aging at a compounding rate. March felt like a year. This past week has felt like a month. I've absorbed more information in the past seven days than I usually do in a whole month. I've been combing through research studies, listening to health professionals on the front lines—both in my family and around the world—and now I could practically teach a crash course on mask types, uses, and DIY methods. One week ago, I had never used a sewing machine. Today, I taught myself how to make masks. Time itself feels strange, distorted, untrustworthy.

When I was asked to write about my perspective, I hesitated—but then I realized how valuable it could be to process all of this in writing. I'm a biotechnology student at a community college in Southern California, living in a modest neighborhood. Before this pandemic, I already lived a fairly isolated life, dividing my time between schoolwork, my fiancé, our plants (he's jealous of how much I love them), our nine-year-old cat (he's clearly her favorite), and our close-knit circle of friends.

I moved here to be near my parents and help care for them. One of them has only one lung left and is severely immunocompromised. Every COVID risk factor you've heard about on the CDC's PSAs—they have them. So, needless to say, I worry.

To everyone staying home: thank you. My parents thank you. I'm sure someone you don't even know is thanking you, too.

I've been limiting my outings to essential trips only—mostly zero lately, since we stocked up weeks ago. My partner's job is still considered essential, so he's been handling our errands. But when my parents' bed frame collapsed, it became clear: we had to fix it immediately.

That meant a trip to the hardware store. Asking for help was tough. The staff was exhausted, stretched thin, trying their best. One woman looked at me like I was out of my mind trying to get wood cut during a global pandemic. And I understood. She didn't know those two sheets of plywood would help two elderly people sleep through the night and ease their pain. She didn't know how much it mattered.

It was the last place I wanted to be. But I'm grateful the store was open, and that people are still showing up—for strangers, for families, for fragile bodies, for love.

April 8, 2020 – Jeddah, Saudi Arabia – "Dreaming of a Dancefloor" (Sarah Rollinson)

How did I get here?

It's not all that complicated. Woman meets man in Ottawa. Woman dates man in Ottawa. Man gets a fantastic job opportunity and moves to Saudi Arabia. Woman stays in Ottawa but hangs onto the long-distance relationship. Eventually, LDR isn't enough. Woman marries man. And just like that, I start spending a third or more of my time living in Saudi Arabia, with the rest back in Canada. That was before COVID-19. Now you're caught up.

I was supposed to fly out in January 2020, but there were delays with my permanent residency card. I'm a UK citizen, born there, and I'd never gotten around to applying for Canadian PR. I'd just shipped my passport to complete the paperwork when everything shut down. Now, my passport is stuck in Riyadh—and I'm stuck in Makkah province, which is under full lockdown.

To clarify: Makkah is both the name of the province *and* the city (also known as Mecca, Islam's holiest city). I'm still confused about the distinction, especially when officials announce "Mecca" is under a 24-hour curfew. Either way, I can't leave. Not that there's anywhere to go. No transport in or out of the country. No passport. No options.

For now, I'm living in a gated community, which means I can still leave the house during the day—as long as I stay within the province and return before the 7 p.m.–6 a.m. curfew. It's a nice neighborhood, quickly developing, and oddly calm. No panic. No hoarding. Our grocery store is still well-stocked—except for masks and hand sanitizer, which are long gone.

What *does* bother me? People discarding masks and gloves right in the parking lot. This kind of biowaste littering defeats the whole purpose. It drives me mad. It's not just irresponsible—it's disgusting.

Here in Saudi Arabia, the call to prayer rings out five times a day. When it's time, shops close for at least 15 minutes, and you'll see people roll out prayer mats and begin to pray—out loud, in Arabic, all over the city. I'm currently living with my in-laws, who are stuck here and unable to return to Russia. That means I can't exactly crank up the music and dance around the house like I'd love to. Instead, I'm surrounded by two elderly Russian relatives complaining about everything and anything. Thankfully, I don't speak Russian. Still, I'm lucky to live near the sea. The air is fresh. The scent of the ocean is sweet and salty and endlessly more pleasant than the sticky humidity, litter, and smog of the inner city.

I've found comfort in cooking and baking again. We've been sampling my creations, and every so often, we treat ourselves to Starbucks or Baskin-Robbins (takeout only, of course). Other than my husband, the only things I touch are ingredients, my bike, my notepads and sketchpad, and my beloved Nikon D7200 camera, which I still bring along when I venture out—though those outings are few and far between now.

I see reports of people around the world refusing to wear masks and wonder if they've read a newspaper, seen a screen, or listened to *any* decent human being. I think back to when I used to travel alone and would see Chinese passengers wearing masks on flights. I'd ask my husband, "Are they sick? Or do they think *we* are?" Eventually, I started getting sick—every time I flew. Colds that lasted a week and ruined the beginning of every trip. I began to understand. I didn't start wearing masks then, but I did carry hand sanitizer and finally broke my nervous habit of finger-biting. It made a huge difference.

Also, alcohol is illegal here. So for those of you sipping wine or cracking a beer during lockdown... just know, you've got that going for you.

April 8, 2020 – Turin, Italy – "Sirens Breaking Crisp Mountain Air" (Alessia Martino)

Everyone's take on "quarantine" looks different these days, depending on where you are in the world. In northern Italy, the impact was swift and severe. As cases surged, the entire country was placed on lockdown March 10—for the world to watch and pray.

I don't find the quarantine terrible, per se. But one of the most frustrating restrictions is the rule that prohibits us from walking more than 200 meters from home. As time passes, more limitations have been added. I haven't left the perimeter of my property—except for the thrilling task of taking out the garbage—since March 9. Even before that, I was mostly staying in, already aware of how serious things were, even if many others hadn't yet caught on. Sadly, too many people here underestimated the risk early on.

Now, people are only allowed out for grocery shopping (for themselves or elderly parents), for essential work, or in case of emergencies. Restaurants, bars, and all non-essential businesses are closed. Nobody is allowed to leave their town without official documentation justifying the need. I don't go out shopping—my sister handles that, including groceries for our mother. I haven't seen Mom in over a month, but as long as she's safe at home, I'm at peace.

In truth, I'm lucky. I live in the countryside and enjoy a bit more breathing room than those stuck in city apartments. At first, I felt imprisoned. Now I don't. I try not to dwell on the past or worry too much about the future. I'm learning to live in the moment, in my own little bubble.

I wake up around 7:30 every morning. On weekdays, I help my father on our land. Agriculture doesn't stop for pandemics, and I'm legally allowed to pitch in as family without a formal work contract. My hands are blistered, but I'm grateful for the excuse to go outside. Soaking in sunshine—even through some late March snowfall—has kept me grounded. After several years living in China, snow feels almost exotic again.

The rest of my day is a mix of YouTube, TV series, and maintaining some structure through yoga twice a week and writing daily—sometimes in Italian, sometimes in English, sometimes in a joyful bilingual mix.

My quarantine diet hasn't changed much, though pizza delivery is definitely a lifeline. I do worry about costs, as I'm not the one selecting the groceries and prices can be steep. Some supermarket items have become harder to find—baking ingredients like eggs are in high demand as Italians discover their inner pastry chefs. There's no toilet paper hoarding here, though. The bidet is a national treasure. But disinfectants and alcohol-based products are like gold.

Non-essential goods were banned for weeks, including—bizarrely—colored pens, though that rule has since relaxed. Face masks remain scarce, so most people still don't have them. Scarves and other coverings are accepted alternatives, and supermarkets now require staff to wear gloves and masks, while encouraging customers to do the same. Stores often provide disposable gloves, and a one-meter distance is mandated for all interactions.

These days, I've come to realize: I'm not stuck at home. I'm safe at home. I'm lucky to have a clear view of the Alps, fresh mountain air, and a supportive family. But peace is fragile. From my attic room, the sounds are amplified—cars passing, occasional voices—but nothing slices through the calm like the sirens of ambulances, breaking the silence like a shattering glass bubble.

April 9, 2020 – Buenos Aires, Argentina – "I'm Scared of What's Coming" (Josette)

Day 24.

There are so many aspects of daily life we once took for granted. Listing them now seems pointless—we all know they've changed or vanished altogether. It's incredible how, in the blink of an eye, the world you knew disappears, and another emerges.

I wonder if this is how people felt during the Great Depression, or the Cold War. I can't even imagine what those who lived through the World Wars experienced. And now here we are—living through the next historical moment. Decades from now, students will study this pandemic, take tests on it, and write essays. And I'll be able to say: *I was there.*

If I thought 2019 was rough—well, welcome to 2020. Do **not** pass GO. Do **not** collect $200.

PANDEMIC? ... What?

If it weren't for the helicopters flying overhead several times a day or the 9 p.m. applause for healthcare workers, maybe it wouldn't feel quite so apocalyptic. (Aren't we all saving each other in some way?)

I double-mask now—one regular, one fake leather over top. I had to go to the ATM today. I didn't think this would become my reality. I miss hugging people. I miss not being afraid of every stranger on the street. Being asthmatic, stepping outside is now a panic-inducing challenge.

We've been in quarantine for four weeks. Yesterday, I had to go to the pharmacy and the bank—I couldn't put it off any longer. Part of me expected to find a ghost town: shuttered businesses, empty streets, maybe some boarded-up shops. But I was wrong.

YEAR OF THE RAT

Let me fill you in without writing a novel about Argentina's past three weeks.

Our president, newly elected in December 2019, made a bold move by locking down the country **before** we even hit 100 confirmed COVID-19 cases. That single decision likely saved thousands of lives. It was crucial in slowing the spread. In a country like ours—warm, social, physical—it's no small feat. People here love to gather. To share everything. *Mate,* food, stories, space. You can't be close anymore.

The numbers are rising slowly, but not slowly enough. The bigger problem? Ignorance. The kind that says, *"This doesn't apply to me."* So the government cracked down. Hard. Breaking quarantine is now a criminal offense. You can go to jail for 6 months to 2 years. Last I checked, over 30,000 people had been arrested, and 900 vehicles impounded. That was a week ago—it's likely higher now.

Then came the disaster at the beginning of the month.

Pension day. The day retirees and seniors collect their benefits. Hundreds—**thousands**—of elderly people lined up outside banks for hours, some overnight. Waiting. No social distancing. No masks. Just hunger, fear, and desperation. These are the very people most at risk—and they were on the streets, side by side.

The government hadn't foreseen it. Their fix? Open the banks on weekends. Split the lines by ID number. We'll see if it helped. I know this much: the virus is now sweeping through nursing homes and elder care facilities.

And I'm scared.

I'm scared all this sacrifice—this month of isolation—will be for nothing if others don't follow the rules. But maybe it won't be for nothing. *Maybe it's the reason I don't die.*

So for now, one day at a time. Today, I go to the ATM. Tomorrow, I get cat food.

Did I mention I caught a cold? Let's hope it's just a cold. But even a sniffle feels terrifying now. Every tickle in the throat has a different weight.
Wish me luck.
I wish you luck too.
—Josette
Buenos Aires, April 8, 2020

April 9, 2020 – Chicago, USA – "Animals on Lockdown, the World Will Be OK" (MC ZULU)

I shouldn't be writing this, and you probably shouldn't be reading it.

My point of view is more cynical than most, with a terminally alarmist bent. Over the past decade, I've littered the airwaves with hundreds of songs, remixes, and YouTube updates—each one alienating a new fan who finally understood what I was actually saying. I sing reggae, mostly over party beats, but somewhere along the line, I got the bright idea to slip in a social message.

I live in the Heart of Babylon. They don't get this stuff. No one realized they were dancing to the beat of their own indictment... until they did. After being booed off stage in my own hometown, I took the show on the road. And thanks to technology, I could stay on the road—even while raising children, even during a global pandemic.

These are the observations of someone who still hopes art can save humanity.

The world will be OK. Humanity? Maybe not. And if not, it's no one's fault but our own. We let economics upset the evolutionary apple cart. We rewarded greed and glorified apathy. Life-affirming values got sidelined while death-driven incentives were dangled in front of our youth like candy. Chasing wealth became the only valid form of self-worth.

How long did we think this could last?

When the dot-com bubble burst around Y2K, investors realized you couldn't just slap a catchy name on a dream and call it value. Substance became key. A company needed a business model. A reason to exist. And now, as austerity sweeps the globe, we're learning the same lesson: substance is the key to survival.

Needs are overtaking vanity. But societal decay feels inevitable. The powerful still guard their thrones, and the rest of us get reshuffled like cards in a rigged deck.

By now, you're wondering: what does any of this have to do with the coronavirus?

Everything.

It could've been a natural virus or a manmade one. A computer glitch (remember the Y2K bug?) or an asteroid from space. Every so often, decadent societies get a wake-up call. This is ours.

We in the "First World" grew too complacent. Our luxuries depend on someone else's misery, and that system needs resetting. The common folk remain powerless, and yet—regardless of origin—people are dying. Of something.

COVID-19 precautions are not a joke. And we shouldn't expect a return to "normal"—whatever that was. A world born of 1980s Wall Street slogans like *Greed is Good* turned into a haven for organ traffickers, tiki-torch Nazis, and inner-city kids trained to shoot at each other before they turn 18.

So now, we lock the animals—good and bad—inside their cages (homes), until we can find a better way forward.

You worship wealth? Fine. Now you'll take orders from the super-rich. Who did you think ran the governments all this time? Your life has three instructions:

Go to WORK.
Go to WALMART.
Go HOME.

Welcome to 21st-century civilization. And while you're absent, watch how nature thrives.

The only way out of this mess is to re-center your spirit. Reacquaint yourself with old human traits like empathy. Resist hatred. Resist greed. Stop trying to survive—and start making yourself necessary. The world will be OK.

April 10, 2020 – Prince Edward Island, Canada – "I Pray for My Fellow Humans" (Dara Mac)

A quiet, gentle spring snow falls today. Quite the contrast from yesterday's grinding, painful chainsaw slaughter—Maritime Electric seems to have it in for my beautiful 30-foot spruce trees. But it doesn't take much time spent with the news to realize what an elite problem I have. I own my land, have trees to protect, live in a tiny mansion, and enjoy good health and nutritious, delicious food. My family, friends, and community are all staying home and, to my knowledge, remain safe. I'm deeply grateful.

To date, here on PEI, 25 people have tested positive for COVID-19. Seventeen have recovered. There have been no hospitalizations and no deaths. The Chief Medical Officer even took time to reassure the children of PEI that the Easter Bunny is an essential worker, healthy and immune. The Land of Anne feels like a dreamlike refuge amidst the hardship and heartbreak unfolding across the world. I pray for my fellow humans.

I continue my daily walks—sometimes just up and down my road, sometimes along the Confederation Trail, and occasionally to the nearby village of North Rustico when I need a change of scenery or to refill water jugs. The other day in Rustico, walking the boardwalk and harbor, I saw the lobster and crab traps stacked along the shore. I spotted a fisherman nearby. "I guess fishing's a go!" I called. "We have to be ready just in case," he replied. The season usually opens May 1, but some fishermen have voiced concerns about maintaining distancing on boats. The season was officially postponed until June 1 after provincial and federal intervention.

Last May, I made a point of making Mother's Day special for my 90-year-old mother in Ottawa. Though she's lived most of her life off-Island, she's never lost her love for PEI lobster. I flew from Charlottetown to Ottawa with a box prepared by local fishermen—fresh lobster and scallops. Minutes after I arrived, she devoured one without even sitting down. She enjoyed one lobster each day while I visited. What a contrast to this year. It's hard to believe.

Our mother-daughter relationship hasn't always been smooth. A while ago, my mother told me my brother-in-law was considering retirement from OC Transpo, but my sister was against it. She took my sister's side, wondering aloud why he should "just sit at home." I sharply replied that retirement was personal—and none of my business. That was before COVID. Amazing how a crisis shifts perspective. Months later, I heard he had retired from driving the city bus.

I was devastated to hear of Jason Hargrove, a 50-year-old Detroit bus driver who died of COVID-19. Just days earlier, he'd gone on social media to vent about a coughing passenger and how little some people seemed to care. Four days after that encounter, Jason fell ill. A week later, he was gone. Black Americans are being hit disproportionately hard—another reflection of systemic inequities, race, poverty, and injustice.

This pandemic has forced all of us to rethink everything. There is no "normal" to return to. This is it. Each of us must find new ways to live, cope, and survive. My son Kai often talks about the contrast between Chinese and Western culture. In the West, people are largely left to fend for themselves. Social distancing only amplifies that reality. Yet, people are reaching out. I've seen beautiful gatherings bloom on social media.

I attended a live concert on Facebook by Bill Coon, a brilliant jazz guitarist in BC. I was at his CD release "Too Much Guitar" with Kai over ten years ago, when he lived in Vancouver. I'd flown from Cape Breton, where I was working with the Eskasoni First Nation and studying jazz guitar with Joe Waye Jr. in Sydney, NS. Music is medicine. I miss our weekly Island Jazz nights at Baba's in Charlottetown—they feed my inspiration to keep practicing drums. I still sit at the kit daily. I've watched lessons with trumpet player Sean Jones on setting up daily routines, and John Riley on the fundamentals of jazz drumming. No, I don't want to be a one-armed drummer—coordination and independence in my left hand remain a challenge.

One of my "sushi and a movie" friends called in tears. Her beloved cat, Webbie, had died suddenly from a mysterious respiratory illness. Five minutes from first symptom to death. He'd been healthy before. I wonder how much silent transmission is happening all around us.

Another friend told me her daughter, a 30-year-old nurse in NYC, had tested positive for COVID-19. Thankfully, her symptoms were mild, and she recovered. Luckily, she didn't return to PEI, where her mother and 94-year-old grandmother live.

I have a phone counseling session in a few hours and need grounding, so I drive to Hunter River and walk the Confederation Trail. A social distancing sign greets me at the entrance. It's beautiful and peaceful, though I've never felt fully safe walking alone on the trail since that young woman was murdered there a decade ago. Still, I manage a 50-minute walk and feel better.

Three Canadian women have been murdered in their homes in recent weeks. Many more live with abusers, enduring mental, emotional, sexual, and physical abuse. It's unbearable to think about for too long.

So I return to gratitude—for all that I have, and all that I am. I am free.

I'm practicing daily mindfulness. Meals are more carefully prepared and slowly eaten. I savor the punchy taste of my morning coffee. I'm deeply grateful to breathe fresh country air and let

YEAR OF THE RAT

thoughts pass through. But the real challenge is finding peace in chaos, presence in uncertainty. I've never been good at that—but this may be the moment to learn.

I listen to the news and hear about the devastation in Ecuador—graveyards replacing hospitals, families keeping bodies in their homes for days in the heat, hundreds of unidentified dead. Hunger trumps distancing. Life goes on, even in terror.

I'm out of onions, apples, carrots, and nearly out of peanut butter. But I have grains, beans, blueberries, and microgreens. Shopping is madness, and I heard the stores are out of onions anyway. On my hardest day, a care package arrives from my local GF producer. After dinner, I bake a small gluten-free chocolate cake. No frosting needed—just warm, comforting sweetness. A perfect end to a heavy day.

I am blessed.

April 10, 2020 – Toronto, Canada – "Entry of a New Time" (Rhett "The Jett" Morita)

Day 34 of Social Isolation
(*...six trips to get food and supplies*)
Last time I saw friends in person: 37 days ago.
Has anyone else noticed how different time feels now? Especially if you've been home from work for over three weeks?
All those scheduled check-ins—breakfast meetings, lunch dates, afternoon pitches, dinner brainstorms—suddenly feel like relics of a world structured by the Industrial Revolution. A world run on fixed rhythms of productivity: clocking in and out, punching timecards, chasing the sunrise and sunset with assembly-line precision. But now? Now we work when it feels right—or when it's simply possible. We eat, clean, play, plan, create, sleep, or zone out... according to rhythms that are more intuitive than imposed. Are you a morning person? A night owl? Are you most productive at 2 p.m. or 2 a.m.? When do you clean—7 a.m., 11 p.m., or never (lol)? Have you lost yourself in a Netflix vortex at 4 a.m., or started a book at 10 and found yourself two-thirds finished by nightfall? Have you organized a closet after dinner, only to step back and admire it at 3 a.m.? Did you catch your baking ingredients nearing expiry and suddenly decide to whip up 140 cookies in a four-hour bake-a-thon?
Where did the time go?
I've learned to appreciate the small things—those you can only truly savor when you're no longer being chased by the world. Even handwashing, now a ritual repeated 20–30 times a day, has become meditative. Each rinse a reminder of cleanliness, care, and inten-

tion. It takes three or four times longer than it used to, but I don't mind. I've slowed down.

Every meal is more considered. Every fresh fruit or vegetable I wash becomes an act of mindfulness. The 25-minute wipe-down of groceries I once would've balked at? Now, it's a quiet ritual—a way to protect my family and remind myself why I do what I do. It's not a chore; it's an act of love.

This *new time* is more than a schedule shift. It's a chance to spend our most precious commodity—**time**—with intention, with presence, with soul.

No hurries. No worries.

Cheers,

Rhett "the Jett" Morita

April 11, 2020 – Jeddah, Saudi Arabia – "We Got This!" (Sarah Rollinson)

It's only been two or three days since the curfew was enforced here in Jeddah—at first, we weren't allowed to leave our homes between 7 p.m. and 6 a.m., and now it's been tightened to 3 p.m. to 6 a.m. I understand why. I do. But I've got some thoughts...

Curfews help limit transmission by keeping people home, especially those who may be carrying the virus unknowingly. They also cut down on contact with contaminated surfaces. But ironically, what I've seen is that these restrictions have created more crowding outside stores. Grocery lines now stretch longer, with only 41 people allowed in at a time. Everyone wears masks and gloves—which is good—but many in the queues are not social distancing. "Too close," I'll start saying next time, in Arabic or English, to make the point.

To be honest, I've never really felt accepted here. I'm not from Saudi Arabia. I'm here for my husband. Sometimes I worry people already know who's sick and want us to share the same fate because we don't belong. Maybe I'm being overly sensitive—but these feelings rise up, and I do my best to bury them and stay positive.

Now, grocery store queues have been split into two lines: one for men, one for women. Today, I didn't even see the women's line—because I was the only one. They brought me to the front of the men's line, took my temperature, and let me in.

Life under curfew hits different. It's not just "only go out for essentials." If you're caught outside after 3 p.m., you face a 10,000 SAR fine (roughly $3,500 CAD). So now, I'm reclaiming my space. I blast my music. I dance. This is my house, and I'll do what I want.

Today I came home and mowed the lawn with the sad excuse for a plastic mower our landlord left behind. It was annoying, but I

focused on the positive. I love mowing the lawn. My dad used to praise the crisp lines I made. I found some fresh basil growing—what a gift. Now we've got herbs for cooking.
Looking back, there were times I was nearly homeless—and times I felt on top of the world. I've lived both ends of the spectrum. I've seen beauty, fear, chaos, and grace. This is just another chapter. I don't know what tomorrow holds, but I keep going.
It's strange being in isolation while living with people. I think I do better, mentally, when I have space to myself. I tried to be a good host, but now I'm just living. The music is up. I'm dancing. This is our home.
These are trying times—for so many reasons. I keep telling myself: keep your head high, don't sweat the small stuff. I told my husband: pick your battles. Not everything's worth fighting over. And hey, there are only so many *ucks to give. If someone's pressing buttons... well, honey badger don't give a *uck.
In all honesty, I'm scared. For us. For the world. For the people who still don't understand. I'm scared this won't go away, and we'll try to act like everything is "back to normal" when it's anything but. Still, I'm a realist. I'll face it head-on. I won't curl up and give up. I hope we all find that kind of strength.
When I was 13, I designed a tattoo. Years later, I had it inked: *There is hope.* That's what I've always believed.
Don't lose that. Hold on to hope. Stay mindful. The rest will fall into place.
This is a moment to rediscover the small joys: the smell of freshly cut grass (and the surprise of finding basil in it), music echoing off the walls, soaking up sun on the rooftop. I see my DJ friends sharing mixes again—keep going, fam.
It's our chance to reconnect, re-center, and bring our best selves to the table.
WE GOT THIS.

April 11, 2020 – Chongqing, China – "Dude, Where's My Towel?"

Part 1: The Continuum

My heart is full of avocados. My mouth hasn't tasted them in weeks. That's how busy I've been. But I'm not complaining—this work matters. I'm proud to have this chance to share something of value with the world.

A doctor on TV says it's not healthy to promote self-mastery or productivity during quarantine. How full of shit is that? Everyone moves at their own speed. Some of us need to pause and grieve. Others need to move, to build, to create. Wherever you are on the continuum, know that you're strong, and you can adapt when you're ready. It helps to know there are other options besides panic.

This weekend, I take a rare step away from the grind and spend the day with Shaolin and her family. Baby Ethan is a blur of energy, so we carry and chase him around all afternoon. In the sun, under my mask, I'm sweating—Chongqing's famous heat is starting to bear down.

We go to the river and take in the sights. I shoot a short video that I later use as a promo for a union conference on COVID-19. Midway through, I get a call from my boss at iChongqing.

"We've set up a press conference," she says.

"Already?" I ask. "But the book isn't even out yet."

"That's okay," she says. "This is just a warm-up."

Later that night, Principal Wang—the new head of the international department—congratulates me. The press conference will be held in the large academic hall. I'm surprised, but I take it in stride. One foot in front of the other. That's how we move forward.

YEAR OF THE RAT

In a rare broadcast, Queen Elizabeth encourages us to picture ourselves in the future, looking back on what we've achieved. She's a time traveler too, it seems—beaming in from 1999 just when we need her.

Meanwhile, Boris Johnson is in the hospital with a persistent buildup of symptoms. The man is sick, in every sense of the word.

And the Revel Alliance? We're nearly 500 strong now. On busy days, I can barely keep up. Hundreds of notifications whirl by, and I either click through them mechanically or trust that the ecosystem will maintain itself while I focus on the real world—on family, food, and flesh-and-blood connections.

I deleted a thread that one person reported, only to spark backlash from another. I imagine this must be what it's like to be an intelligent creator—one who, somewhere between the Dark Ages and the Renaissance, was told by their significant other, "I was all well and good with you creating life, but maybe it's time to strike a balance at home."

Maybe the good ones go mad, too.

Part 2: The Towels of Time

The Top 10 herbs for the lungs, they say, are ginkgo biloba, mullein, licorice, rosemary, eucalyptus, Irish moss, echinacea, slippery elm, hyssop, and coltsfoot.

Two years ago, I discovered Kickstarter—a platform for inventors, entrepreneurs, and creatives to launch their dreams with crowd support. I became a super backer, pledging to over 100 projects in the first six months. I helped birth movies, novels, shoes, pants, dice, headphones, cable cars, and more. These little boxes of inspiration still trickle into my quarantine zone like time capsules. My 'Ultimate Travel Onesie' became my de facto space suit for my sixty days in lockdown.

And then... the towels.

Self-cleaning, fast-drying, Polygiene Stay-Fresh technology—the world's most practical towel, they claimed. I was in. The creator, Chris, was so chill he sometimes vanished for three months between updates. Somewhere along the way, I was banned from Kickstarter for a month after tracking down his family to ask where the hell the towels were, and whether the USD 150,000 we collectively pledged had evaporated into a black hole of bamboo fiber and broken promises.

Is this real life? Or just fantasy?

The first year was fine—sporadic updates, an ETA of 2019. But then we rolled into 2020, and two years for towels started to feel excessive. Even if they were magic. When they finally admitted they'd spent the shipping funds on more towels—and they were now stranded in a Hong Kong warehouse—we began to wonder if we'd ever see them. I contacted FloShip, their fulfillment company. Despite my generous USD 210 contribution, I wasn't even on their list.

Meanwhile, in Ecuador, reports rolled in of bodies burning in the streets. Things were grim. Civilian populations, I thought, need to become astronauts. That's our only shot.

We went for a walk. Picked up some snacks. Shaolin fed Baby Ethan some spicy Xinjiang meat skewers, and he loved it. The sun beat down. It was warm—already summer in Chongqing—and our vitamin D levels soared. We felt good.

If we rewind a century to 1918, everyone was outside in tents. Everyone wore a mask, even a cotton one. Was it the fresh air? The UV light? The wind? Vitamin D? All of it?

But today, when we see hikers and joggers huffing and puffing, we need folks to cover up those moist emissions—as my cousin, Dr. Theresa Wood, superstar poet, physician, and philosopher, reminded her followers. Trudeau's "don't speak moistly" remix? Still gold. Get me a lossless file. I'll give you a drum & bass version that'll make your lungs dance.

Part 3: Hot Water Without a Towel

The Top 10 herbs for the lungs are ginkgo biloba, mullein, licorice, rosemary, eucalyptus, Irish moss, echinacea, slippery elm, hyssop, and coltsfoot.

Two years ago, I discovered Kickstarter—a platform for inventors, entrepreneurs, and creative types to launch and crowdfund their passion projects. I dove in headfirst, becoming a "super backer," supporting over 100 projects in the first half of the year. I helped produce movies, novels, shoes, pants, shorts, shirts, games, dice, headphones, phone cables, and even cable cars. And now, years later, they still float into my quarantine zone like gifts from a past life. My "Ultimate Travel Onesie" became my space suit during 60 days of lockdown. And then, finally, after two long years, I got the call: my "self-cleaning, fast-drying, stay-fresh guaranteed" towel from the Kanso + Polygiene Stay Fresh line had arrived in Chongqing.

Chris, the towel creator, was so "chill" that sometimes he went three months without an update. At one point, I got banned from Kickstarter for a month after I tracked down his family and asked them to tell us backers how he was spending the USD 150,000 we'd given him. Were we ever going to see a towel at the end of all this? Is this real life? Is this just fantasy?

At first, it all looked promising—sporadic updates, optimistic ETAs. But when we passed into 2020, a full year behind schedule, people got testy. Two years to make towels? Even magical ones?

Eventually, they admitted Chris had spent the shipping funds on more towels, and the existing ones were sitting in a warehouse in Hong Kong. After some digging, I contacted his fulfillment team at FloShip and discovered I wasn't even on their delivery list—despite backing the project with $210. Ouch.

Meanwhile, reports out of Ecuador were apocalyptic—burning bodies in the streets. The only way forward, I kept insisting, was for

YEAR OF THE RAT

civilian populations to become astronauts. That was our shot at survival.

We took a walk. Shaolin shared some spicy Xinjiang meat with Baby Ethan, and he loved it. It was sunny, hot already—summer in Chongqing. Our vitamin D batteries topped up. We were okay.

Looking back to 1918, people wore masks and camped outside in tents. Maybe the fresh air, the UV light, the wind helped stop the spread. The century had come full circle, and here we were again, trying to breathe through cloth. And now, when I see joggers panting through parks, I hear Justin Trudeau's immortal words: "Don't speak moistly." A remix of his speech had already dropped and gone viral. Find me a lossless file, and I'll spin a D&B remix: "Ramen."

Let's put a pin in this: hemoglobin attack theory—COVID-19 binding to iron, blocking oxygen absorption. Blood type correlations. Experimental treatments in animal trials. Trudeau warned us we may be living like this for another 18 months. Meanwhile, the U.S. was poised to melt down forever.

All of this, while Ben Ben shuffled around the house wheezing like a chain-smoking grandpa. My poor pup. But he was still hanging in.

And—miracle of miracles—after a hundred emails, Chris from Kanso finally got me back on the list. In the middle of a global pandemic, a towel arrived in Chongqing. Shaolin was unimpressed.

"Chinese towels, made in China, for Chinese prices," she said, raising an eyebrow. "Why would anyone buy a Chinese towel, made in China, sent to Hong Kong, and then mailed back to China, but more expensive?"

She had a point.

China Post agreed. They hit us with a re-importation tax of $150, reasoning that only someone truly insane would pay over 1000 RMB for a couple of towels. However, if those towels were "worth" less than 1000 RMB, the tax would've been about $20. A much better plan.

So I reached out to Chris again. To his credit, he offered me a "discounted" receipt showing the towels were only worth $129. Since technically I hadn't purchased anything—only supported his venture—and technically he hadn't sold anything—just sent me a gift—it was a clever workaround.

Unfortunately, the Chinese postal bureaucracy is more Vogon than human. Try telling them money is imaginary, time is a construct, and these were simply gifted interdimensional towels—and you'll find yourself, as I did, in hot water... without a towel.

Part 4: Press Tour Realities

I wake up early, take care of a few lingering tasks, and teach from 9 to 9:40. It's the first day I'm going back inside the school since January 15, the end of last semester, and now, we're off to the Academic Hall for my first official press conference.

To my surprise, there's my name on a sign, media vehicles parked all around, and an excited buzz from the school staff. I'd pictured four or five local reporters. What I get is a sea of media—over twenty different outlets. Local and national networks, TV crews, newspapers, web journalists, and even government leaders have turned up.

The conference kicks off with a professional host who makes me feel like some kind of rockstar, and I speak at length about exponential growth, the importance of masks, and what we've learned here in Chongqing. Shaolin stands by my side, offering expert translation and support, especially when the questions veer into highly technical territory. Principal Wang and Catherine jump in, too, to highlight the educational and scientific contributions of the project.

I catch a few raised eyebrows in the audience. Some of my school leaders, perhaps unaware of the full scope of what I've been working on, are clearly surprised. "Kai did what now?" I can almost hear them whisper. It reminds me of when I was five years old and the police came to my door to thank me for stopping a robbery. My mom thought they had the wrong house. But I had lobbed water balloons out the window and scared off a cat burglar. Left to my own devices, apparently, I have good devices. And now, decades later, left to my own devices in quarantine, I've written a book.

Part 5: Home Invasions and Noodle Triumphs

After the press conference, a few of the journalists want to follow up. Which is fine, until they show up at our house.

Our house! Full of strangers. Oh, the humanity.

They keep their masks on, thankfully, and don't touch much. We've all been code green for a month, so it's probably okay. But still—it's strange to let the outside world in after months of carefully managed quarantine. The walls feel thinner, like the boundaries we've built are suddenly porous.

Later, when the cameras are gone and the tension fades, we walk to a little noodle shop and eat outside. For the first time in months, we sit in the sun, masks off, slurping noodles like it's just a normal day. It is so not a normal day—but that only makes the moment more precious.

People look over and take photos, recognizing me from the morning broadcast. It's weird. But it's also wonderful. We're trying our best, and somehow, weirdly, it's working.

Even in a world turned upside down, sometimes you still get your towel.

April 12, 2020 – Toronto, Canada – "Meeting a Stranger" (Rhett "The Jett" Morita)

Day 36 of Social Isolation

Okay—unprecedented, uncertain, and unknown "new times" aside—this is a strange new world of social isolation. So much time spent at home with your closest circle of family, a significant other, or maybe just yourself. We've all now met a microscopic "stranger" who introduced itself with a firm handshake that, for some, never lets go. Thanks to its unwelcome arrival, we've been forced to adopt new rules of engagement, new social etiquette, and new ways of relating to the world—and to ourselves.

The biggest shift, perhaps, is the near-total absence of physical social interaction. As social beings, we're used to hugs, handshakes, high-fives, and close conversations. Now, even our most essential in-person encounters must take place within the confines of a cautious two-meter bubble. And only if they're deemed legally essential.

So here we are—spending more time than ever in the company of ourselves. For many, this is the first time they've been separated from friends, family, or even strangers for more than a few hours. Very few of us have ever gone on a silent retreat—no human contact for two weeks, or a month. **WILSON!!!** Yeah, it's like that.

And in this silence, something happens: you start to meet a stranger. That stranger is you.

Like any new encounter, it takes observation, patience, and a touch of compassion. Slowly, the layers start to come off, and maybe—just maybe—you get a glimpse of yourself, raw and unfiltered. It might take a month. It might take a year. For some, it may never happen. But if it does, be gentle. Be curious. And don't look away. This is a version of yourself that everyday life might have hidden from you for years.

I once heard a saying: *Walk a different path home, and you might meet a stranger.* I've come to realize that stranger lives inside.

Lately, I've been dressing in the most bizarre and wonderful ways. I've rocked some long-forgotten black-and-white zebra-print leggings I found while cleaning out a storage bin, thrown gym shorts over thermals, channeled a masked-up post-apocalyptic bike courier, played cowboy with a hat and handkerchief, and styled myself like a silent film star in baggy pants. I've grown out my facial hair longer than ever before, while actively shaving my head again after a long hiatus.

It's wild. It's weird. And I've loved every second of it.

This is the freedom I didn't even know I was missing—the freedom to be myself, without fear of judgment, without the burden of social expectations. It's liberating to dress, act, and exist however feels right in the moment—not what's expected or "professional" or acceptable. Some days it's all black. Others it's sportswear for days. Then, suddenly: flowered shirts and zebra leggings.

This is a once-in-a-lifetime opportunity to discover the you that's been buried under deadlines, button-ups, or business lunches. The you that got lost in hustle and habit. Yes, safety and survival must come first—but amid the fear and chaos, there may also be a chance to meet a stranger. It could be like speed dating. Or it could turn into a lifelong love affair.

Happy meetings.
—Rhett

April 12, 2020 – Antigonish, NS, Canada – "The Sun Is Shining" (Lisa)

The sun is shining. I've opened the kitchen window, and the cats immediately perk up. They know it's the sign that their mother—the caretaker—is awake for the day. For them, that means fresh water, topped-off food bowls, treats, morning snuggles, a clean litter box, and the beginning of their daily routine—and mine.

The apartment is quiet. I sit in the stillness and remind myself to breathe, to prepare for what I'm about to ingest today. And I don't just mean food—I mean the thoughts, the emotions, the reality of a world that's going to get worse before it gets better.

So, I wait a little longer.

I practice gratitude.

Today, I woke up. Millions didn't.

Today, I have food. Some people haven't eaten in weeks.

I have clean water. Some must fight for every drop.

I have a roof over my head. Some sleep in the streets.

My home is safe. I am not stuck—I am safe.

I repeat this until I believe it. For others, their home is not a sanctuary, but a personal hell.

The more I am thankful for, the more I remember.

I am blessed.

I turn on the internet. Once, I welcomed the news each morning. Now, I dread it.

Still, I try to be optimistic. Maybe this will change things.

HEADLINER:

Nova Scotia has 21 new cases, bringing the total to 428 confirmed COVID-19 infections. No media briefings over the Easter weekend, but daily case updates will continue.

It baffles me that our borders weren't completely shut to non-essential travel until just days ago. Now there's clear evidence: it's not just from travelers. We have community spread.

People still aren't taking this seriously. My blood boils. I can hear Premier McNeil and Dr. Strang scolding us like disappointed parents: *You're grounded. Go home and stay there!*

I chuckle at my own sense of humor.

Am I losing it? Have I already lost it?

Breathe, Lisa. You can't control others—only how you react.

Tears fill my eyes. I knew what I was preparing for. Why am I letting this weaken my immune system?

I grab some water and an apple, turn on music, and dance around the apartment.

Raise those vibrations.

I've been alone for 31 days now. Just me, my three cats, and seventy-something houseplants.

I'm thankful for their company. Without them, the loneliness would be unbearable.

My partner is an essential worker. I miss him.

He stays away to keep me safe. I'm immunocompromised.

It's hard—not to hug, not to kiss, not to be touched.

Just like that, your whole world changes.

31 days without human contact.

31 days of silence.

31 days of solitude.

The quiet drowns out my thoughts. Silence can be deafening, but I embrace it—like sunshine on my face, warm and fleeting.

I am okay. I am safe. I choose happiness today.

I have six mashed bananas in the fridge. A friend sent me her secret double chocolate banana loaf recipe and swore me to secrecy. I laugh—her humor is a balm. I'll make one for myself, and one to share. Sharing brings me joy. It seems to do the same for others.

YEAR OF THE RAT

Cat #2 climbs up for his morning snuggles. I greet him with a soft pat on the head.
I haven't been inside a store or any public space in over a month.
And for that, I'm grateful.
The stories I hear from others about what's happening outside make me uneasy.
This *Invisible War* has never felt more real.
I see it through my phone, but I dare not venture into it.
I don't have a mask yet anyway. So, I stay home. My backyard is my world—where I stretch, walk, or sit in stillness.
My cat kneads me—"making biscuits," as we call it. It hurts. Time to shift positions.
My morning routine is complete.
Maybe I'll plant more seedlings.
Maybe I'll just sit outside and listen.
There are signs of spring in the garden beneath my window. Signs of life. They make me hopeful.
Today seems like a good day to enjoy the fresh air.
I pause to admire my plants, my paintings, my cats, my cozy home.
I truly appreciate the little things.
I hope everyone can—especially now.
Maybe tomorrow I'll write again.
Maybe tomorrow we'll have fewer new cases.
Maybe tomorrow holds something beautiful.
Until then, stay safe. I'm rooting for you.
Join us in the Revel Alliance with Jorah Kai, fighting the *Invisible War*.
Stay safe, friends.

April 13, 2020 – Hamilton, Canada – "Lifestyle My Cheese Pie (It's Almost a Quiche)" (Cadence)

It's super, super easy.

- Pie crust (I use premade)
- 2 cups shredded cheese (I went with marbled cheddar and Havarti)
- 3 eggs
- 3/4 cup whole milk
- Salt and pepper to taste

Mix it all together, pour it into the pie crust, and bake at 425°F for about 25 minutes, or until the top is golden and crispy.

It's more cheese and less egg and cream than a traditional quiche, so the texture is a little denser—but I like it that way. It's quick, comforting, and kid-approved.

(From a Canadian Burlesque Hall of Fame legend turned supermom, trust me: it's fabulous.)

April 13, 2020 – Chongqing, China – "Never Trust a Vogon"

Part 1: Bureaucracy, Bagels, and Biodomes
Armed with a receipt from my local print shop—which felt entirely too reasonable to hang out in, even masked up—we jump in a cab and head toward China Post. The driver threads through the government district, past the old Coppola pizza joint where I used to throw lounge events. That place dropped 25 million RMB on decor, including a 1-million RMB Mona Lisa made of felt-covered pushpins. They had great pizza.
Now we're on our way to a meeting with destiny, with RZA in my headphones and Shaolin beside me, radiant with wisdom. We land on the wrong side of the compound, of course, and hoof it for 20 sweaty minutes until we find the right entrance.
I'm thinking about my book cover again. The publisher doesn't want the Mona Lisa in a gas mask. They worry it'll offend the French. "Si vous avez peur d'offenser les Français," I mutter under my breath, "restez au lit." They don't speak French, so I take solace in the full-page Mona Lisa inside the book. Tabernak.
People everywhere are having wild dreams. Quarantine dreams. Cosmic dreams. I've been astral traveling. This weekend, I spent time in President Sanders' New York. I can still taste the bagels.
But closer to home, reality bites. There are five new mystery cases in Chongqing—cases not linked to travel. That means community spread. Again. The authorities are scrambling to trace contacts and lock it down. Shaolin and I are playing it safe, sticking to home. Meanwhile, one of my younger coworkers and his girlfriend are still going out to eat every day, often without masks. We think they're foolish. They think we're paranoid. Time will tell.

I stumble across a study in *Nature Medicine* from scientists at Scripps, Edinburgh, Columbia, Sydney, and Tulane. They've been studying the infamous spike protein on the SARS-CoV-2 virus. Picture a medieval mace with spikes. That's the virus. And it's terrifyingly good at bonding with human cells—too good for even the best biotech labs to have made artificially. It's proof to the science-minded that this virus is natural. Of course, the tinfoil crowd just thinks it means it's from the future.

Meanwhile, George R.R. Martin is in a bunker somewhere finishing *Winds of Winter*. Or maybe writing about towels. Either way, good for him.

Speaking of PPE: why haven't we invented health armor by now? Spray-down decontaminating suits for nurses and doctors? Come on, Ironman was 2008.

Part 2: Strange Dreams and Spiky Truths

People in record numbers are having wild dreams. All that pent-up, cooped-up energy is making the dreamworld weird and vivid. I've always been out there, but lately I've been vibing through the Metaverse like an astral-traveling wizard. This weekend, I swear I spent time in President Sanders' New York. I can still taste the bagels.

Today, there are five new mystery cases of COVID-19 in Chongqing. "Mystery" means local, not imported — community transmission. Despite our best efforts, there are still embers smoldering in the dark. The government is working to trace every restaurant, train, and alleyway. Anyone who crossed paths with these ghost cases will need to get tested, maybe quarantined. Shaolin and I are mostly staying home. Meanwhile, our young American coworker and his girlfriend eat out every day, sometimes maskless. They think we're uptight. We think they're reckless. Time will tell. Time. What a thing.

There's more good news for science lovers — or for the tinfoil hat crowd, who'll probably tune out anyway. A new study in *Nature*

Medicine makes a compelling case: SARS-CoV-2 evolved naturally. Scientists from Scripps, Edinburgh, Columbia, Sydney, and Tulane decoded the virus's spiked protein structure — those medieval mace-like protrusions that help it invade human and feline cells. They look like alien docking hooks. These spike proteins are so precisely evolved that it's hard to imagine any human tech could have engineered them. It's scary news for cat owners. Lock those outdoor kitties up tight.

And yet, even though it wasn't made in a lab, it's so bizarre, you could almost believe it came from the future. Almost.

Part 3: Billionaires, Masks, and Mad Science
Speaking of sci-fi, remember when I asked where all the billionaires went? Where was my invite to the clean island after I posted that photo with the mountain of toilet paper? Well, looks like George R.R. Martin found a mountain fortress somewhere. He's not the only one—but that's a tale for another time. Maybe even another book.

With all the PPE shortages, I'm still wondering why no one's made reusable sci-fi health armor yet. I'm talking crazy cool space suits. Decontamination chambers. Spray-and-go. We should've had Dr. Ironwoman prototypes by now.

I swap some good vibes with a plucky journalist and an old dance-floor comrade turned Canadian government administrator. We've both traded rave lights for bureaucratic battles. She stays calm and patient in public; so do I. But sometimes? Sometimes, I wish I could grab these COVIDIOTS and shake some sense into them.

As of April 11, Canada had repatriated 14,526 citizens on 110 flights from 60 countries. The world is on fire, and still, the dance continues.

Part 4: Press Tour Realities
The next morning, I wake early, groggy and tense, but focused. I handle a bit of business and teach from 9:00 to 9:40, my new pan-

demic rhythm. Then Shaolin and I head off to the Academic Hall. It's the first time I've been back inside the school since January 15, the day the last semester ended.

As we approach, I see my name on a sign. Media vehicles are parked out front. School staff look excited. I'm bracing myself for a quiet little warm-up—maybe four or five strangers in an empty auditorium.

Instead, I walk into a whirlwind.

There's a professional MC. Rows of dignitaries. My school leaders. At least twenty different local and national networks: TV crews, newspapers, online news outlets, livestreamers. Government officials. All gathered for...me?

I blink. Breathe. Walk slowly to the podium. This is not a drill.

I speak at length, trying to walk them through the concept of exponential growth and how every moment of delay costs lives. Shaolin is heroic, translating my technobabble in real time. Catherine and Principal Wang help clarify when needed. It's a dense conversation—my bread and butter—but I'm struck by how surreal this is. Somewhere in the back of the room, I picture one of my school's principals looking up, totally baffled. "Wait—Kai did what now?" It reminds me of being five years old, when the police came to our door to thank me for stopping a robbery. My mom thought it was a mistake until she learned I'd been tossing water balloons at a cat burglar. Left to my own devices, I've apparently now written a book. I guess I have good devices.

Part 5: Home Invasions and Noodle Triumphs

After the press conference, some journalists come to our house—our house. Full of strangers. {oh, the humanity}

They wear masks. They don't touch much. And really, we've all been code green for a month now, so I guess it's fine. But it still feels weird to have people wandering through our space like it's an exhibit. A few years ago, I was just a guy writing stories in a corner of the internet, and now I'm the tour.

After they leave, Shaolin and I go for noodles. We sit outside. We take our masks off.

It's so normal, it's revolutionary.

Sure, people are still snapping photos of me like I'm a sideshow curiosity, but I slurp my noodles and laugh anyway. The sun is warm. Shaolin is smiling. We've made it through another wave of chaos, and somehow we're okay.

I don't know what the future holds, and honestly, I'm too tired to speculate. What I do know is this: I've got towels. I've got noodles. I've got a story. And I've still got Shaolin, for now.

It's weird, but we're doing our best.

And maybe—just maybe—that's enough.

April 13, 2020 – Tokyo, Japan – "Olympics Postponed, But I Hope for the Best" (Ken 2)

Hi everyone,

I'd like to share a little bit about the situation here in Japan.

The Tokyo Olympics have been postponed and are now scheduled to begin in July 2021. It's disappointing, but we understand why it had to happen. I still hope for the best.

Right now, the Japanese government advises people to leave home only for necessities, but we don't have enough masks. That's a big problem.

In Tokyo alone, more than 200 people are testing positive for COVID-19 each day. And many others are getting infected in other prefectures across the country. My information is mostly about what's happening here in Tokyo.

As of today, Japan has reported 7,370 cases of COVID-19, with 123 deaths. There are currently 6,463 active cases, and 129 are considered serious.

Japanese schools are scheduled to reopen on May 7. I really hope it will be safe by then.

Most companies are asking people to work from home, and many are doing their best. Trains and buses are still operating on normal schedules, even though fewer people are riding. They're ready in case of emergencies.

I hope everyone out there is staying safe and healthy.

– Ken 2

April 13, 2020 – Ottawa, Canada – "Woodland Wanderings and Edible Plants" (Corrie Lee Lemoncat)

I wake up at the crack of 10 a.m., as I usually do during this pandemic. I just can't fall asleep before 3 or 4 in the morning. I start the day the same way I have every day for the last month—with a hot cup of coffee and a doobie.

Other than quick supply runs, I barely leave the house. Most of my time is spent outdoors, but in the woods—scouting for wild edible plants and mushrooms, which is one of my greatest passions. My daily routine is a cycle of reading about permaculture and foraging, working on the garden behind our apartment building, checking on our window gardens, creating art, or wandering the forest trails. I'm lucky to have access to nature, thanks to my car and my bike.

In the last month, I've only gone grocery shopping three times, always wearing a mask. I've sewn about 20 of them for my family so we can keep clean ones in rotation. Fortunately, everyone's been really on board with wearing them. We're a very pro-mask, pro-safety household.

A few weeks ago—before COVID really hit here—I slipped on some ice and fell right onto the healing incision from my recent hand surgery. The skin split slightly. It didn't seem serious at first, but unbeknownst to me, a small pocket had formed under the scar tissue where the surgical forceps had gone in. Something must've gotten in during the fall, and despite cleaning the area, I didn't realize it had gotten infected.

At first, I didn't notice anything beyond the usual post-op swelling. But when the inflammation worsened and the pain increased, I set up a video call with my amazing surgeon. He confirmed it was infected and needed to be drained—but also warned it might be tough to get into an ER under the current conditions. With my brother being immunocompromised, going to the hospital felt like a bad idea for both of us.

I told him I felt comfortable handling it myself if needed. While he didn't officially approve, he also didn't tell me not to. So, I steeled myself and used a sterilized scalpel to drain the abscess. It wasn't a big deal—something I'd usually go to a doctor for, sure—but in pandemic times, it felt like the safest choice. I cleaned and dressed the area, and it's been healing well since.

Being a type 1 diabetic, healing takes longer—especially when stress and upheaval mess with my blood sugars. The timing of all this couldn't have been worse, coming right after surgery and the start of the lockdown, but I'm getting back on track.

I'm grateful to be staying with my parents while I heal—especially since it was my dominant hand that needed surgery. If I'd been stuck alone at my place in Hull, Quebec, I don't know what I would've done. The borders are being monitored now, and my car just died. There are no grocery stores near my apartment, so staying here has been a blessing.

I've also been spending less time online for my mental health and more time learning how to become a mushroom farmer—something I've always dreamed of. I built a mini colonizing room in a closet and inoculated a batch of homemade straw logs. It's a full-time project, and honestly, it's doing wonders for me. Way better than endlessly scrolling through news and social media.

—

Editor's Note: As of April 12, Ottawa reported 586 confirmed COVID-19 cases, including 11 deaths and 25 new cases that day. The median age of infection is 48. There are currently 13 outbreaks in institutions. Infection sources: 27% from close contact, 23%

from community spread, 20% travel-related, and 20% pending investigation. – JK

April 13, 2020 – Chongqing, China – "Don't Panic"

Day 81

We're walking outside, enjoying a sunny day, when it happens.

The hairs on the back of my neck tingle. Six teenagers are heading toward us, still 15 meters away. Their masks dangle lazily around their necks. One lifts his face and—sneezes into open air.

Time slows. I can see the trillions of virus particles bursting forth like tracer fire.

PANIC.

Where's my towel?

Ten meters now. Too close. I hold my breath, turn my back, yank my HEPA-filter mask snug, and cover the straw in my strawberry juice—one fluid motion.

Half a second too long? Or just in time? I bark at Shaolin to mask up. She's a few steps behind me, possibly out of the sneeze zone.

The teens, embarrassed, fumble their masks into place. I give them a glare that could sterilize metal.

"Criminals. Terrorists. Sneezing in the open air…" I mutter. Shaolin shakes her head.

"Anger," she says, "is like holding a hot coal and hoping someone else gets burned."

She's right. Doesn't make it easier, though.

At China Post, we've crossed our T's, dotted our I's. Time to retrieve the mystical towels. We pay the import tax, inspect them—wavy, grey, enigmatic. Seem normal. That's the trick, isn't it?

Boxed again, taped up, and off we go.

Police inspect us on the way out. I present papers in quadruplicate. We are immaculate. We are allowed to leave.

YEAR OF THE RAT

Back home in time for some TV and print interviews—China, Canada, the usual circuit. Afterward, I wash the towels with lavender softener and hang them to dry. Magical or not, they deserve pampering.

Meanwhile, a Virginia pastor has died of COVID-19 after holding a packed church service. Who could've seen that coming?

Everyone.

Canada is doing better—sending out checks, basic income, and emergency funds for all. It's the right move. The U.S., meanwhile, is confiscating PPE from blue states and redirecting it to red ones. It's dystopian. It's deliberate. It's evil.

Trump is the perfect storm of malice and incompetence.

So now, state governments are smuggling PPE under the radar like contraband—just to protect front-line workers. What kind of empire is this?

One doctor says, *"COVID-19 punishes our narcissism."* I get that. There are endless think pieces now—on philosophy, psychology, the mythos of the plague—but sometimes, it's simpler than that. This is a lesson in discomfort. In humility. In making peace with uncertainty.

Pearl TV cancels an interview with me—sensitive about a negative Western diary on Wuhan. I offer them my own story as counterbalance. They agree. Good. I'm tired, anyway.

Meanwhile, my publisher wants me to remove the "e" from "Doctore."

"But it's Italian," I protest.

"Are you Italian?"

"No," I say. "But I'm not Danish either, and you're not giving me grief over that."

I may lose patience, but I'm grateful to anyone who tolerates me. Jiggity Jorah Ka-ka-ka-Kai has been a lot lately—teacher, loud voice, pandemic procrastinator. I like that term: *procrastinate the pandemic*. Flatten the curve... eventually.

What happened to me? Part of me died from the fear. What's left is fearless. Reborn.

A plucky novelist versus a novel virus.

Bernie Sanders has bowed out, and while part of me is relieved he doesn't have to shake hands anymore, the other part is gutted. We're officially in the wrong timeline. The Hadron Collider glitched us in 2012. Next time I'm there, I'll try to stop it.

I'll visit Bernie's America in my dreams. I'll bring back what I can. I love you, Uncle Bernie. You are a lighthouse in the darkest night.

South Korea reports that recovered patients are testing positive again. Antibodies seem inconsistent, especially among the young. Some people might be fighting this off without antibodies—T-cells? Cytokines? Macrophages?

We may need multiple vaccines. Herd immunity may be fantasy. Secondary infection is a very real possibility.

One study even suggests reactivation: that the virus may lie dormant, then strike again.

Fauci says they're discussing immunity cards for Americans. Not as elegant as our Chinese "Youkan" app, but still. The West worries more about privacy than saving lives.

You're asking the wrong questions, folks.

Dylan's working with the *3Hands Project*—young, healthy people doing groceries for the vulnerable. I love it. That's what astronauts do. Suit up, save others.

Mental health and long-term care are in crisis. I'm proud I got one CTV interview about mindfulness. It matters.

It's been 100 days since the first reports of the virus. 96,000 dead. 1.6 million infected. Billions locked down.

YEAR OF THE RAT

New York City is burying the unclaimed dead in mass graves. My friend Marley's grandmother might be among them. We cry. We rage. We grieve.
In Ecuador, they burn bodies in the streets. India is welding infected communities shut. Oil reserves will be full in 4–6 weeks. Doug Ford is making more sense than usual. The UK's Boris Johnson is out of ICU. The Finns have hired necromancers: -1 daily deaths.
It's all real. It's all now.
My job keeps the lights on. Shaolin has been amazing. We've closed my second class so I can finish the book. I send back 44 corrections. We go for a walk. It's 30 degrees in April. The first day of summer.
My editor wants to change the title from *The Invisible War* to *The Invisible Danger.*
No. I say no.
Call it something else in China, fine. But the English version is mine, or I'll give it away for free. I win. I'm suspicious, but I win.
I take a shower with my Kanso towel. It's light as air. Still dry. Still magic.
We go out for more sun. I've answered 36 editorial questions and feel good about it.
Near the school gate, two guys in full hazmat suits appear. Shaolin backs up. I snap a photo. We brace for impact—
It's a drill.
As the school prepares to reopen in May, changes are underway: handwashing stations, thermal scans, quarantine plans.
The "safe isolation dorm"?
Yeah. It's our building. The foreign teacher dorm.
Great. I'm going to need a longer mixtape.

April 14, 2020 – Lunenburg, Canada – "Plant More Seeds" (Sasha)

Catapulting through life like the Velveteen Rabbit served me well this year. I've been out of the matrix for a while—radicalized by a laundry list of chronic illness diagnoses and (thanks to two-ish years of bed rest) a lot of time to read. I am a woman, mother, wife, friend, and daughter.

Together with my husband Chris, our two children, two cats, and a fish, we are quite the unit. Our home looks like a small tropical tree and plant nursery.

Moving our family to the middle of nowhere, Nova Scotia, has brought me great peace. We traded home ownership in the HRM for a piece of paradise. We remind ourselves often to check our privilege.

Fast forward to now: day 38 of self-isolation. I woke up this morning with a quiet, creeping sense of dread. Am I desensitizing? Just tired? The numbers on the news aren't shocking anymore. The death toll climbs. Over a million infected—closer to two now. Health workers still don't have enough PPE.

I pour myself a cup of coffee. It smells better than delicious—but it came from the city, a city where, reportedly, some people are following isolation guidelines, and others are not. I wonder what kind of coffee we'll have when our specialty beans run out. I tell myself it doesn't matter. I'm the same woman who once filtered coffee grounds through a sock while camping. I'll survive.

I repeat it to myself: "I'll survive."

Then, like a bullet train from my anxiety brain:

"Will I survive?"

Halfway through my morning medication, Chris emerges from his home office with a stack of printed worksheets—a glorious list of suggested activities from our eight-year-old's teacher. I want to do all of it. I want to win the Mother of All Mothers Award—if only this soul-crushing existential dread and very disabled body would give me an inch to work with.

The smiling face of our youngest gives me Herculean strength (that I'll surely pay for tomorrow), and we dive into the list until it's time for lunch.

We typically follow a dairy-free, gluten-free, low-sugar diet, recommended by our doctor. But that's gone out the window lately; the local grocery stores are slow to restock gluten-free items. Today, the kids get mini pizzas and apple slices. Chris and I have potato, bacon, and leek soup.

The gentle scent of leeks and bacon fills the house. I literally lean into it. From my bar stool by the stove, I'm able to cook for my family. And I'm thankful.

Food insecurity is a major trigger for me. I try not to think too far ahead while making sure our seeds are tucked into their trays, germinating under plastic domes in our indoor greenhouses, waiting for spring.

Don't burn the leeks.

Those were the explicit instructions from the friend who gave me the recipe.

I still don't know why I never thought to sauté leeks in bacon fat before. As the soup simmers, my inner child creeps in again. Will the food supply chain break down?

"All chains are meant to be broken," she tells me.

Food security is in our hands—in our relationship with the land, with animals, with one another. If this soup turns out well, I'll bring a bowl to my neighbor. If not, our chickens will happily take care of it. They are my most loyal fans when it comes to kitchen scraps.

Of course, they also get proper feed and oyster shells from the farmer's co-op, but as free-range chickens, they enjoy a varied diet.

A few days ago, Chris installed a camera inside the chicken coop so JP could check on them more often. Today, he skips across the lawn in full rain gear, humming happily on his way to collect eggs and refill their food and water.

The soup is good. Whew. Thanks, Heather.

After lunch, JP and I drive up to the community mailbox. Usually, we'd find a few neighbors lingering for a friendly chat. But today, it's just us—and I feel relieved.

Still, when I touch the mailbox, my panic response flares. It's like I've stuck my hand in a sharps container. JP squirts a blob of sanitizer onto my hands and the keys.

This is our new normal.

Nova Scotia's chief medical officer recently said the province doesn't have the funding for rapid virus modeling—so we don't yet know how many are predicted to die. Ontario's modeling says to expect between 3,000 and 15,000 deaths. "Morts," Chris and I say, as a soft euphemism for the kids' sake.

Grief hangs heavy in my heart—for the (now over 119,000) lives lost globally, for healthcare workers without PPE, for essential workers who risk so much for so little.

I decide to plant more seeds.

April 14, 2020 – San Diego, USA – "The Bourgeoisie Are Speaking Moistly" (Kait Marcelle)

This week in my corner of the world, $1,000 fines are now being enforced for anyone in public without a mask. Most surrounding counties are following suit. And here, in this moment, is where the two types of people diverge in this pandemic: To mask or not to mask, that is the question.

In the working-class neighborhoods where I live and shop, everyone is masked—somehow, some way. Thankfully, I live just a block away from a major craft store, but the line to get in is always fifty to a hundred people long, waiting to access the 25-person-max occupancy. By late afternoon, an employee is stationed at the back of the line just to turn people away—no time left in the day to serve them. These employees are being worked to the bone. You can see it in their eyes. I want to give them a hug, but what good would that do? If I could afford it, I'd buy them lunch daily.

While waiting for my bulk fabric to be cut, I watched one poor employee juggling ten ringing phone lines. Ten. Nonstop. The entire thirty minutes I waited. "We apologize for any delay," she repeated again and again. "You'll receive an email as soon as we have your order ready for pickup." The sheer volume of times she had to say that is astonishing. You could hear the exhaustion and the apologies from a person who has no control over any of this. Please. Be kind.

In line, there's a strange, gentle camaraderie. As people rush in, find their materials, and begin queuing to leave, the social distance eases by a cautious foot or two. We start talking—about elastic, stitches, patterns. The experienced sewers demonstrate to the newcomers. I'm grateful. The moment felt almost normal—strangers in a craft store, politely talking. Those without masks were there to get supplies to make them. Those with handmade masks were trying to make more, for themselves, for their neighbors, for anyone in need. It was heartbreaking and heartwarming all at once, watching a community come together under pressure.

But driving through the more affluent neighborhoods, I noticed a very different trend. Few masks. Sometimes none. I saw multiple neighbors chatting by their mailboxes, patting each other on the back, standing far too close.

Now, maybe they live in shared households. Maybe they're already co-exposed. Maybe that was their only moment of human contact for the day. I don't know. But it's hard not to notice the pattern: this casual disregard always seems to show up in higher socioeconomic neighborhoods. Correlation doesn't equal causation, I know. But it nags.

Personally, I hope I can endure whatever else is coming, so I can be here for the people I love. I've been relatively unaffected economically. I have low overhead. I have no children. My heart aches for those who have lost jobs, who are barely treading water. Our social safety nets are fraying fast. People have been trying to access unemployment benefits for weeks with no success. What are they supposed to do?

I wish there were something more I could do for them.

April 14, 2020 – New York City, USA – "I Am No Hero, I Am Not Ready to Die" (Anonymous Nurse)

Disclaimer: The words below are my own and reflect only my views and experiences as an ICU nurse. My intention is solely to express my lived experiences throughout this pandemic. I do not speak on behalf of the hospital where I am employed, nor do I intend to misrepresent the experiences of other nurses in the city. I speak only for myself—and I hope others may resonate with my words.

Yesterday, I considered writing a will.

I am 24 years old. I am an ICU nurse in New York City. I am in good health. I should have no reason to be thinking about wills. But yesterday, I had to accept the terrifying truth that my death now feels statistically plausible. Even likely.

When I graduated from nursing school in 2018, this—*this*—was never the future I imagined with barely two years on the job. I thought I was prepared to see death. I had seen plenty in my first year alone. But in the last two weeks, I have watched more people die than most people do in a lifetime. And now, I'm not sure if I'm prepared to see any more.

Because death is different now.

Death could pick me.

Last week, a daughter called to check on her mother. She thought her mother's condition was stable. No one had updated her. Family members aren't allowed inside anymore. The hospital is sealed. So I told her the truth: "If I stop the IV pump right now, your mother will die."

I was blunt. There's no time to sugarcoat anymore.

She broke down, sobbing over the phone. And there I stood, awkward and robotic, clutching a bundle of supplies in my gloved hands—meds, tubes, vials, syringes—ready to enter the room where her mother lay dying.

Every time I walk into a COVID room, I expose myself. So I tell myself: *Anything you forget that forces you to go back in... might kill you.*

As she cried on the phone, I listened. But my mind raced: *Did I bring the right meds? The tubing?* My mask was half on, my sweat beginning to soak the PPE, my humanity fraying at the seams. I wanted to comfort her. I didn't know how.

How do you apologize for not being enough?

They say I'm on the front line. But the truth is—I'm the last line. I'm one of the final faces a patient sees before death.

That's not heroism. That's a burden. A sacred one, but a crushing one.

Outside of this pandemic, the ICU ratio is one nurse to two patients. Now it's three to one. In some hospitals, it's worse. Some days, I'm *lucky* to only have three patients.

Those days break me.

ICU nurses are trained to be precise. We sedate, titrate, medicate, paralyze, intubate. We wash your body, feed you, and care for you when no one else is allowed near. And now, as your body fights for breath and your loved ones can't be here to see you, I hold up the phone so your family can say goodbye. They see your face swollen, lips cracked, feeding tube in your nose, blood on the sheets I haven't had time to change.

I feel like a thief in a sacred moment.

Still, I stand there. Exhausted. Ashamed. Because I am the only link you have left.

Some days, my patients lie in their own stool longer than I want to admit. But what do you do when one patient codes in the next room? When the heart monitor flatlines and I have to choose?

YEAR OF THE RAT

Even when I leave the hospital, I can't escape the plague. It follows me home on the soles of my shoes, on my raw, bleeding hands. It lives in the sirens outside my window. In the texts that say another coworker's parent has died. In the phantom ventilator alarms that echo through my apartment long after my shift ends.

Until now, I never knew silence could be so loud.

I spend my off-days reading everything I can—new studies, drug trials, plasma treatments, cytokine storms. But every day I clock in, I feel underprepared. And every day I clock out, I feel like I failed. Like I could have done more. It is never enough. *I never feel like enough.*

That is why I ask you—please—don't call me a hero.

To me, it feels like a lie.

I don't feel brave. I feel broken.

I am not a martyr. I am not ready to die.

Most days, I run nonstop for twelve hours. If I have time to eat, it's a miracle. If I pee more than once in a shift, I consider it a blessing. But I don't know anymore if I should be thankful for a decent lunch break—or just for the fact that I'm not the one in the ICU bed.

This is not the version of healthcare I signed up for. Yes, I accepted that I might get sick helping others. But I didn't sign up to die because I didn't have a proper hazmat suit. I didn't sign up to wear the same N95 mask for 12 hours straight, praying the virus didn't slip past the frayed elastic or into the creases of my paper gown.

If I die, I want people to know it wasn't fate. It was failure.

America failed its essential workers.

The system is broken. It was always broken.

This pandemic has simply shown us where—and how deeply.

When I was in college, I used to go weeks without calling my parents—immigrant nurses from the Philippines still working in Chicago. I blamed schedules, time zones, exams. But now, I call them almost every night. Because every time I read a chart, I see their names. Their faces. I hear their voices in my dying patients. Or maybe I hear my own.

I am still so young. I want to go home. I want to eat my mom's cooking. I want to see my nephew grow up. I want to fall in love, get married, have kids. I want my parents to spoil their grandkids like they spoiled me.

So please, don't clap for me if all you offer are cheers.

Cheering doesn't change the outcome.

Personal protective equipment does.

Policy does. Universal healthcare does. Basic preparedness does.

If I have any plea left in me, it is this: *Do not forget what this felt like.*

Don't forget what it meant to fear the breath of a stranger.

Don't forget the sound of ambulance sirens in the quiet streets.

Don't forget the empty shelves. The ice trucks. The faceless deaths.

Don't forget us.

This should never happen again.

April 15, 2020 – Toronto, Canada – "Thinking the Unthinkable" (Rhett 'The JETT' Morita)

Weird, strange, stupid, silly, ridiculous, daft, deranged, loco, psycho, impractical, mental, batty, meshuga, haywire, wacko, bonkers, ludicrous, certifiable, cracked, cuckoo, unreasonable, fucked-up, mad, nutty—and my personal favorite: *foolish!*

These are the typical responses when someone presents a radical *new* concept. Something that rocks the boat, shakes the foundation, flips the script, turns the tables. Something revolutionary. Something... *inconceivable!* (Thank you, Wallace Shawn.)

So today, as we slowly—perhaps awkwardly—backpedal into the future, we may find ourselves groping for footing on a never-before-trodden path. A strange new place. Some of us are beginning to think thoughts that feel alien, untested, or even heretical. And the moment we speak them out loud, we're met with scoffs. Eye rolls. Laughter. Resistance.

Imagine you're one of the 0.0001 percent of the population—say, 75,000 people on the planet—entertaining a paradigm shift. Trying to point out the emperor has no clothes. How do you make your voice heard through the roar of the crowd? In America, that's 33,000 people versus 330 million. In Canada, 3,600 versus 36 million. The numbers are stacked against you. And yet... *you might still be right.*

So I say: don't dismiss the unthinkable too quickly. Yes, we must weigh new ideas against the principles of safety, compassion, and science. But we also need to keep space open—space for the weird, the wild, the not-yet-provable.

Consider the history of germ theory. Ideas that were dismissed for *centuries*—by the brightest, most respected minds of the time—turned out to be the very foundations of modern medicine. Avicenna (Ibn Sina) spoke of contagion in the 11th century. Ibn al-Khatib expanded on it in the 14th. Marcus von Plenciz was ignored in 1762. Miasma theory ("bad air") reigned supreme until Pasteur and Koch arrived *hundreds of years later*. Even when vaccines started working, we had no idea *why*.

Same with Alfred Wegener and continental drift. Laughed at in 1912. Taught in elementary school by the 1980s.

The point is: the world changes when someone dares to *think the unthinkable*—and when others are brave enough to listen.

So here's my invitation: think about what this pandemic might be asking of us. What *new alignments* can we create? What *collective dreams* could actually move the needle?

Because I believe the future won't be shaped by solo saviors or lone wolves. It'll be shaped by teams. Tribes. Communities of visionaries. Some will dig with shovels. Others with spoons. Some with massive front-end loaders. All good—as long as we dig *together*.

Now is the time to dream the impossible dream.

Be aware. Be cautious. Give and take care.

—Rhett the JETT Morita

April 15, 2020 – Antigonish, Canada – "Hold On, We Got This" (Lisa)

The windows are open, letting in the scent of damp earth and the chatter of birds.
My fur children take turns making their demands—love, treats, attention. They've got me well-trained, and I don't mind.
They remind me I'm not alone. I have responsibilities.
I need structure—and so do they.
This morning I woke up feeling... weird.
Not *bad*, exactly, just untethered—like I'd lost time, sleep, ambition, and any sense of the clock.
Wait. Is time even real?
Then I read the news. Another punch to the gut: reports of the U.S. government, under Trump, intercepting medical supplies and rerouting them for partisan gain.
It makes me sick—uneasy in a deep, soul-wracking way.
Money, power, and greed are winning again.
Also? I noticed my last diary post didn't go up.
So I poked the big bear—yes, *that* bear: Jorah Kai.
He's busy, of course. Too busy saving the world. ♡
I turn my attention to today's update from Dr. Strang and Premier MacNeil. I brace myself.
I *feel* things are about to get worse.
(I'll be right back after the numbers drop.)
1:05 p.m.
I'm back. Did a little more research. Turned up the music and danced while enjoying a medicinal joint.
And, yes. Just as I suspected. Our numbers are up again—29 new cases, and one more death.
My heart sinks.

It's frustrating to watch our sister provinces, PEI and New Brunswick, doing a better job than we are.

Time to reset. Time to plant seedlings—always my go-to when the anxiety builds.

I'm not just planting for myself. I'm planting for friends, neighbors, anyone in my little circle.

Yes, I'm a seed hoarder. *Give me all your seeds!*

(That's a cry for help *and* a mantra, thank you very much.)

A dear friend just told me her husband is building me a raised garden bed and bringing it next month.

This fills me with such joy—something to look forward to.

I pray I'll still be able to garden in the backyard, like always. It's one of the pillars that helps keep me sober.

A recovering addict in the middle of a pandemic... yeah, it's a test.

People say: "Only go out for essentials."

I agree. But what's *essential* is different for everyone.

For me, things like potting soil, canvas, compostable pots—those *are* essential.

They help me stay grounded. They help me *not* spiral.

And mental health *is* health.

Today, the sky is grey. The air is heavy.

It's the kind of day where it's tempting to sleep until this whole thing is over.

But I won't.

I've got messages to send, seeds to plant, people to check in on, and ideas to scatter like dandelions on the wind.

My thoughts are with my province. With the family of the person we lost today.

We're small here, and every loss cuts deep.

Please—start listening. Take this seriously.

The worst may still be coming.

To those grieving, those who've lost someone and couldn't be with them—my deepest condolences.
To those struggling with dark thoughts: *please hold on.*
You matter. We need you.
You are not alone.
Stay safe. Stay kind. Stay stubbornly hopeful.
We *got* this.
Love,
Lisa

April 16, 2020 – Lunenburg, Canada – "Tough Choices" (Sasha)

Yesterday, my husband, Chris, went to the emergency room (ER). One of the last places anyone wants to be right now is a rural hospital ER. My appreciation goes out to all the staff who somehow work miracles with ancient tools that are crumbling and underfunded.

Have you ever wondered where the weak points in your COVID-19 protocols are? A trip to the ER has to be high on that list. Which helps explain why Chris toughed out septic bursitis over his kneecap for several days. It came out of nowhere—no injury, no warning—and it's never happened to him before. He hoped it would just go away.

Despite barely being able to walk, Chris drove himself to the hospital. The ER doctor told him it was a good thing he came in, then stuck a giant needle into his knee and drained two ounces of fluid. Some of it was sent off for testing. The needle hurt. His knee was a burning balloon. I'm glad I wasn't there to see it. You can't unsee that kind of thing. Still, I wish I could have driven him, held his hand, and looked away when they brought out the big needle.

They hooked him up to an IV and started Cephazolin. He came home with prescriptions for oral antibiotics and anti-inflammatory meds. Thankfully, he wasn't admitted.

He decontaminated, curled up on the couch, and watched reruns of the Masters tournament he's always wanted to see. I was just relieved he was home.

Still, no matter how cautious he is—masked, glasses, hand sanitizer in hand—I worry that trip to the hospital (and any future ones, if it flares up again) might have put our immunocompromised family in danger. But to be clear: *his life was in danger.* It was a tough choice. I think many families are facing these decisions now.

I try not to dwell. I grab a disinfectant and go after every high-touch surface I can find. Fear gives me more energy than usual, and I use it—knowing full well I'll pay for it later. My mitochondrial energy is like an old phone battery. No matter how much I charge or rest, I top out at 2% battery life. I'm still working on the "use it wisely" part.

Chris is doing better today. The pain is less, the swelling's down, and he's moving more. For someone who's usually nonstop, it was scary seeing him so still, so hurt.

It's harder to clean with the kids home from school. The isolation part is easy—we live in the middle of nowhere, Nova Scotia, with a lake in our backyard and loons that just returned this week. Their haunting, beautiful calls feel like the perfect dusk soundtrack to pandemic living.

I'm looking forward to the frogs joining in this year's choir. You wouldn't believe how big the frogs get out here. I've attached a photo of our son JP holding one from last year. If you're going to catch a frog, go big or go home. (And no, I'm not going to eat them. Probably.)

Still, I find myself daydreaming: rotisserie frog thighs, glistening, juicy. That's the food insecurity monster in my mind, whispering. I vow not to eat my favorite green choir, no matter how bad the shortages get. But deep down, I know I'd feed my kids like a mother bird, no remorse. Am I a monster? Depends who you ask. Ask the frogs, cows, pigs, and chickens—and I'm death incarnate.

One love.

–Sasha

April 16, 2020 – Chicago, USA – "Social Distancing—The True Death of Society" (MC ZULU)

It was all a dream...

I used to post pictures to Facebook and bask in the wonderful cyber-acknowledgment we all crave. It was a virtual popularity contest, and my generation hit just the right age to actually care about each other's accomplishments. Technology had finally done something good—linking distant family members and giving former classmates the opportunity to smirk at each other's lack of success. Follow-up questions included: "Who got old? Who went grey? Who got fat?" And when they said, "Wow, you look the same!" they were really saying, "God damn... what happened to you?!" Maybe not. But I digress.

It was called *social networking*, and for a while, it did just that. Until the advent of the "Filter Bubble." Eli Pariser's 2011 TED Talk explained it well: our online experiences were being tailored to give us *more of what we already want*. Algorithms quietly removed the people who challenged us, replacing them with those who agreed. The result? Echo chambers. Closed loops. End users trapped in the infinite mirror of their own opinion.

This is the same condition that leads celebrities to nervous breakdowns—they never hear the word "no." It's the foundation of every corrupt regime. And online? You're always right, as long as you stay on the platform.

We got addicted to "Likes."

Facebook built a virtual skyscraper to house billions, and then walled us off from one another like inmates in a digital prison. That wasn't social networking. That was our first taste of social distancing.

Then came the smartphone revolution. Human interaction shifted from enjoying the moment *with* those around you to capturing the moment *for* those who weren't. Don't believe me? Try talking to someone glued to their screen. You are now socially distanced.

And what followed? Ugly.

Trust eroded. Xenophobia and nationalism were weaponized. Entire regimes toppled, and power vacuums yawned open in unstable regions. No matter your belief—however hateful—you could promote your post and find an audience. Hate-speech chat rooms flourished. Misguided thoughts turned to groupthink. The result? School shootings, terror attacks, suicides, Tide Pod challenges, mass hysteria—and people calling it "community."

Fast forward to 2020. A respiratory virus spreads across the globe. Doctors advise universal "social distancing." But why "social"? I'm a writer. Language matters. "Physical distancing" would have been more accurate. Or "physical spacing." But "social distancing"? That's become *cowardly cringing*. No nod, no eye contact. Just avoidance.

And when you're Black? That flinch hits different.

Yeah, I said it. Hold up while I silence the race card alarm. Yes, there are problems in China. We all saw the videos. But it's not just China. It's everywhere. In Africa, Chinese racism sparked equal backlash. In the U.S., Asians are attacked. In Hong Kong, dissidents are beaten in the streets. In America, Dr. Fauci announces that African Americans are more likely to get COVID-19. Well... take a number. Join heart disease, COPD, hypertension, PTSD, and the rest of the comorbidities we're blamed for.

Social distancing has taught people not to have compassion. I've seen people online brag that they "have no sympathy" for those breaking quarantine—as if everyone lives in comfort, with a pantry full of food and space to isolate. What if you don't? What if you live in a crime-ridden neighborhood, with low wages, no nearby health food, and closed schools and support systems?

Sound familiar? Maybe you didn't think it could happen to you. But now the whole U.S. is in lockdown, and suddenly everyone's experiencing what was once someone else's "normal."

Yes, physical contact is risky. But social connection is *essential*. And we've been losing that for years.

The Filter Bubble was great for advertisers. But it made us little dictators. How many times have you read: "If you believe [x], unfriend me now"? That's not discourse. That's entrenchment. It's critical that we *disagree*, that we challenge each other, and still stay connected. It's what makes us human.

Social distancing should never mean spiritual isolation.

No person is an island.

Let's remember that.

– MC ZULU

April 18, 2020 – PEI, Canada – "Stay Home, Don't Lose Your Head" (Dara Mac)

The 35-foot black spruce stand tall, majestic, stoic—until I scream profanities in horror. Why? Because I'm from Montreal, and that's just what we do.

The Maritime Electric crew did their dirty work. They ignored our agreement and beheaded my beauties. I consider myself a peaceful warrior, but today it wouldn't seem so. The message from our Chief Medical Officer is: *Stay home!* Yes, and enjoy the sounds of screeching chainsaws, the grinding of sacred trees, and trucks belching diesel. Who can even drum with all that racket?

Mindfulness is easier when pleasant things are happening—like watching a live Q&A with one of my favorite jazz drummers in his pajama bottoms, streaming from a tiny NYC apartment. His advice? *Stay home and practice. Focus. Cut the random crap.*

Before each session at the kit, I sit in mindfulness and meditation. Here. Now. With each breath, I release what I cannot control.

"Sit and relax. Close your eyes. Imagine looking at your life with joy, excitement, and anticipation because you don't know what's coming. As you accept whatever comes, your life becomes truly exciting."

—Kenny Werner, *Effortless Mastery*

I have access to several online drumming education groups now. There's no shortage of material. The challenge is always the same—planning, focus, not getting overwhelmed by the sheer volume of what's out there. The best advice I've received? Picture where you want to be in five years, one year, one month, one week... and let that guide what you practice *today*. When I sit at the kit, I don't set a timer. I pick something I want to learn, sit with it, integrate it, and make it mine. That's how you find your own sound—the stuff that makes *you*, you. (Thanks, Aaron Edgar.)

Time for my daily walk. *I am so lucky to live on this beautiful, peaceful island,* I think, as I wander the unpopulated shoreline. Until I stumble upon a headless seal. The eagle circling overhead reminds me: I'm not alone in this pandemic pandemonium.

Heading back, I spot a few people ahead with two dogs off-leash. I wait at a distance, giving them time to leash up or adjust. I think it's safe to pass—until I hear, *"Don't worry! He's friendly!"* Famous last words.

A muddy, drooling mutt barrels toward me. I freeze. A flashback: the Great Dane from Cape Breton, clamping my arm in its jaws, waiting for the order to rip it off. This encounter doesn't go well. Mr. Snowbird, returned to his cottage for the good weather, seems to think social distancing, mask-wearing, and basic courtesy don't apply to him. It's not uncommon for this breed to claim the entire beach, as though it came with the deed. Welcome to Holiday Island.

PEI declared a Public Health State of Emergency on March 16, 2020, when our first travel-related COVID-19 case was confirmed. Strict control measures followed—social distancing, staying home, washing hands, two-week self-isolation for travelers, testing, and contact tracing. Entry to PEI is now limited to essential travel. People are being screened, and some are turned away at the Confederation Bridge. Returning to your cottage? *Not essential.*

So far, 23 of the 26 cases have recovered. No evidence of community transmission. Our collective efforts are working. But we're warned: *We can't slack off now, or all will have been in vain.*

In addition to the Public Health Emergency, PEI has declared a full State of Emergency. What that means? Even tighter border control—not just at the airport and bridge, but beaches and ports. So no boats, no yachts, no private jets from wherever. Maybe no tourism season this year. But you know what? Our government is prioritizing *health* over *money*. That's something. That's *everything*. And it's quite the contrast to our neighbors down south.

This global pandemic is forcing each of us to rethink how we live, how we sit with ourselves, how we relate to others. It's waking us up.

I've always found the hardest part of fasting isn't the hunger—it's eating again. The most difficult part of a silent retreat isn't the silence—it's learning to speak again. And even harder? Hearing others' voices again.

So when this is over, I wonder... *How will we be together again?*

April 19, 2020 – Turin, Italy – "Quarantined Celebrations: Trading PJs for Dresses" (Alessia Martino)

Quarantine life goes on, and while everyone awaits the elusive flattening of the curve, mind-movies of the post-lockdown "return to normal" start to play. But it's hard to picture the future clearly. For now, quarantine *is* the new normal.

Here in Italy, bookshops have just reopened—though not in every region. Each region holds a certain degree of autonomy, so while people in one part of the country can go outside and even get tested, others remain in stricter lockdowns. My own region remains closed, but I did sneak out for a solitary walk by the river, my first since February. I stayed within the 200-meter limit from home. The sun was shining, the grass was green, and the river ran higher than usual—something I don't often get to see, since I'm normally only back here in summer.

I'm an April baby, and this was my first April birthday in Turin since I was 19. I thought about those past birthdays—homemade cupcakes, laughter, friends gathered around a table. This year was different: a quarantined birthday. Bitter, but also sweet. No guests, no parties, and yet—heartfelt birthday messages poured in from around the world. I felt surrounded by love. My family was with me, and we had not one, but *two* cakes: apple pie with chocolate chips, and blueberry cheesecake. I even pampered myself with a South Korean face mask and, for once, swapped my quarantine PJs for a real dress. Happy quarantined birthday to me.

Soon after, Easter arrived. I wasn't ready to let it pass unnoticed. Thankfully, everyone in the family got an Easter egg. Mine? A double-layered dark chocolate Ferrero egg, with a surprise trio of Ferrero treats inside. We played board games and ate lasagna. It was cozy and fun—something simple and special.

A minor injury to my right hand has made some everyday tasks harder. So, I gave myself permission to slow down. I took a week off from my morning work routine and surrendered to the timeless drift of quarantine. I often forget what day it is, though my body clock still nudges me awake between 7 and 8 a.m., and I settle into bed around midnight. I've had some of the best sleep of my life during this lockdown.

And lately, I've started helping my younger sister with her English. Before the pandemic, I worked abroad teaching English, so this has been a welcome way to bond and stay connected to the work I love.

April 20, 2020 – Jeddah, Saudi Arabia – "Supply Chain Issues, and Serenity, Now" (Sarah Rollinson)

And the beat goes on.

How is it that the days are flying by when I'm doing almost nothing at all? We're two-thirds through April, and the start of the month feels like it was yesterday.

It's been especially difficult for me to ground myself in all this. I haven't even been home to my son—or anywhere I truly consider home—since before COVID-19 entered the global conversation. I'm stuck in a surreal space, living through a pandemic not even in a second home, but in a place that still feels foreign. My dreams are always a little strange, but now I wonder if my subconscious even remembers where "home" really is.

Today, we went to Thuwal—a small town about 25 minutes from here—in search of eggs. For some reason, they've become a rare commodity. I always wear my abaya in these smaller towns, and I try to cover up as much as I can. Still, the looks I get fall somewhere between disgust and the kind you'd imagine a sex worker might receive on her first night out. Either way, it's exhausting.

Turns out, they were out of eggs too. A shame—eggs are my go-to breakfast, especially since pork products are illegal here. But it could be worse. Much worse. I could be out of toilet paper. ;)

Honestly though, the disappearing items on the shelves are beginning to unnerve me. I hope it doesn't get any worse.

3 p.m. curfew: all humans now must stay inside for the rest of the day.

The humidity's gotten unbearable over the past few days, so now my rooftop has become my sanctuary. During the day, I sit up there to write and reflect. At night, it becomes my workout space. My

YEAR OF THE RAT

husband managed to haul our treadmill up three flights of stairs last week, and now I finally have a way to work off all the stress-snacking. My pre-pandemic "exercise" was biking... to the grocery store to buy chips. Not exactly peak performance.

But this is different. I *need* the movement. The endorphins. The serotonin. It helps.

So I crank up the treadmill to a brisk pace and gaze out at the sea. I wish I had my Bluetooth headphones so I could vibe to some music, but I settle for my own thoughts. The warm sun, the breeze on my skin, the glittering blue water just a kilometer away—off-limits, but still mine to look at. I feel grateful. I have family, friends, safety. I have what I need.

Each day, I check in with my parents and friends. Sometimes to lift their spirits. Sometimes to lift my own. Staying connected matters—especially now.

I just got a clothing order delivered from a Dubai store. I'm trying to dress a bit more conservatively, knowing I'll be here longer than expected. Still, I couldn't help hacking one sweatshirt's neckline with scissors and carving a little leaf-shaped design into it. It's comfortable enough to wear around the house—and honestly, I'm not too concerned about what anyone else thinks anymore. I like what I like.

Good news: my sewing machine just arrived! All I need now is some fabric, and I can start making things again. It gives me something to look forward to.

Bad news: the grocery store in our compound is temporarily closed due to "government regulations," whatever that means. It's a logistical nightmare. The next nearest store is 25 minutes away, we're only allowed out until 3 p.m., lines are long, and my husband has meetings all day. And I don't drive.

Serenity now.
I miss home.

April 20, 2020 – Chongqing, China – "Krakatoa Erupts"
Part I – The Ash Cloud

Day 88. I am a volcano. Krakatoa is dormant no longer. What was once a mountain—long silent beneath the smelly feet of climbers, ropes, and other bindings—has roared to life, spewing smoke and fire, launching molten rage. I'm hot around the collar. I'm incinerating friends who wander too close. Our chat history is a time capsule, a plaster cast, frozen in ash like the people of Pompeii—mid-breath, mid-word, obliterated.

There's been a tragedy layered atop tragedy in Canada's Maritimes. A man disguised as a police officer went on a rampage in rural Nova Scotia, murdering at least 16 people. My friend on the ground says the body count is now 19 and climbing. It's horrific. My first thought is how terrifying it must be to flee a uniformed killer. My second thought: for rural white communities, this may be the first time they've felt that brand of fear—terror from those in authority. My Black, Indigenous, and Latino friends know it too well. Some of us have been living tragedies for years. Others, for centuries. RIP to the lost. Love to the torn-asunder. Peace to the broken.

I brew strong Italian coffee in my French press. I'm down to my last half kilo of beans, so we order two more. I hope they arrive in time. A surreal story circulates: a German zoo says it may need to feed some animals to others to survive the economic crisis. The seals and penguins alone need huge quantities of fresh fish. "We've listed the animals we'll have to slaughter first," said Neumünster Zoo's Verena Kaspari. Yes, I got that from Fox News—but still, my heart aches. German zoos are asking for €100 million in government aid.

YEAR OF THE RAT

If YouTube comments are any gauge, 10% of listeners think I'm a slave—to positivity, to China, to the CCP—for saying Chongqing did a good job. I guess I'm a slave to nuance. I'm not new to this—Day 88 offers plenty of time for reflection. Myagi, one of the sharpest minds I know, says I have a high adaptability quotient. Maybe. Or maybe I just think things through.

I'm a philosopher, and so I'll sit on your stoa and ask: Are we not all slaves? To ambition, hunger, lust, ego? To the need to be loved or remembered? If so, is death the only freedom? Or is it found in our choices, in our reactions—or better yet, in our pro-actions?

Part II – Signal Fires and Street Songs

I pick up a box of tiny, rock-hard avocados. They might become breakfast in a few days. Hope is delicious.

Shaolin's already back on the subway. She trusts the thermal scanners and contact tracing protocols. I'm more skeptical—especially about crowded, low-ventilation spaces—but it's been a month since Chongqing reported a new local case. In Chongqing, we trust.

Meanwhile, scientists at the Scripps Institute used high-resolution X-ray crystallography to map how the CR3022 antibody binds to the coronavirus spike protein—targeting a hidden site that only reveals itself when the virus shapeshifts to infect a cell. Antibodies are just 10 nanometers wide. One-billionth of a meter. And yet we're fighting for survival on that microscopic battlefield.

Today, I cried on national TV. I'm sorry if that disappoints the warriors. But we were talking about Dash's tribute song to frontline workers. When they asked about Wuhan, Italy, Spain, New York... it all came flooding back. I've felt plugged into something massive lately—cosmic batteries. But all it took was that one listen. The weight of sacrifice and loss, the beauty of defiance and courage—it cracked me open. Art is therapy. Music, medicine.

Dash and I polish our three-pronged release strategy:

1. **Radio:** We pitch to every station from campus to syndicated. Canadian content is gold.
2. **Producers:** Bedroom beatmakers around the world will remix it. Kids bringing sandwiches to their parents while they make something new and necessary.
3. **Street Stories Challenge:** Rappers drop 16 bars about their COVID-19 experience. Agency through expression.

Shaolin sends it to her ex—he's too busy filming his fifth COVID-themed ballad on a "Voice of China"-style show. My former student, however, is all in—eager to shape a beautiful Chinese version. We're tossing spaghetti at the wall. Some of it will stick.

This is busywork. Hard. Thankless. But this time, it's different. I feel the gratitude of my tribe—500+ strong. They listened. They prepared. And now they're leading their families, their friends. Ripples skipping across the world. One Canadian screaming hope and warning from a distant hilltop.

I rest. Regroup. The volcano quiets. I am a mountain again—solid, silent, resolute.

Part III – The Ash Settles

China quietly increased its official COVID death toll by 50%, now at 4,632. Many still say it's low, but perhaps it reflects more of the truth—deaths outside hospitals, hidden losses. Wuhan has reopened, but the people there will carry fear for years.

In 2008, the roadrunner looked down and realized the economy had already crashed. Somehow, the music played on for 12 more years... until this virus stopped it cold.

The Fed is printing trillions to buy junk bonds, rescuing billionaires while tossing crumbs to everyone else. These trillions? They'll be paid back by us. A tragedy within a tragedy. Sharpen your pitchforks. Dust off your guillotines.

If we're lucky, the rebooted economy will move from empty promissory notes to tangible assets and bartering. You can't hold 1/100th of a gold coin in your hand. But land? Food? Seeds? That's real wealth.

A friend gave me a metaphor. Imagine the world's leaders pub-hopping. China enters first, trips, spills half its beer, and quickly dances to cover the mistake. The others—Italy, Spain, France, UK, the US—follow. They all trip. Then, flat on their backs, they yell at China for not warning them. It's absurd.

Next week, I return to school. Masked kids, me in a gas mask, air purifier humming by my feet. None of us feel ready. Chongqing is calm, but whispers of new cases from Russia and possible lockdowns in Wuhan keep us on edge.

A McDonald's in Guangzhou made headlines: "No Black people allowed." The company shut the store and apologized. Still, it laid bare a current of xenophobia and fear. China, like many places, is looking outward for blame. But fear turned to hate never helps.

YEAR OF THE RAT

I'm being recognized more now. On the street. In fruit shops. "That foreigner guy. The writer." It's weird, but it's fine. The work is more important than my ego.

A new friend tells me: research is more useful than marketing. She tells me to watch the *One World* concert. "You know Coldplay, right?" Shaolin loves Coldplay. Ironically, I don't know Coldplay—but Chris Martin once called me out on Facebook and had Jacky Murda—legendary drum & bass producer, label boss of Chopstick Dubplates, my old dubplate partner—tripping out. Back in the '90s, I used to drive from Ottawa to Montreal, cut plates with Jacky, then headline a rave for 3,000 wild kids. Funny how the world spins.

I've been sleeping again. Spending time with Shaolin and the RZA. Recharging. Finding center.

The NIH says a vaccine will take 12–18 months to develop. But now, a new mutation found in an Indian sample may weaken the virus's binding ability—and possibly render vaccines ineffective. "This raises the alarm," the study says. If more mutations follow, our efforts may be in vain.

China feels normal again. Some people aren't even wearing masks. But Foxconn still screens workers daily. So we remain cautious. The death toll worldwide is 2.5 million cases, 165,000 dead—and those are just the ones we know. The poorest countries haven't even begun counting. That doesn't mean they're safe.

Stay sharp. Stay safe. Stay kind.

The mountain breathes.

April 20, 2020 – Cagayan de Oro, Philippines – "I Pray for the Front Line" (Cindy)

I wake up at 6 a.m. in Cagayan de Oro—CDO for short—a highly urbanized city and the capital of Misamis Oriental. First things first, I'm hungry for some strong coffee. After that, with clear eyes, I make breakfast for the family: eggs, sausages, dried fish, and fried rice. I love to cook for them, especially now that I have the time. When I'm working, I don't usually get to do this.

I drink a lot of water, not juice, to stay hydrated. Every morning feels so quiet—nothing like before the lockdown, when the house was buzzing with everyone getting ready for work and school. That first hour of silence is my favorite. It's the only time I get to sit with myself, think, and plan how to be productive. And, of course, figure out what to cook next.

Today, I decide to go out for groceries. I make sure to pack my mask, alcohol, and hand sanitizer. I grab my shopping bags and list and head out. It's strange. No friends, no one to walk with, and you have to follow social distancing rules with everyone. It's a big change for me.

Here in the Philippines, you can only go out if you have a quarantine pass—one person per family, just to buy food or medicine. I believe that's a big help in stopping the virus and lowering the infection rate.

Walking through the streets into the city feels surreal. My once-busy home has become a ghost town. People wear masks, but you rarely see anyone in full protective gear or with eye protection. Most of it just isn't available here, and a lot of people can't afford it. But I'm glad to see people staying calm and not panicking.

At the grocery store, there's a long line. Security guards check temperatures before anyone is allowed in, so the wait feels endless. I'm grateful to have a mask on—but not everyone else does. Panic buying and hoarding are not allowed, so you're only allowed to buy limited amounts of food. For example, only two loaves of bread per person. Prices are rising, too, which is hard for many people. I hope the government will do something about that soon. A lot of people are really suffering.

Later, I come home, put away the groceries, and rest before dinner. I feel sad and bored. Sad, because I can't work. My flights and appointments have all been canceled. I've been trying to find online work, but it's not easy.

I'm a model and makeup artist. My whole industry is on pause. Many of us have no income right now and are depending on friends and family to get by. There's little to no help from the government. It's stressful. It's hard not just here, but all over the world.

I hope I'll be able to travel this summer, but I know I have to wait for the go-ahead. It's better to be patient and make sure everything is truly okay before anyone starts traveling again. That's the only way we can stop the virus from coming back.

I really hope we find a vaccine soon—but I know it's not that simple. In the meantime, the best thing we can do is **pray for the front line workers**, follow social distancing rules, and **stay at home**. Don't spread the disease. Enjoy the time with your loved ones. That's what I try to do.

April 20, 2020 – Antigonish, Canada – "I Hope You Smile" (Lisa)

Happy 4/20 to those of you who indulged in the green medicine. I'm awake. The sun is shining. There's a strange calm in the apartment today. I didn't sleep well—tossed and turned, even though I fell asleep early.

Today is a day of mourning—and for some, of celebration. I can't figure out which one I belong to. Maybe I'll just sit still and listen. There's a sadness in me today that isn't mine. And I can't seem to shake it.

I'm Lisa. I'm 31, soon to be 32. I'm from the middle of the woods—between two cornfields, rivers on all sides. And today, I wish I were there. Anywhere but inside my own head. Anywhere but this town. There are too many people. I need the critters and the chainsaws.

Yesterday was a sad day for us in Nova Scotia. I cried for the victims—and for the shooter. I mourned the lost lives, and yes, I grieved for his too.

How much isolation and trauma can one person take before they snap?

I'm not defending him. But I'm not condemning him either. I didn't know him. I don't know what he'd been through, or what made him snap. It's not my place to judge. We're all capable of darkness. It's how we carry it that matters. Unfortunately, he didn't carry it well. And now lives are lost and families are broken.

Let's change the subject.

Good news? I woke up. I have food, a roof over my head. My fur kids are happy (they stole my bed before I could make it). I have a fiancé who loves me and stays away to keep me safe as an essential worker. It sucks being apart, but he does it for me.

I have friends, family, and community that keep me grounded. I'm more blessed than most.

For the first time in 37 days, I went into a store. It felt like the twilight zone.

I wore my mask. Pockets stuffed with sanitizer and wipes. I walked in, didn't touch anything I didn't need. Followed the arrows on the floor. I felt like a kid again. Hopscotch. Floor is lava. The air is poison. People are the virus.

Just breathe, Lisa, I whispered to myself, again and again.

My friend helped keep me safe—loaded everything from the cart to the cash herself, placed the bags down for me. I just paid. I'm so thankful for her. She doesn't have anyone to do errands for her. She doesn't get to watch the chaos from a phone like I do.

I see her, and I see the world differently now.

Then—I scratched my eye.

One little itch. Instant fear. My stomach dropped. What had I done?

I rushed outside, slathered sanitizer on my eyelid. Felt so stupid. That's why I don't go out. I was so prepared, and one tiny mistake could've gotten me infected. Next time? I'll stay home.

Some good news—I've gotten orders for paintings. That's exciting. It keeps my hands and mind busy. That's what I need. Idle hands and an overactive mind aren't good for a recovering addict during a pandemic.

Lying on the couch, proofreading what I wrote—it sounds like ramblings. Maybe that's what this is. I'm definitely not myself these days. But the only constant in life is change.

Today, I will enjoy the sun streaming through the window.

Today, I will smudge and keep everyone in my intentions.

Today, I will appreciate people and moments.

Today, I will be the tree. I'll sway, but I won't break.

Today, I hope you smile.

I hope you love.
I hope you turn the music up and dance.
I hope you create something beautiful in these trying times.
And most of all, I hope you aren't too hard on yourself.
It's okay to not be okay.
If you need me, I'm here. Reach out. I'll always listen.
Yesterday, alongside the mass shooting, we lost two more souls. That brings the Nova Scotia COVID-19 death toll to nine—five from the nursing home. We have 675 confirmed cases and 200 recoveries.
In Canada, the numbers are 35,056 infected, 11,843 recovered, 1,587 deaths.
Worldwide, 2,416,135 confirmed cases. 632,983 recovered. 165,939 deaths.
So if you're going to mourn, pray, smudge, set intentions, or celebrate—keep those numbers in mind. Think of the people and their families.
We are all one. This affects us all.
Please stay kind. Stay humble. Stay patient.
We're all struggling. We all need understanding.
This isn't over yet. But we *will* get through it.
This is *The Invisible War*.
—Lisa

April 21, 2020 – Toronto, Canada – "I Champion the Slow" (Rhett "The JETT" Morita)

Day 45 of Isolation

"Does anyone remember that classic line from *Top Gun*—'I feel the need... the need for speed!'?" That pretty much sums up the mantra of modern technology and the hyper-capitalist world behind it. The faster you release new tech, the more you can earn. Speed equals dominance.

I saw it firsthand. From 2006 to 2008, I worked on Nokia's international video production team, flying all over North America to shoot promos. In April 2007, I was invited to their annual conference in Helsinki, Finland. It was a big deal—135 top executives and lead researchers gathered to celebrate Nokia overtaking Motorola as the world's top phone company. They were on top of the world. The vibe? Triumphant. The president grinned ear to ear, practically radiating pride. The entire event was one long back-pat about crushing Motorola. Sony Ericsson was barely mentioned, and Apple? Not even on the radar. They weren't making phones yet.

Five months later, Apple announced the iPhone. Within two years, Nokia had lost everything. That's how fast the world turns. Even for tech giants, evolution waits for no one. They never saw it coming. And I lost one of my best gigs.

That kind of obsession with speed isn't limited to the tech world—it's embedded in the medical and scientific communities, too. First to publish gets the credit, the funding, the fame. Speed is rewarded. Competition is the norm. Nobody gets a medal for coming in seventh, right?

It starts early. Medical students are trained to move fast, recall faster, and always be ahead of the pack. Who wants a doctor who finishes last? Who speaks slowly? Who fumbles the names of bones? We're conditioned to equate speed with competence. The world tells us: time is money.

But now, in this moment—this global pandemic—millions of lives hang in the balance. The race for a vaccine, for a treatment, is on. And I say: let's pause. Let's reward the slow, the steady, the careful. Let's not rush into half-baked science or panic-fueled politics. Let the researchers cross-check, peer-review, and verify. This isn't a sprint. It's not about beating the competition. It's about saving the world.

I stand with the slow.

This isn't just about doctors and scientists, either. Every one of us has a role to play, regardless of race, background, class, or education. Whether you're sewing masks, delivering food, socially distancing, or just staying home and keeping spirits up—you matter.

Yes, the frontliners are in the trenches. But behind them, the careful thinkers are building the scaffolding for what's next. It might take 18 months. Maybe two years. But change is coming. We've entered a new domain. The world after this will look as different as Nokia did two years after the iPhone.

And we all need to be ready.

I know I'm not the fastest. I'm a slow adopter. I learn gradually. But I prepare. I start early. I train behind the scenes for years. And when the time comes—bam—I'm ready. Like a ninja. Silent. Swift. Decades of quiet discipline beneath the surface. That's my way.

So yeah—I champion the slow.

—Rhett "The JETT" Morita

Toronto, Canada

April 23, 2020 – Buenos Aires, Argentina – "On the Inside Looking Out" (Josette)

I don't know what day it is anymore. The body is starting to feel the repercussions of a cooped-up mind—a cooped-up being. My system is all out of sync: nightmares, racing thoughts, irregular sleep, demotivation, and bursts of mania.

After this, I think all zoos should be shut down. Every animal set free.

It's incredible, when you stop to think about it, how many things we used to take for granted: a walk down the street, waiting in line, taking a bus, visiting someone, going... anywhere. What I wouldn't give for a hug.

The New Fashion Trend

Welcome to 2020, where the latest fashion statement is how funky your mask is.

As an asthmatic, going outside is now a completely stressful, anxiety-ridden ordeal. It didn't used to be this bad. We have several small neighborhood supermarkets within a two-block radius of my apartment—normally a blessing. But not anymore. Let me explain. In Buenos Aires, the city made face masks mandatory the moment you step outside your door. Honestly, I was relieved—before that, too many people, especially the elderly, were walking around unmasked. I started wearing a mask even before quarantine began, more to protect others from me. People used to stare. Now, they copy me.

Despite the mandate, maybe one out of every ten people still refuses to wear a mask. They say things like, "The police won't catch me," or "I'm not going far," or "Nothing's going to happen to me." The worst part? The ones who *are* masked seem to think that's enough—so they'll stand right beside you, breathing down your neck in line, as if the mask grants permission to forget social distancing. One guy even lowered his mask to smoke beside me.

No Social Distancing Here

As someone with a respiratory condition, let me be clear: the masks alone aren't enough.

In one narrow-aisled market, an older man brushed past me instead of walking the long way around. I called him out—"Excuse me, you cut in line, and you're too close"—but it was already too late. If he had anything, I'd already been exposed. He then tried to smooth things over by asking if the flour he was holding was good for making pizza. Really? That's your follow-up?

In another shop, I was picking out veggies when a woman stood *directly* behind me. I turned and said, "Could you please back up? I'm asthmatic." She immediately understood and stepped away. I appreciated that. But why do I have to announce my medical history just to get personal space? Should I wear a sign around my neck? You never know who has a condition. Just keep your distance.

It's fall now, and this is the time of year I usually get sick—bronchitis or something like it. That makes me even more cautious.

Two days ago, I ran out of food. But I'm too afraid to go out. Delivery? That's a whole story in itself—we'll save it for later.

Heroes and Hypocrites

Every night at 9 p.m., we clap from our balconies for health workers. It's beautiful. But some of those same neighbors are leaving notes on the doors of doctors, telling them not to come home. One woman who contracted the virus had her car torched by her neighbors. They didn't want her living in their building. This is what fear does.

Remember when crowds of elderly people broke quarantine to line up at the banks for their pensions? No masks. No distancing. Now the virus is sweeping through nursing homes. In one residence, 19 people tested positive just yesterday. This was predictable. The government should have seen it coming.

And now? Non-violent prisoners are being sent home under house arrest to prevent prison outbreaks. In other prisons, where nothing has been done, protests are erupting. If COVID gets into the prison system, it'll be catastrophic.

Economics and Uncertainty

Argentina's economy has always been unstable. And now? Inflation is out of control. The black-market "blue dollar" is back, trading at a huge gap from the official rate. Merchants can charge whatever they want. At least rent increases have been frozen for now.

Every country has its pros and cons, its heroes and hypocrites. It's heartening to see new medical centers being prepared, stockpiled with supplies for the peak. It's encouraging that no one's rushing to end the quarantine early. People's health matters here. But this pandemic has also revealed people's true colors—both good and bad.

One of my friends is doing volunteer work, buying groceries for the elderly and calling to check in. I can't imagine being truly alone through this. I'm alone, yes—but I have my cat.

I hope people start taking this seriously. I hope they stay home and protect themselves. If not, this will drag on indefinitely.

Are you waving at the future? I am.

—Josette, Buenos Aires

April 24, 2020 – Chicago, USA – "Where Ya Going, Honey? FK YOU!! That's Where" (MC ZULU)

Because by now, you've had your fill. You're utterly fed up—not to mention sick and tired—of the person(s) you're quarantined with. Doesn't matter that you'd move mountains for these people. Right now, you'd settle for moving a mountain in between you and them. Picture it: a family of lions in the Sahara. One lion always wakes up starving and devours the entire food supply. Another stays in pajamas all day and barely speaks. A third takes hours to get dressed (to go nowhere) and locks everyone out of the bathroom. Now trap this pride of beasts in one cage and call it "sheltering in place." That's reality TV gold.

But here's the point: Lions weren't meant to be caged. They're made to roam—to join the rat race, grab overpriced lattes, flex on Instagram, and conquer distant lands one filtered selfie at a time. This is no way for a lion to live. Lions need space... or they will lose their minds.

So here's MC ZULU's advice on clearing space—especially in a global pandemic.

Start in the mind.

Any human experience begins upstairs. You might've been born into chaos, but the ending? That's more likely shaped by what you dared to dream. People escape poverty, launch empires, write their way out of pain. You can survive quarantine. No, scratch that—you *must* survive quarantine.

And more than that, you need to emerge better. This isn't a vacation. Some folks have to work *twice* as hard just to keep their heads above water. For them, positivity might feel irrational. That's okay. Irrational hope is powerful. Speak your future into being. Rewrite the code. Tell yourself you're rich, healthy, grounded—even when it feels like a lie. That's how change begins.

Then, clear physical space.
If you haven't touched something in six months, send it to another realm. This is no longer your cage. It's your *universe*. Clear the clutter. Only an empty vessel can be filled. Your current vessel is full of yesterday's traps—designed to support a reality that no longer exists.

Some of that clutter? Might be people. Be bold. Release the wrong ones. Affirm: *I am drawn only to what benefits me, and I enhance the lives of those I meet.* It's not about selfishness. It's about usefulness. We've evolved past hoarding. Now it's about *need*—not *want*.

And with that mindset, prosperity is no longer greed.
You're not chasing success to outdo the neighbors. You're moving from your spiritual center. Suddenly, trends don't matter. The mob doesn't matter. You live for *you*.

Oh—and unless it's business? Stop *lending* money. Give what you can afford to lose. Not to look noble, but to *clear space*. That one dollar you cling to, miser-like? It might block blessings worth thousands.

Here in Illinois, Goodwill is still accepting donations. Yes, they're for-profit. Yes, the Salvation Army has religious baggage. Choose whatever feels right to you—but make the choice. Clear the space.

—MC ZULU

April 25, 2020 – Montreal, Canada – "I'll Keep It Up Until My Fabric Runs Out" (Harriote Lampe)

My name is Harriote Lampe, and I live in Montreal, Quebec. I'm a proud Inuit woman, 30 years old. I spent my childhood in northern Labrador, moved to Nova Scotia as a teen, did some traveling, and now I've been living and working as a cook in Montreal for six years.

It's typical springtime Canada—sunshine to freezing rain, hail, snow, sunshine again every half hour. A lovely time to quarantine.

Mornings start with one of our three cats meowing bloody murder. Then come the obligatory kitty snuggles until my roommate wakes up. We make coffee, roll a joint, and Skype with a few friends to share news, joyful memes, video game goals, or the occasional "Today on Jess's Cooking Show!" Around lunchtime, we sign off and each make something to eat. Having a roommate helps—makes the food feel more worth it. I've had no trouble getting groceries lately. Early March was rough—eggs, rice, pasta, sauce, and toilet paper were scarce—but now the only real stress is the lineups.

Our grocery store is inside a small mall, and there's almost always a huge queue. Thankfully, in Quebec we have dépanneurs everywhere—convenience stores that sell everything from wine to frozen veggies. We call ours "The Big Dep." It's run by a sweet little family, never a lineup. We do almost all our shopping there now. Only downside: no pierogies. Luckily, we've got a 'rogi hookup—a friend who manages another store gives us next-day delivery.

I'd been working and saving for years, so when the restaurant closed its dining room back in March, it didn't hit too hard. Three of our bosses had just returned from Italy, so they quarantined and shut down operations. Our last dinner service felt momentous. Joe Beef and other big names closed right after. A couple weeks later, we learned the reopening would be delayed indefinitely. That shook me. Numbers were rising fast. It got real.

Echoes of the Spanish flu and how it devastated my ancestors in Labrador haunted me. Misinformation was spreading, fear was rising, and resources were thin—especially for Indigenous communities. Friends said they felt sick and needed testing. Others worried about rent or talked about rent strikes. For three weeks, it felt like no one knew what to do. Then the government started offering benefits.

That part was frustrating too. I'd already applied for EI before the national lockdown, but only for the two weeks they initially told us. Then they extended it—but how do you *extend* EI? I called 80 times a day for a week, trying to reach someone. I kept hitting weird errors online. Finally, I found a workaround. Boom—access granted! I inspected every tab. Filed my report. Signed up for CERB. Two days later, my friends and I were screaming on Skype: "The government works! The government works!" We ordered groceries and smoked a fatty.

A couple of our Skype crew are immunocompromised. My roommate and I help by delivering groceries or running laundry since laundromats aren't always an option. I'd been thinking about making masks, but didn't start until I came across some cute kitty-cat fabric: 100% quilter's cotton. A little spark lit up in my brain, and I couldn't ignore it. I struggled with the first few masks, trying to overcomplicate the design. Eventually I found a no-sew pattern in a Facebook group that was perfect—just cut, fold, and insert a filter. I got to work.

As a cook, I thrive on efficiency. Once I got the flow down, I was making 40 a day. Then another 40. I used my boyfriend's foodsaver to seal each one in its own clean pouch. My roommate posted on our local Facebook group, *Solidarité Hogan*, and we hung the masks outside on our fence. Anyone could grab what they needed without contact.

People asked if we could mail some. We brought others to our favorite Big Dep for customers. The owners told us people were grateful. We got messages, gifts, masked selfies. It felt good. It felt right. So I kept going.

Today, I punched out another 45 masks sitting on my floor. My back ached, my knees were stiff, but I was proud.

I'll keep it up until my fabric runs out.

April 25, 2020 – San Diego, USA – "Letting Go of Bad Habits, Holding Onto Hope" (Kait Marcelle)

This week has been rough. Despite having all the tools, I still manage to be failing at several things at once. Two steps forward and one step back is still progress, I remind myself.

Over the weekend, people in nearby beach towns took to the streets to protest public health measures. At first, it seemed absurd—really, we've only been home for a little over a month. Surely staying home a bit longer will save more lives than it harms, right? But even I, a proud homebody, have started to feel the ache to socialize, to see people again.

At first, most people around here seemed to accept the lockdown measures, but as time went on, cracks began to show. When you can't access social safety nets because the systems are overloaded, fear takes hold. Some of my friends have been waiting six weeks just to hear if they'll get any financial assistance. I don't blame anyone for feeling afraid, angry, or desperate to return to work in the face of losing everything. But still—I don't think we should end social distancing measures anytime soon. Try again next year.

Letting Go of Smoke

In the meantime, I've been rearranging my priorities. I quit smoking this month, and I'm now rounding out my fourth week as a non-smoker. It was a terrible habit—something I reached for at every sign of stress. But COVID made it real. I found myself chain-smoking more than ever, terrified of what the virus could do to already-compromised lungs. So I started to prepare—downloading self-help books, talking to friends who had quit, researching techniques—and finally, I took the plunge.

I quit smoking for myself this time, not out of guilt or fear for someone else. Not even when my dad was diagnosed with lung cancer could I bring myself to stop. But this time was different. I already had a smoker's cough, after starting at 14. I imagined myself needing a ventilator... and maybe taking one from someone healthier. That haunted me.

So I quit. It's one of the few things I feel good about this month.

Weddings and What-Ifs

I never imagined I'd be planning a wedding in the middle of a global pandemic. Even though the date is still months away, I'm already fielding questions, trying to make plans amid chaos. But everything feels trivial now. All I want is for my loved ones to make it through this. Forget the dress and decorations—I just want to marry the person I've loved for over half my life.

What breaks my heart is knowing that if I end up in the hospital, my fiancé has no legal right to see me. That alone has changed everything. I used to dream of a big, dramatic wedding, but now... I'd be fine with a drive-through Vegas wedding officiated by Elvis. He does love Elvis, after all.

Tiny Seeds, Real Hope

We've been growing veggies from seed and scraps. It's a small thing, but it helps. My mom, a government worker, plugs away in her favorite sweatshirt at the kitchen table, doing what she can. We're all doing what we can.

These days, survival isn't just about staying safe. It's about shedding what no longer serves us and holding tight to what truly matters. For me, that's letting go of cigarettes, and holding onto my health, my relationship, and hope for a better tomorrow.

April 26, 2020 – Turin, Italy – "Every Day Can Be an Adventure, Even in Quarantine" (Alessia Martino)

Every day can be an adventure, even in quarantine—especially now, when the time we always said we "never had" is suddenly ours to take.

Midweek, I decided it was time to declutter—not just physically, but mentally too. A radical reorganization of space. I opened every drawer and box to see what I could do without. I thought I knew what I'd find, more or less. I was wrong. A simple cleaning task quickly turned into a voyage of rediscovery.

The best surprise was hiding in plain sight: my old passport. I'd thought it lost, but there it was, undisturbed. I started traveling through its pages. Time folded in on itself as I wandered across borders—ten years younger in the United States, then Australia, the UK, Cyprus, Greece, the Czech Republic, and beyond.

I miss traveling. I can't wait to start again. But even now, I find I'm grateful for the pause. I don't know what travel will look like in the future. I only know that every step I took, every memory made, is mine to keep. Pandemic or not, those experiences live on.

(Editor's note: Alessia is a time traveler too!)

My quarantine adventures now play out on screen—TV shows, movies, worlds beyond mine. It was finally the right time to catch up. I even started the Marvel Cinematic Universe marathon in chronological order. I think I've watched eight films in the past week. Action is good medicine.

Life remains enjoyable, but there's one thing I miss more than anything: the taste of variety. I'm not used to eating food from the same flavor spectrum every day. I love Italian food—deeply—but even that has its limits. Before the pandemic, I'd made a habit of eating food from different countries. Each bite was a portal. Each spice a passport. Now, I miss the flavors of the East. The supermarket near me doesn't offer many international ingredients. Thankfully, my brother found non-instant noodles to help satisfy my craving for fried noodles. I'm hunting for the rest of the ingredients to make the sauce—an adventure in its own right.

Italy plans to begin easing the lockdown on May 4th—phase two of reopening. It's a relief. But truthfully, I'm not sure I'm ready to leave my safe abode. So far, I've only had to wear my mask once, during a socially distanced meeting. But when the other person took off their mask midway, I lost a bit of faith in public precautions.

When I got home, I washed everything—mask, glasses, face, outer clothing, hands. I do my part. But sometimes, it doesn't feel like enough unless everyone else does theirs too.

April 26, 2020 – Prince Edward Island, Canada – "Love and Forgiveness" (Dara Mac)

The sun is setting on this quiet little rural Atlantic Canadian community. Like a hush falling over the land, neighbors are packing things up, calling it a day. Everything feels so calm, so peaceful—yet I find myself anxious and close to tears. My heart aches. At any moment, a gunman could appear in a fake uniform, in a fake police car, and do us all in—then laugh, and move on to the next quiet road, the next peaceful, loving home and community. So what makes us any different?

Just one week ago, a few neighbors here decided to have a party. Was that their first mistake? Hosting a gathering during a pandemic, when social distancing was still the rule? Or was it inviting the wrong people—neighbors prone to arguing and causing scenes? Either way, they couldn't have predicted what happened next. They didn't deserve that untimely, tragic end.

I started out the week with a promise to myself: to stay positive, to laugh more, and to do a little personal experiment. I've learned that the brain is like an engine—it carries out the orders it receives from the body and mind. So, if I laugh, if I smile, my brain will release chemicals and hormones that support joy. But the same goes for imagined fear: if I focus on worst-case scenarios, my brain responds as if it's real. That's anxiety. That's how panic attacks start.

As a therapist, I remind myself: those fearful thoughts are not real. We are safe. Everything will be okay. It's just anxiety talking.

A gunman killed 22 people in 13 hours across rural Nova Scotia. Twenty-two more have died of COVID-19. But that horror is not happening *right now*. There have been no new cases of COVID-19 on PEI in ten days. On May 1, social distancing restrictions may begin to lift. Maybe I'll be able to make music with my friend again, share a pizza with her and her mom, and walk my best doggie friend, Taz.

I've only been to Charlottetown once since this all began. I miss it. I miss walks on the boardwalk, having tea with a friend, going to the gym, sipping a Guinness on jazz night at Baba's.

Yet these horrid events have brought me closer to those I love and cherish—including my two beautiful cats, both rescued from cruelty and violence in their early years. It's hard to imagine how anyone could hold so much anger and hatred that they'd shoot a tiny pet, a creature that loves so unconditionally.

And yet, from all I've read, the victims of the Nova Scotia shooting were remarkable people—zestful, selfless, compassionate, community-minded. Two of them had posted music to the Ultimate Nova Scotia Online Kitchen Party shortly before their untimely deaths.

I lived and worked in rural Nova Scotia for many years. The places attacked were all familiar to me. Shubenacadie—Shubbie, to the Mi'kmaq—once housed a residential school that burned down in 1986. My friend, Pi'Kun Poulette, a musician and survivor of that school, recorded a song called *Forgiveness*—a path through trauma and horror, toward healing.

"They tried to break my spirit, I wouldn't let them see me cry.
They held my head underwater until I almost died.
I can still hear screaming deep inside of me
For the sins of the residential school in Shubenacadie."
"To find love, I had to forgive.
With forgiveness, I found love again."

In this time of trauma, our Mi'kmaq friends—who have known centuries of grief—offer Sacred Fires and Healing Dances. They remind us that *love and forgiveness* are the way of the Creator. That healing is possible.

Be safe, my friends.

Find your breath.
Open your heart.
Smile.
Know you are not alone.

Correction: The fishing season on PEI begins May 15, 2020, not June 1, as previously reported.

April 26, 2020 – Chongqing, China – "Haters, Jean-Claude Van Damme, and a Guru for The New Normal"

Day 94.
Part I – Fear Is a Virus Too
A Chinese businessman on YouTube calls Kenyans in Nairobi and their leader "monkey people." He beams into the camera like he just won a dare. His restaurant is shut down for enforcing a "no Blacks after 5 p.m." policy, but the damage is done. A Canadian oil worker wants to kick First Nations protestors off "his" land. An American president floats injecting bleach into lungs while protestors wave Confederate flags, screaming at doctors.

Are Chinese racist? Canadians? Americans? I think... we're all afraid. And fear, as I've said before, is a motherfucker.

This fear is everywhere. It's in the air, on the news, in the streets. The same fear that makes us point fingers, blame each other, and feed misinformation like it's a new form of currency. And somehow, it all gets twisted—China gets blamed, then turns around and blames foreigners. Fear rebounds and refracts like light through a cracked prism.

It's exhausting. It's dangerous. And it's not helping.

I want to shout: Love is greater than fear.

But some days, even I struggle to believe it.

Part II – I'm Not a Guru—Jean-Claude Van Damme Just Thinks I Am

So, I try to help. I write, I speak, I do what I can. I warn my friends. I publish a book. I give away the audiobook. I cry on live television talking about frontline heroes.

And what do I get for it?

A friend tells me: "Just because you've been quarantined the longest, done a thousand hours of research, and warned everyone first doesn't make you a guru, okay?"
Okay. I'm not a guru.
But then I get an email 10 minutes later. I'm booked to speak at the Canadian COVID-19 Sustainability Conference. And headlining alongside me? Jean-Claude Van Damme. Childhood hero. And the Lion Whisperer. Is it possible that JCVD thinks I'm a guru? Honestly, that might be enough for me.
I'm not trying to be anyone's savior. I'm just trying to help people understand what's going on. I never claimed to be an expert—just someone who pays attention. But the backlash? It's real. People lash out because they're afraid. And I get it. I've been there.
But the difference is—I didn't stay there.
Part III – KUMITE! (Or, How I Outran Spicy BBQ and Global Collapse)
Let me tell you about last night.
We made Korean BBQ. It was glorious. Thirty minutes into our walk, my stomach turned into a lava pit. Public bathrooms? COVID traps. I had two choices: risk a fatal virus or shit my pants. I chose... KUMITE.
Benben and I sprinted through the streets of Chongqing, my belly roaring like a demon. I saw JCVD's Bloodsport montage flash before my eyes. I was blinded. Drenched in sweat. I leapt over cracks in the pavement. Dodged coughing toddlers. Made it to the gate. Two stairs at a time. Threw off my shoes, folded them neatly (Shaolin would frown otherwise), and—glory of glories—I made it.
The bathroom. The bidet. Salvation.
Was it COVID? Probably not. But it's 2020, and diarrhea is one of the symptoms, so now I have to wonder.

We wash the dogs. I cook dinner. I field questions from friends across the globe: "Is it safe to go to the clinic?" "Should I be scared?" "What else can I do?"

Stay home. Wear your mask. Be kind. That's what you can do.

Now, I prepare for my return to the classroom. Gas mask or N95? No air conditioning—just neck fans, open windows, and cautious optimism.

I still fight the system—Chinese bureaucracy, Western ignorance, the global news cycle—but I also remember to stop. To walk. To love. To laugh. To buy Shaolin a flower. To sit in the sun.

We are not just surviving this. We are transforming.

And maybe, just maybe, we're all gurus now—teaching through our actions, through our presence, through the simple act of showing up for others.

Ask yourself: What class are you teaching today?

Ramen. ◈

April 28, 2020 – Twente, Netherlands – "Krom Laughs from His Mountain" (Camilo Sons of Leonard)

None of us truly expected the land to fall under quarantine. It came swift as a northern wind, chilling the bones and emptying the streets. For weeks, I could smell the fear hanging heavy in the supermarket aisles, ripe and sour. As a humble follower of Krom, I sought to pretty that stench with my noble dawdling. I foraged with honor, lingering from item to item so as not to further disturb my fellow noodly citizens. We all knew the smell—it was panic, baked fresh daily.

The elderly roared across the streets like beasts reborn, their scooters screeching, their spirits undaunted by the invisible enemy. It was beautiful. Here in the Netherlands, masks are rare—understandable, yet still strange to see. Shops shuttered like frightened turtles until just last week, when some dared to open again. It's life as usual, only the shops were closed and the streets stretched wide and hollow as a bard's empty coin purse.

On sunny days, the Dutch take to their bicycles, singing birds in the trees, children in tow. It's picturesque—like a fever dream with stroopwafels. Meanwhile, the youth leap, roll, and somersault through parks and sidewalks, turning quarantine into a light cardio adventure.

Any barbarian living long enough in this kingdom would grow soft from their kindness. Even the Prime Minister, Rutte, did his best, though he couldn't provide enough masks for the healers. Other parties, like Baudet's crew, ventured into the northern wastes to bring back quality mask treasure hoards. Strange, testosterone-drained men speak in riddles now, maneuvering their way into power as the herd stumbles blindly after them.

Krom laughs from his mountain.

Elder care continued, virus be damned. I quit my job voluntarily—what warrior wants to be responsible for the death of another man's granny or pop-pop? But the virus stayed distant, like a legend, told often but never seen.

The sun grew stronger. The people crept outside. Rules declared no groups larger than two, and all must keep the sacred 1.5-meter distance, lest the wrath of the municipal watch descend. Schools will soon open their gates again, but all great gatherings and feasts are canceled until September. After the 20th of May, most businesses shall return to life—reborn under strict sanitary codes.

Of all the hardships faced, the greatest crisis was the brief weed drought. Coffeeshops closed, and stoners wept. For two long weeks, the land was dry, and the people restless.

I pray vaccines remain optional. I hope 5G does not deplete our precious air supply. The rumors of adrenochrome-addicted Hollywood fiends and high-level sex trafficking swirl like dark clouds over the Internet peaks. It's like that old Korgoth the Barbarian pilot—arthritic wizards, twisted science, the fall of empires.

Who knew it was prophecy?

Thank Krom there are still opposing forces. Go now—spread the word, draw your sword, and do something useful for the sake of humanity, if you dare believe you know better.

April 29, 2020 – Chongqing, China – "Lifestyle Easy Bake Peanut Butter Banana Bread with Oreo Ice Cream"

You will need:

- 3 ripe bananas
- 1 cup of sugar
- A heap of patience
- 1.5 cups of flour
- Thick skin (because it's 2020)
- 1 tsp baking soda
- 1 tsp salt
- A mask for when you go outside
- A handful of ground nuts
- 1/3 cup melted butter (unsalted or salted, your choice)
- The ability to share good science for 100 days without being stopped by skeptics
- 1 large egg, beaten
- A healthy dose of belief in science
- One large scoop of peanut butter
- Optional: 1 tsp vanilla extract
- Empathy and kindness to survive

Method:

1. Preheat your oven to 350°F (175°C) and lightly grease a 9×5 inch loaf pan. Trust your experts on this one.
2. In a large bowl, combine the flour, baking soda, and salt. Don't scoff at academics.
3. In a separate bowl, cream together butter and brown

sugar. Reopening society without mandatory mask legislation is a disaster waiting to happen—so bake with purpose.
4. Mix in the beaten egg, mashed bananas, and peanut butter (and vanilla, if you're feeling fancy).
5. Bake in the preheated oven for 60-65 minutes, or until a toothpick inserted into the center comes out clean. Trust what works—masks in public prevent the spread of infection, just ask China, South Korea, the Czech Republic, Morocco, and Germany.
6. Once done, let it cool, and top it with a dollop of Oreo ice cream for a cool, delicious treat.

Stay home, stay kind, and enjoy the bread.

April 29, 2020 – New York City, USA – "Be Grateful for Your Breath" (Kevin)

Day 97.
You're going to hear, "We're trending down," or "It's easing up."
You're going to start thinking it's okay to relax a little.
You're going to listen to the news you trust—the one you think tells it like it is—and think it's either overblown (it's not), that the malaria drug is a miracle cure (it really, really isn't), or that we're in Armageddon (we are not).
Truth: This virus is with us for a while.
Truth: It will come in waves.
Truth: Life will not be what it was two months ago, not for a long time.
Even mild COVID-19 means mild pneumonia.
All those posts about how bored you are, how hard homeschooling is, or how much you're working out... they're tough to see when you're in the room with what I've seen.
My patient today, a teacher four years younger than me, is steps away from being unable to breathe on their own. Every kind of oxygen support is in play, short of a vent. They said, "Kevin, I'm so scared. Can you stay here with me for a little bit?"
They would *love* to be teaching your kids.
Another patient—a nurse, fit as a fiddle, who three weeks ago was training for a marathon—looked at me today and said, "I... I... I'm having... I want to catch... my... breath."
I sat beside them and we closed our eyes. We visualized next year's race: the sun on their face, the strength of their breath carrying them forward.
They'd *love* to be working out like you.

Then there's the patient who got sick the same day I did. They can't get up to use the bathroom without their vitals crashing. I placed a bedpan under them. Just wiping themselves leaves them drenched in sweat and totally drained.

They told me, "I'm so hot, sweaty, and uncomfortable. I don't know how to get comfortable."

I asked if I could cool them with a bed bath.

They said, "Aren't you worried about catching this?"

I said, "I've had it. It was bad. I was hot and sweaty, short of breath, and scared too."

I sat with them, and I wasn't scared. I was there.

The common thread is breath.

Be grateful for yours.

I'm lucky—lucky to have some immunity, lucky to stay in the room, to comfort patients, to ease their fear, to touch them without fear.

So remember this the next time you're bored at home.

The next time you're tempted to go out.

The next time you take a deep breath without even thinking about it.

Right now, many people are wondering if they'll make it through the night.

They're not worried about a curve or a press conference or the latest rumor.

They're worried about surviving.

Wash your hands.

Be grateful.

Stay the fuck home.

YEAR OF THE RAT 169

Transformational Fair Use Claim

This speech by Jean-Claude Van Damme, delivered at the COVID-19 Response & Recover Virtual Conference, is included here as part of *The Invisible War* to provide historical context and insight into the global dialogue during the early days of the COVID-19 pandemic. Both Jean-Claude Van Damme and the author, Jorah Kai, were invited as headlining guests, with Jorah Kai being billed as a 'COVID guru' alongside JCVD and other prominent figures. The inclusion of this speech, presented in its entirety, serves as a critical component of documenting this unique moment in history.

While the speech is transcribed verbatim, it is also analyzed within the broader thematic framework of the memoir, which reflects on the pandemic's impact on global society, nature, and human behavior. This work transforms the original public address by offering a reflective narrative that ties the speech's themes of ecological responsibility, human interconnectedness, and philosophical reflection into the ongoing global discourse around COVID-19. The inclusion of this speech serves an educational, documentary, and historical purpose, contributing to a broader understanding of the pandemic's cultural and emotional effects.

April 30, 2020 – Los Angeles, USA – "Respect Nature, Respect Ourselves (The Yin and the Yang)" (Jean-Claude Van Damme)

Backstage at the COVID-19 Respond & Recover Virtual Conference & Expo
Day 99

Jorah Kai finishes his speech, arms pumped in the air as the digital crowd erupts into applause. He stands tall for a moment, basking in the virtual cheers, a sense of accomplishment settling over him.

"Remember, folks—Vitamin D!" Kai calls out, his voice firm yet light. "Get your sunlight and vitamins in every day—4,000 international units at least, and you'll be much stronger. I promise you that."

He smiles wide, his hands still raised in the air. "Thank you, that's my time. Good night..."

The crowd erupts, their digital avatars clapping, sending bursts of virtual energy his way. Kai pumps his fists, the rush of adrenaline still surging in his veins. He takes it all in for a moment before turning and ducking back into the holographic green room, the flickering virtual walls shifting around him.

Kai grabs a bottle of water from the table, chugging it down in one go, the cool liquid refreshing his parched throat. His pulse slows, but the energy of the event lingers, the glowing digital space humming with a quiet, electric buzz.

Across the room, Jean-Claude Van Damme is sitting on a glowing virtual sofa, his posture calm, almost meditative, as he holds a tablet in his hands, reading through the holographic notes for his upcoming speech. He's dressed simply, wearing a form-fitting, black athletic jacket—lightly textured with subtle geometric patterns—and loose-fitting jogger pants that offer comfort yet still maintain a sense of sleekness. His feet are in low-top sneakers, casual but functional for the virtual stage. The low lighting of the green room casts gentle shadows over his chiseled features, his expression focused as he reads.

He looks up, catching Kai's gaze through the flickering virtual atmosphere. Without a word, a mutual recognition passes between them. There's an understanding that they're both about to speak to the world in their own unique ways. With a small, knowing nod, JCVD places the tablet down on the side table, his eyes meeting Kai's once more, ready to take the virtual stage.

"Go kick some butt, JC," Kai says, flashing a grin.

"That's what I do," Jean-Claude responds, his voice gravelly yet warm, the playful grin he offers for a moment bringing back the boyishness of Frank Dux in *Bloodsport*, his eyes twinkling with the same fiery spirit that made him a global action star.

JCVD steps into the spotlight, and I follow closely, lingering at the door of the virtual green room to listen in. His posture is calm but resolute, his eyes scanning the crowd of avatars that have gathered to hear his words. His presence, even through pixels, radiates strength and peace. It's like his aura is larger than the virtual space itself.

"I would like to say hello to everybody with lots of love," he begins, his voice carrying a soft, yet powerful resonance. "From my mouth and my heart to you all. Some people ask me a question about this virus... what it will bring and stuff like that. I don't want to make a joke about it, but the only answers I can give are the following: What happens is supposed to happen."

The crowd buzzes for a moment, and JCVD holds their gaze, watching their avatars fall silent under his steady stare. Then, with a knowing pause, he continues.

"It's a disaster on one side of – I would say – the metaphor of the yin and the yang. I'd say right now, we are in the yin, it's a kind of disaster, it's sad. And on the yang side, if I can find somehow, somewhere, to forget some pain, or to appease something..."

He smiles, looking up as if his thoughts drift to another place. The holographic image flickers for a second, blurring before resolving back into focus. For a moment, JCVD is somewhere else, deep in thought.

"I see blue skies around the world. I see animals, females, mammals, in the waters, having been stressed, having a newborn in the water, knowing that she will not be harmed, being imperiled. Lots of animals are now free and have less stress in exchange for that very bad virus who is stopping us from going forward."

Kai exhales slowly, aligning his breath with the pace of JCVD's words.

"But at the same time, it looks like some sort of mathematical balance, that I cannot explain, but we're all aware deep inside ourselves that we did go a little too far, and what's happening is a result of being organically there. Forgive my English... while it's there for that, and that's why I'm thinking that virus is kind of happening the way it was supposed to happen. I love people, I love children, I love animals. But when I see them and the way we treat them, not all of us, more people love animals than people don't like animals..."

There are a lot of good people in the world, I think, loving people, but why do we have this bizarre disconnect in the West between animals and meat? We love this one, we kill that one, but we don't want to see the dirty business. In China, when I have to go to a supermarket and point at a chicken and they kill him in front of me – it's surreal, but someone, I feel, it's honest, it doesn't coddle my sensibilities.

I lose myself in thought for a moment, but he's continuing, and I have to race to catch up.

YEAR OF THE RAT

"Why don't we have the capacity to do something without hurting them? And maybe nature, including that painful virus, will get us to talk to our bodies and leave us (and them) alone."

"That's why I'm thinking like a child, that picture is brighter. But at least, it feels good that you ask me that question. Because for years, I've been suffering, like many children, an emotional, sensitive guy like me..."

Yeah, I say, and clap, then feel foolish and stop. I'm a sensitive guy, too.

He looks at me for a moment, and I gulp. My eyes say, "Sorry JC!"

"...about the killing and eating of species that we don't need to touch. Even though in China, they're having a very, very, very hard time, they're eating the seam of a tree as tea." (What? I think? Does he mean tea leaves? Maybe, yeah... but doesn't everyone drink tea?)

"Let's not forget pop culture. I love America. I became *Bloodsport* because of that. I love China. I shot *Bloodsport* with American money and Israeli producers in Hong Kong. So I love all countries. All I'm saying is take care of the environment. Respect it, and nature will help us heal this disease."

"Thank you. I love you all. I'm sorry about my emotions. Thank you. I am Jean-Claude Van Damme."

The crowd cheers, avatars flooding the virtual space with applause. The virtual stage lights flicker and dim as the applause fades. I wander off to the side, caught in my thoughts. The coffee tastes like air.

Speaking at the COVID-19 Respond & Recover Virtual Conference & Expo, April 30/May 1, 2020

Note: This entry is transcribed from Jean-Claude Van Damme's public keynote speech at the COVID-19 Response & Recover Conference, which he headlined alongside Jorah Kai. The words here are used under Fair Use (17 U.S. Code § 107) for documentary and educational purposes, with respect and gratitude for his contribution to the global pandemic dialogue.

May 1, 2020 – Buenos Aires, Argentina – "There Is a Before and an After" (Josette)

There are several things on my mind this week – as usual, never a dull moment in this cranium.

Psychological distress.

I am becoming concerned at the number of people in my circle who are expressing evidence of psychological distress – feeling down, depressed, moody, angry, anxiety-ridden, having insomnia.

I, as an unlicensed psychologist, am torn sometimes with how to help them. I do make sure I listen and empathize – probably the best and most important way to be there for others without dictating what they should do or feel or tell them – anything, really. It's not the time to be "telling."

Current studies are showing that changes in daily routines, sleeping patterns, and eating patterns, as well as the stress that being in a pandemic has caused, are contributing to a worsening of chronic health conditions, mental health conditions, fear and worry, and increased consumption of tobacco, alcohol, or other drugs. Different risk groups and age groups will also experience these feelings and situations in different ways: children, elderly, parents, health care workers... all these diverse populations of people have their own set of worries and concerns. The task would be to help manage the specific stress for each of these different populations. What everyone is experiencing is particular to that person as well as that group – no one has written the book on this, so, in a way, we can be excused from many behaviors that perhaps in a "normal" situation (what is normal?) may not be ideal.

My cognitive training would tell you to write down your thoughts and look at the truthfulness in said thoughts. Are they true or not? And if they are not truthful, is it helping you to think that way?

I wanted to go outside, but this looked extremely suspicious (ha! A little bit of humor)

I often say to people that no one can tell you how or how not to feel during this time because not one person alive today has experienced it before (unless they have found the source of immortality). It is not the time to feel ashamed, disappointed, or any other type of negative emotion toward oneself; think, "Oh, I was supposed to do this today, and I didn't" kind of mentality. It is not time for self-punishment. Taking care of your mental health during this time requires, in my opinion, giving as much place to negative thoughts and feelings as positive ones, or accepting that you don't want to do anything, accepting that you want to eat junk food, accepting that you want to cry, accepting that you're in a bad mood, etc. Accept how you feel in that moment rather than suppressing it.

- Take breaks from watching, reading, or listening to news about the pandemic
- Do breathing exercises, stretch, meditate
- Try to get some sunlight each day
- Exercise
- Sleep well and regularly
- Eat healthy, well-balanced meals
- Connect with people
- Try to divide up your day
- Try to divide up your week – the week is the week and the weekend is the weekend

I do believe that it is particularly important to make sure your week is still defined as a week, and your weekend still defined as a weekend. Doing activities on the weekend that you wouldn't do during the week will help to give you a break from the new routine that you have established for yourself.

Boxing at home

The latest here lately has been what to do about the prison population in Argentina – the most talked-about prison being one that is a few neighborhoods over from where I live. As I mentioned in my last post, the prisoners were causing riots, which has been resulting in a clash with both those who manage the prison and the politicians behind it.

It really is rather a controversial issue – do you keep them locked up to serve their time but with a high risk of contracting the virus – or what do you do? I suppose that if the government had anticipated this issue (much like they did with the elderly covering their pensions *sarcasm*), there would have been facilities set up to account for social distancing or some protective measures in place to prevent this virus from sweeping through this population.

Conspiracy theorists would argue that the prison population is one of the populations that are not useful to society – that the virus was designed to take out those populations who are "a drain on society" and not useful (quoting a girl I know).

However, I believe that everyone should have a chance to live – in whatever way that may be. And it is too bad that the government did not anticipate this issue. So, what happened?

1900 prisoners in prison not far from my apartment were "released under house arrest"...

"Well, that's not so bad," you may think.

So, what do you think about a man who was locked up for sexually assaulting a young girl and is now under house arrest next door to her?

The news has been filled with the police having to recapture these criminals because, despite demanding that they be put under house arrest, so they don't succumb to the virus, have gone out, and contributed to recidivism – robbing, stealing, creating mischief. Quite a few have also, upon release, gone after their significant others. I really wish law enforcement didn't have to deal with this on top of everything else they have going on these days – that WE have going on.

I'd like to mention that during these 6 weeks of quarantine (we have 2 more weeks now), there have been over 30 femicides.

#niunamenos

(*ni una menos* means "not one woman less" – and is the slogan for violence against women)

sigh It's a double-edged sword. Someone is going to suffer no matter which way the pendulum swings.

There is a before and an after...

What that after may be, no one knows. But the road to it is not paved with gold. A pandemic with a resulting epidemic in crime? I hope not.

But we can hold on – even when we feel like letting go. Just remember why you are here and those that love you – you have to be safe and healthy, and if you can't do it for yourself, do it for them.

Josette

May 1, 2020 – Antigonish, Canada – "Hold Your Broken Back Together" (Lisa)

Broken? Let's talk broken...
My heart, it's broken, my shell it's very much so broken as I lay here and listen to the constant pumping of fluids and medicine going through my veins and the never-ending sound of the IV pump, trying to save my broken shell.
I'm tired, not just the normal tired either.
I'm talking about my soul, always fighting with my body and mind for peace.
I've been in this hospital for almost a week.
It's been a blur.
In the last two days, I've been healthy enough to be coherent and move around a little more.
Which I am grateful for, it was pretty scary for a while.
I am grateful for getting better, but as I get better, the more impatient I get to get answers, to go home...
Patience has never been one of my strongest virtues when it comes to myself and medical issues.
Hospitals make me uneasy. I've spent most of my life in them and avoid them at all costs. Especially in the time of a pandemic.
I am confined to this unit, (keep telling myself I'm safe).
My Covid test was negative, but we still don't know why I'm so dehydrated, why my creatinine level is so high and why any of this started?
Why can't I just be patient?
Why can't I accept that I am here, I am safe, I am COVID-free, and these nurses are trying to help me?

YEAR OF THE RAT

Maybe it's from the years of trauma and isolation I spent in The IWK Children's Hospital from 12 until 18 years of age.
I don't know any of these answers, or maybe I do.
All I am being asked to do is sit in a hospital bed and get hydrated, take my medicine, and do the daily routine.
Somehow at age 14, I found myself getting dialysis training, as to take that responsibility away from my parents and give them a break.
To become more independent and knowledgeable.
By 15, I was hooking up my own machine, hooking myself up to my own machine, etc.
Now 32 in 3 days, grown-ass woman, sitting in a hospital bed crying like a child because she wants to go home and is sad.
Grow up, Lisa, this isn't anything new, it's life, and you're lucky you're still here, and you've overcome so much.
This is what I tell myself, and I know it's true, but today I want to cry.
Today I am vulnerable, today I am tired of it all. I just want this kidney to be okay.
I've watched the virus from behind the comfort of my phone screen in my own home since it has started.
I kept telling people that it's better than being stuck in the hospital during it.
Boy, was I right.
When I got into the hospital, I could barely keep my head up.
I suffered for 3 days before I ever gave in to my own stubbornness and asked my fiancé's sister to wake him.
He came and got me. The look on his face was wearisome and scared. I thought this may be the last time we see one another.
I tell him I love him and to look after himself and our cats. Whatever happens, they will need you.
It was quite sad and maybe overdramatic but as is life.

The rest of the night was a blur, I got seen, they admitted me. The next day they sent me to a ward, and now for the last two days, I am starting to get back to myself.

There have been many questions as to why I got sick, why my kidney function went down, and still what is causing some of my problems.

I think the doctors are just as hopeful as I am, that it was viral, and now it is passing, and I am on the mend.

It's like a twilight zone in the hospital.

You're not allowed to go anywhere off the unit, you can't go outside to get fresh air. The nurses and doctors look scared and uncomfortable and yet still try to ease their patients' troubled minds, bodies, and hearts.

I've grown even more fond of how they are presenting themselves with their masks, gowns, tired and scared eyes, and over-washed hands.

As I lay in my bed with no mask, getting waited on hand and foot. How selfish of me to shed tears for myself.

These heroes in their uniforms, masks, gloves, have to go home after this.

They have to worry if one of their patients like "me" has given them something that they could take back to their families.

I will put my big girl persona on now. I've cried enough.

It will all be okay.

We will all be okay.

I haven't watched the news in almost a week.

I couldn't tell you if the numbers have climbed, stayed the same, or any of that.

Maybe it's a good thing I haven't. It was starting to take a toll on me.

I am hoping Nova Scotians have heard Dr. Strang and the HONORABLE Premier Stephen MacNeil's plea and have stayed the blazes home since I've been stuck inside the battlefield walls.

I am ready to go home now.

I am ready to put this behind me but never let it slip my mind as it can all be taken away so fast.

I will wait for my doctor to come to my room and bring me the good news.

I hope you all rest.

I hope you all find peace.

I hope you all find a little something to hold your broken back together.

-Lisa

Postscript:
After Lisa's last journal, she got fed up with COVID restrictions and masking rules and decided to cut ties with the Revel Alliance and live her best life without the worry of COVID-19. Living in a fairly low-density area, she is thriving, happy, and enjoying her life.

May 2, 2020 – Toronto, Canada – "20/20 Vision (Leave No Trace)" (Rhett Morita)

These three words are part of the protocol or code of conduct for Burning Man: *Leave No Trace*. They represent a respectful and aware sentiment towards the value and sanctity of this finite planet that we all share, graced by the wealth of her vast bounty.

In these times, 'Leaving no trace' could easily describe my day-to-day process, as I'm continually cleaning surfaces with disinfectant wipes. I have become like a seasoned criminal, either wearing gloves (which I still disinfect after touching things, with wipes or hand sanitizer), and I'm always removing my fingerprints. I jokingly say that if a detective were to check my premises for fingerprints, they would come up empty-handed or "fingered."

It would be like I was a ghost or invisible. Funny enough, I often think about how I can look like the classic invisible man when wearing a hat, glasses, and a face wrap or bandanna. To me, the scary aspect of the invisible man is that 'You cannot see him.' It's the simple, classic fear of what cannot be seen or sensed. It's an extension of the classic childhood fear of the dark, the fear of something just beyond our range of perception. The realization that our senses are limited, and that we cannot get security from the limitations of what we can see—or, in the case of the dark, what we cannot see. Our imaginations fuel our fear, and we 'fill in the blanks,' creating our worst nightmares in our 'mind's eye.' That's why children want nightlights—so they are not filling the darkness with imagined fears, mostly due to lack of experience and reference. This learned childhood behavior might explain some of the strong reactions people have to the onset of this virus. Since they lack proper reference, experience, and understanding, they 'fill in the blanks' and live 'daymares' of fright, anger, and anxiety. It's like our brains really hate 'voids.' They would rather put something in there (like conspiracy theories) than leave it empty. Look to flotation tanks for more elaborate examples of that process, as it can 'fill in the blanks.'

Now we can overlay asymptomatic carriers as a metaphor for the 'dark shadows' of the Coronavirus, which, by human sense capabilities, is still unseen. Its microscopic size is basically invisible to the human eye. These silent but deadly 'ninjas' appear to have no external symptoms or visible signs but still have some degree of viral transmission (data is still sketchy and controversial). What we cannot see might hurt us.

This is a tricky and potentially stressful situation to cope with. (My own personal stance) You might as well assume everyone you deal with has it, including you! The self-inclusion is, to me, the 'new' important extra bit that I started adapting to my behavior just a few weeks ago. Now, I am fortunate that I bought a half dozen containers of disinfectant wipes nearly three months ago, when I saw that the 'unseen' was going to be a major problem. So, when I shop, I clean the handles of my shopping cart before and after I use it. That is my *Leave No Trace* protocol. It's considerate to others—leaving no trace that I had 'used' it, while being respectful to the next shopping cart user.

I am appalled by the leftover gloves and wipes, thrown around the grocery stores after those self-centered shoppers have safely made their trip to the store, without concern for who comes next.

We are all in this together, and consideration for all of our different approaches and care for the well-being of our fellow humans—and our planet—is something I am trying to be more aware of, as it's too easy to get so self-centered and only self-aware due to our socially isolated conditioning. I noticed, whilst shopping, how our perception goes internal, self-focused, which seems to be a natural inclination when you're all wrapped up, feeling a bit anxious, and maybe even self-conscious. It takes an effort to see outside of your own bubble. In our current lifestyle, I have been trying to 'pause,' take a slow deep breath, and become aware—'pop my head up,' observe my surroundings once in a while. I am attempting to see the bigger picture.

There is a popular term in the filmmaking community that has been gaining hashtag momentum: *'It takes a village.'* It is our global village that needs to adapt, respect, and attempt to *Leave No Trace* as a philosophy to help direct our behavior in these New Times.

Rhett the JETT Morita

May 3, 2020 – Cape Breton Island, Canada – "Lifestyle Spinach Chickpea Burgers" (Dr. Mike)

Thanks for tuning in today! If you weren't able to catch the live session, be sure to watch it on YouTube and share with your friends.

This is a simple, tasty recipe that makes a great plant-based burger. I always appreciate any feedback—there's always room for improvement! The trick with bean burgers is forming a good patty, and it's easier to bake them than fry them. Using parchment paper or a non-stick baking pan helps a lot. As they bake, they'll harden into a nice patty. You can also try a non-stick skillet without oil, but sometimes it's a bit tricky to get the right touch to flip them without falling apart.

Let me know how the recipe works out for you and how you like them! And don't forget to tune in next week when Dr. Chris Milburn will join me to discuss COVID-19 and obesity as a risk factor and what you can do about it. Stay safe,

Michael

Spinach Chickpea Burgers

Yield: 5 4" Burgers
Ingredients

- 200g frozen spinach
- 1.5 cups cooked chickpeas
- 2 tbsp ground flax seeds
- 1/2 lemon
- 1 tsp toasted cumin seeds
- 1 tsp salt
- 1/3 cup chickpea flour

Instructions

(Adapted from Veggie Burgers Every Which Way by Lukas Volger)

1. **Make flax eggs**: Mix 6 tbsp boiling water with 2 tbsp ground flax and stir well. Set aside to congeal.
2. **Toast cumin seeds**: In a skillet, toast the cumin seeds until aromatic.
3. **Cook spinach**: Add spinach with a tiny bit of water, cooking until just thawed and the water evaporates. Be careful not to run out of water. Drain and squeeze out any excess.
4. **Blend chickpeas**: In a food processor, combine 1 1/4 cups chickpeas, lemon juice, flax eggs, and salt. Process until you have a hummus-like consistency.
5. **Mash remaining chickpeas**: Mash the remaining 1/4 cup of chickpeas with the cooked spinach and toasted cumin seeds. Add the processed mixture and mix thoroughly. If the mixture is too dry, add a little water. Add chickpea flour or any other flour needed to create

the right texture for forming patties.
6. **Bake or fry**: To bake, place the patties on a baking sheet and bake at 375°F for 20-30 minutes. If you prefer to fry them, cook in a little olive oil for a few minutes on each side, then bake for an additional 15-20 minutes.

Oven temperature: 375°F
Tips

- You can use either fresh or frozen spinach, but keep in mind that fresh spinach shrinks down quite a bit, so you'll need a lot of it!
- If you don't have chickpea flour, don't worry. Any flour will do, just use a little to adjust the texture. Wheat flour works fine.
- If you're not a fan of cumin, you can try fresh coriander, dill, basil, or any combination you like. For a bit of heat, cayenne pepper is a great addition.

May 3, 2020 – Turin, Italy – "Small Things to Keep the Spirit Alive" (Alessia Martino)

This week has probably been the most diversified of my quarantine so far.

The weather has been alternating between grey downpour skies and cloudless blue ones. It affected my mood from time to time, although I'm generally calm with a positive outlook on life—other than my room lighting. Looking outside the window has been a bit of a fun distraction. The still but ever-changing scenery has given me a front-row seat to a prime show. Sometimes, I just stop whatever I'm doing and sit at the table by the window; I like to contemplate the view of the mountains, watching them change from dawn to dusk, always amazed by their beauty. It can be for a few seconds or much longer, especially when the spring sun comes out and the sky is clear. The afternoon blue sky always brings me the most peace.

Entertainment has been diversified. We started playing UNO and Jenga— I'd forgotten I had them. It was fun to see my sisters getting familiar with Jenga as they'd never played before. I have a mini Jenga set that I bought at Ikea, which has blocks in three different colors and a dice to choose from. The mini version makes it more fun because there's less room to push blocks out of the middle, and the risk of compromising the tower stability is higher. Different towers were definitely harmed during the game, but the laughable outcomes were golden. On another occasion, we decided to put on nail polish. I chose light blue and a salmon-like pink, alternating between fingers.

May Day was the best— we played a civilization board game called *Through the Ages* for over five hours. We were well into it. Small things like this keep the spirit alive.

Getting back to Thursday, yoga was also great. I missed it. I hadn't been able to do yoga for about three weeks, but as my hands don't hurt as much as before, it was worth trying. I need to get back some wrist strength. I wasn't able to do two asanas, but thankfully, I was able to follow everything else because the lesson was slow-paced. The ending meditation was exactly what I needed and missed the most. Just 10 minutes gave me the strength of what felt like 10 hours of sleep. Still had enough energy for a full Avengers movie to continue our Marvel marathon. On May Day Friday, we hit movie number 10 with *Ant-Man*.

When one week ends, another begins, and I'm hoping for it to be just as good. May the 4th be with us as we start phase two. More people will be allowed to leave the house, and more will be able to return to work. Restaurants will be allowed to do takeaway food, people will be able to travel within the region rather than just within town borders, and we can visit close relatives.

May 3, 2020 – Prince Edward Island, Canada – "F U COVID" (Dara Mac)

Phase one of loosening restrictions: we're allowed to do what we've already been doing on PEI—driveway visits, six feet apart. Some people were disappointed the CMO didn't adopt the 'Two-family bubble' model from New Brunswick, where each family picks one other family to spend time with. I worried everyone I'd want to see would have already chosen someone else, and I'd be stuck like the wallflower at a high school dance. But no, our CMO gave us more flexibility—for our personal, emotional, physical, and mental health.

Premier Dennis King was interviewed on a local station when he said, "FU Covid," hoping to boost islanders' spirits. Two local T-shirt makers jumped on it immediately, selling "FU Covid" shirts across the island. It's PEI's version of Nova Scotia's "Stay the Blazes Home." Between Premier King's "FU" and Dr. Morrison's no-bubble PEI, this place feels like a good fit for me.

Within five minutes of my walk into town, a horn sounded, and a car pulled over. Sure enough, out popped my cousin—busted! I never expect to see familiar faces driving, since I grew up in Montreal, where anonymity is the norm. But here, there's no hiding. Love it or hate it!

My mother was born on PEI but left as a teen, living most of her adult life in Montreal, Quebec. That's where she met my dad, a Francophone Montrealer. Though we're all bilingual in English and French, we went to English school, so we were "spic and span" growing up. Montreal had its language wars, both in and out of our home. I left before it became illegal to speak my first language in my hometown.

Montreal reportedly has as many Covid-19 cases as all of Ontario, and Quebec has the highest number of confirmed cases in Canada. Still, a Radio Canada reporter recently asked the PM why PPE is showing up in unilingual packaging when shortages are such a huge issue. If a pandemic doesn't make things real, I'm not sure what will. That said, growing up in Montreal had its perks—exposure to a multicultural society, experiencing different neighborhoods, and a whole range of cultural and ethnic perspectives.

Some beautiful things are emerging from this pandemic, like a weekly online drum lesson with a local drummer/educator and two other PEI drummers I hadn't met before. We receive charts and instructions through FB Messenger and have a Zoom class once a week. It's a great way to connect, though I'm still awkward with video face-to-face after seven weeks of isolation! I'm more comfortable quietly watching talks, lessons, and in-house concerts. I also discovered Emmet Cohen's Trio, which broadcasts weekly from his home in Harlem. What a fabulous jazz pianist with an incredible bass and drum accompaniment. Even with sketchy rural PEI internet, I'm still enjoying great connections.

I went to town this week to print charts and get supplies. I'd like to avoid grocery shopping right now, but I was running low on everything, and my "guru" son warned that things could get worse. Shopping is stressful, especially when some people still refuse to wear masks or respect the rules. They make it clear they're doing things their way, even in these Emergency Measures times.

For example, a senior lady walked down the aisle toward me—no mask, no gloves. I pointed to the arrow on the floor, indicating the correct direction. She let me know she didn't care. So, in my full gear—goggles, mask, and gloves—I said, "Well, maybe you've had a good life, but I'd like to have a few more years." I need to find other shopping options because this whole experience brings out the worst in me.

Afterward, I walked with my friend and best dog, Taz, for the first time in seven weeks. I noticed a bunch of things on the path I usually walk right past. This stay-at-home situation is sharpening my senses and offering a broader perspective. For instance, I used to give a confused look when locals at a nearby fishing village would say, "Oh, you live in the backwoods of Rustico." I'd think, well, there are trees around, but that's about it. Then I started hearing the daily calls of a Barred Owl on my walks, and suddenly, yes, I do live in the backwoods! Wow! Isn't that great?!

Even practicing regular meditation and mindfulness for years doesn't compare to the richness of living through this pandemic. As others have said, it's a journey into the core of ourselves. If we've followed our hearts, we're in luck because we're surrounded by our choices, day in and day out. I'm deeply grateful for all I have, all I am, and all that is becoming. The planet is healing, and humanity has a chance to heal too.

May 4, 2020 – Antigua, Guatemala – "Don't Forget to Live" (Dammien Alexander)

Today feels different. The world outside has grown quieter, yet there's a strange energy in the air. I've been reflecting a lot lately—not only on music but on **life**—and more importantly, on **living** through a time like this. I'm in Antigua, Guatemala now, and like the rest of the world, I've been thrown into a reality I wasn't quite ready for.

The rainy season has begun here, turning the days into a rhythm of hot sun and stormy clouds. The usual hustle of tourists is absent—this town feels **eerily empty**. It's strange, especially because Antigua is usually so vibrant. In some ways, it feels like the world has **slowed down**, but for me, it's also been a chance to catch up with myself.

I caught up with an old friend today, Jorah Kai. We've known each other for years, and oddly enough, Kai ended up in one of my music videos about a decade ago—*Homicide Hottie* and *Bang It Out*. That was back in Halifax, in a spot on Gottingen Street, at the Bus Stop Theatre. Man, that neighborhood has changed. The memories came flooding back as we talked.

Jorah asked me about life here in Antigua. It's different now, he noted, especially with the lack of tourism. The city's charm is still here, but there's a palpable sense of **waiting**, like we're all stuck in limbo. The pandemic's grip has made people more **isolated**, but at the same time, it's pushed people to reconnect in new ways.

I've been working on my album, **Don't Forget To Live**. It started as a single—a song called *Pedestrian Superstar*, recorded in Toronto. But, as I began working on it, I realized the music was taking me somewhere else. I had the chance to work with friends and engineers I respect, like Charles Wishart Austin, who allowed me to compose and experiment in his studio. The whole process has been a mix of patience and determination.

The album blends **Funk, Electro-Soul, R&B**, and **Indie Rock**, with a touch of **House** music. One track, *Sin City*, is from my old band—my brothers. We recorded it live, on the floor, and it's one of my favorites.

As for how the album will be released, there's no big stage to perform on. The digital concert will happen on May 8th at 3 pm, broadcast live from the Tropicana Hostel here in Antigua. There won't be an audience—just the virtual world. It's hard not having the connection of an actual crowd, but I'm determined to make it work.

The whole idea of **living** through this pandemic has really made me reflect on things I took for granted before. I had a sinking heart moment at first, feeling like everything I worked for might be over. But then, I decided I'd rather focus on **creating** than giving into fear.

Guatemala has been relatively safe, with fewer cases compared to other places. But the curfew and mask mandates weigh on me. I've noticed some tension between locals and foreigners, particularly in the border towns. It's uncomfortable. Yet, in the midst of it all, I'm still grateful for this time. It's **forced me** to face my fears and emotions head-on, to meditate more, to just **be still**. And I've started to feel inspiration return.

Jorah asked me how I'm using my downtime. At first, I couldn't even pick up my guitar, but now, I'm back in the groove. It's amazing how much of a difference it makes when you stop fighting the uncertainty and just **flow** with it.

As for how long this will last—who knows. Speculation is a trap. It leads to bad headspaces. I'm just **going with the flow** for now. But I've learned a lot during this time. One thing I can share: **reach**

out if you're struggling. I know the isolation can make things feel worse, but talking to someone, being vulnerable—it helps.

And as for staying grounded, I've found Stoicism to be a life raft. Don't let emotions control you. Feel what you feel, but know it will pass. This crisis has been a **journey** into the core of who I am. The world is changing, but so am I.

In the end, we're all healing, **together**, even if apart. **Love is everything**. It heals everything.

Album Info

Dammien Alexander blends his love for Funk, Soul, Jazz, Hip Hop, and Blues with the vibrant energy of House music. Using live looping, electronic production, and lush soundscapes, his work crosses genres and highlights his soulful vocals. His latest album, *Don't Forget to Live*, is available on Bandcamp. The digital release concert will be streamed live at the Tropicana Hostel in Antigua, Guatemala, on **Friday, May 8th at 3 PM local time.**

May 4, 2020 – Los Angeles, USA – "Discipline and Structure (It's What All of Us Need)" (Nunich)

I was so stoked for 2020. I thought this was the fucking year. I thought it would be *it*. We live in a great artist spot in downtown Los Angeles, our baby Asha turned 1 on the first day of spring, and we were going to throw a huge party for her—but Covid-19 fucked everything.

We had to cancel the party. The whole world had to cancel parties. Here we are, in a worldwide quarantine shutdown. What a time to be alive. Honestly, though, it's kind of awesome. Life's a little beautiful right now. Where we live, it's brighter, cleaner, quieter. Less heavy traffic, less garbage—everything's a little nicer. Overall, it's better. I miss restaurants, grocery delivery, and dressing up for shows. I miss a ton of shit. But at the same time, I love this worldwide hiding out. It's great to work on creating a home, spending time with Asha, playing with her, taking care of her, watching her grow. Not feeling like I'm missing out on the fun beyond. Asha gets both mommy and daddy 24/7. From her perspective, this shutdown is marvelous. For us too, in some ways. But not in others.

Before Asha, I used to make a carefully crafted music mix every month and share it with the world. After Asha, six months went by, and I still hadn't made another. It's hard to get anything done as a new mom. Literally, all your time goes to taking care of your child. It's wonderful, but if you want to be or do anything else, it's an adjustment. It takes time. Six months for me to get back to making a Night Nurse mix. And I think it's pretty good.

Now that Asha's a year old and more functional, I can be more functional too. We've started implementing a bedtime routine, which is difficult but awesome. It's incredible to get some of my life back, to have time for myself. Asha's bedtime struggles are tough, but she's adjusting. Discipline and structure—*it's what all of us need*, even babies. Implementing it and maintaining it is the hard part. But we're doing it. Phew. We'll make it, or we will.

I wonder what will happen next. Will we ever eat out at restaurants or gather in groups again? Will concerts with thousands of people ever be a thing again? 2020, Covid-19—shit. Holler at your girl.

May 4, 2020 – Chongqing, China – "A Breath of Fresh Air"

A breath of air. What can you do with a breath of fresh air? Turns out, quite a lot. Canadian super astronaut Chris Hadfield taught me that any problem in space must be solvable in that breath. It's the difference between life and death. As I've restarted teaching—in person—1000 kids this week, I've had to rewrite my protocols on the fly. I wasn't going to use public bathrooms at all because the risk of contracting the virus in aerosolized particles was too high. But now, I have no choice but to use public school bathrooms. With my mask on, I hold my breath to avoid attracting dangerous aerosolized poop particles toward my face. I carry an air purifier with me. I'll do a lot for a breath of fresh air.

A Dose of Good News
May 4th, always a happy day for Star Wars fans, brings good news. Scientists conclude with some certainty that we cannot be re-infected with COVID-19. Researchers at the South Korean Center for Disease Control and Prevention (CDC) now say that the COVID-19 virus cannot reactivate in human bodies. The CDC added that unlike HIV and chickenpox—which can hide in the nucleus of human cells and remain dormant for years—the coronavirus stays outside the host cell's nucleus. "This means it does not cause chronic infection or recurrence," explained Dr. Oh Myoungdon, the head of the CDC committee, meaning it is unlikely for patients to relapse in this fashion.

Back to Normal
We go visit some friends. Things are basically back to normal. A bunch of friends, masks off, sharing air together. Yaya and her daughter Cherry have bought a gorgeous house, traditional style,

lots of wood. I find a massage chair in the back to write my blog. I'm happy.

As the AC circulates the air, and more friends show up, a voice in the back of my head creeps: *Is this how I die?* But no, in Chongqing, I trust. So we have a dinner party.

Geopolitical Pressure

Geopolitics are heating up—sucking the air out of the room. Some good friends are angry at me, just for living in China, it seems. A dear cousin of mine yelled at me on Facebook for being a journalist during a crisis—and having the gall to get a paycheck for my work—and then blocked me. I know it should hurt and sting and make me fret, but in terms of the barbs and jabs I've taken over the years, I barely felt this one. *'Tis but a flesh wound.*

It's funny though that the FED can bail out the billionaires with their junk bonds on the back of the working class. Yet, we turn on journalists, storytellers, doctors, and other front-line workers. They collect a paycheck for operating in a pandemic, accusing *them* of disaster capitalism, while the global elite use the chaos to profit like never before, while the poor starve. They've got us all bunched up, and until we unite and work together, they'll always float to the top.

I hope he's ok. He must be having a hard time out in Alberta, with the economy and the layoffs. I don't take his anger personally. Before I go on an epic rant, I want to talk about getting back to normal in China. For the early crowd, the idea of life back to normal is what they showed up for. In 10 days, my life has changed for the better. If it's strange, it's still good.

Straddling Two Worlds

I've had my feet in two canoes for a long time: one in China, my new home, my new family—and it's a wonderful life—and the other in Canada, where I was born, where I was raised, and where my parents and family live. For 6 years, I've straddled the world and stood tall, but these canoes are going different ways. I'm about to be tested in my "Jean-Claude Van Damme" epic splits.

A Split Decision

As the anger rages that China should have used bigger flares, sounded a bigger alarm, and told a BETTER WHO that there was a problem, the fact that my life in China is pretty much back to normal—using simple NPIs (non-pharmaceutical interventions) that China told the world about and was mostly ignored—is only going to make the angry finger-wagglers angrier. But I'm here to tell my story anyway. I've never been a stranger to a tough crowd, and don't be afraid to tell me how you feel; most of you know I can take a punch. In fact, it's not the falling down that matters so much as the getting back up. Rocky told me that, and I never forgot it. So here goes.

Back to Life, Back to Reality

One day I went to a tax office, using our protocols to verify I was "code green" (zero risks of COVID), passed a temperature check, and then got a year's worth of taxes/receipts, etc.

Another day we had a picnic because our city has had zero cases, no new infections, and our protocols of social distancing and masks for everyone have worked. Now we can relax and not be so serious about the masks and distancing. Kids play in the park, and Shaolin and I had a picnic, and it was really fun.

I got my hair cut. With masks, it was ok.

Another day I went to get a PCR COVID-19 test, and it was easy to get and cost about $50, and my school paid for it.

My First Day Back in School

I started school on Monday. I had to pick up my test, so my classes were canceled. No COVID! That is good news.

Tuesday, I get up early, make coffee, choose my favorite dress shirt—a grey iron-free "quick-dry" model I bought with my dad in Canada on my last trip, my favorite "Haida Raven Power" red power tie from Vancouver, a NASA-inspired pair of black dress pants with 4-way stretch that feels like PJs but looks like business, and my wheat suede AF1s. I unplug the small headset microphone and amplifier, put it around my neck, and clip the speaker to my belt.

I decided to wear my matching grey 4-filter HEPA face mask with charcoal lining rather than the gas mask because I want to show my students I'm confident in Chongqing's protocols. But I still pack a HEPA filter air purifier in a duffel bag for good luck. I turn the first few minutes of every class into a discussion on "English as an Idiomatic Language" and then show them the literal embodiment of my idiom: a breath of fresh air.

I show them the HEPA filter air purifier I plug in at my feet, creating a bubble of purified air scientifically shown to pick up and destroy 99.99% of circulating virus and other bacteria/dust/mold particles in my vicinity, making the job of my mask easier and more effective and also reducing contamination and spread that may seep out from someone's mask/respiratory droplets.

On the way in, they scan my temperature. I'm ok. I'm allowed inside.

Teaching and Learning

Then I introduce my students to a clip from their old teacher, Ian, who greets them, makes some jokes, and then introduces me to them. We chat a bit. Then I play my Xinhua news clip, which talks about my diaries, my writing, my book and research on COVID, and my respect for the Chinese protocols. The students are aware many people in the world are angry at China. They are upset by it. We discuss the reasons we can imagine and what other people may be thinking. We generally settle on "they are scared and just lashing out, like a drowning person" and not to take it personally if we get jostled by them. In fact, we have a lot of science, experience, and equipment we can share to help a lot of people—that is, if they're willing to hear it.

The Jean-Claude Van Damme Moment
I show them the site and look, the list of keynote speakers: me, the only guy wearing a mask in the lineup, and then they see him: Jean-Claude Van Damme, and it all makes sense. They're impressed: their English teacher is sharing the stage at a big COVID-19 expo with his childhood hero, action movie star and martial arts legend. I tell them that I hope that whoever they thought of today, as their idol, that in 20 years, if they work at their own mastery, that one day they will share a stage with them also, whether it's to fight off an alien attack or repel an asteroid or stop another viral pandemic. Just be their best selves, and they can, too, share a stage as experts with ones who were once their heroes. That's the beauty of growing up and becoming a guru at something you love.
Then we talk about outlines, how to listen well, how to plan for a good class, and actively listen and make outlines before and during a lecture, and then I let them hear my TED Talk. As the class finishes, I get a huge standing ovation: they clap and cheer. I'd say it was a pretty good first class back. I smile and wish them a successful year, and then I pack my air purifier back into my duffel bag and move to the next class.

Back to Life, Back to Normal
I teach a few more classes on Tuesday and go home to relax. At home, I wash up, change into "home Green zone astronaut clothes" after my shower, and feel the adrenaline leave my body. I've just shared breathing space with hundreds of kids, from 1000 people's homes. In Chongqing and our protocols, we trust. But hey, since everyone wore a mask and controlled our own respiratory droplets inside our masks (99.99%) and I stood near an open window, in a zone of HEPA-filtered air that caught 99.99% of ambient particles and my own mask was a HEPA filter 4-stage charcoal-filtered N95 mask that caught most particles... I'd say the chance of catching COVID in that room, even if any of the kids was an asympto-

matic carrier, was pretty low. Still, it was riskier than sitting at home for three months, so the adrenaline had me a bit shook up.

May 5, 2020 – Kampala, Uganda – "Lockdown in Kampala" (Aliker P' Ocitti)

The Price of Escape

Next week, if you pull out 20,000/-UGX (about $4) to pay for anything, no one will give you any balance.

These were the honest words from a trader in a lockup shop during the lockdown in Kampala. I had pulled out 20,000 Uganda Shillings to buy bottled water at 1000/-UGX.

I walked for two hours from Manyangua to Gayaza trading center like a foot soldier, carrying my luggage on my back, to meet the only opportunity to travel to Gulu by my friend, Odong, who was using private transport.

The government had instructed parents to pick up their children from school, which the following week was locked down. It felt like a coup in town—a successful change of government.

The Lockdown Trap

The lockdown meant no public transport, except for cargo lorries and private cars with special stickers. The government permitted only three travelers in private vehicles. I had tried reaching out to newspaper distributors across the country, asking for a lift in their night shifts, but I was unsuccessful. I even contacted my high-profile contacts to help arrange trips back to Gulu, where I'm based.

My school had closed without me. I had prioritized picking up my children from school, which led to the headteacher closing the institution. But there were still pending writing contracts waiting to be completed.

With no work in sight, the lockdown meant a crushing blow to my economy. The 20,000/-UGX I had was a small lifeline, offering me a glimmer of hope in difficult times.

Trapped in Kampala

As I sat in front of a lockup shop, I found myself trapped in Kampala, just like the trader. We were all struggling, looking for a way out.

"Why do you think, next week, if one pulls out 20,000/-, he will not get it back?" I asked.

"We are so many trapped in the lockdown with our families here. We want to leave Kampala, but there's no public transport," he said.

"I'm traveling to Gulu now with a friend," I responded.

"You're lucky. Someone can give you a lift. I want to travel to Mbale with my family, but I have no money, and soon, we won't have food. This coronavirus will make us all thieves," he replied.

"What are you going to do?" I asked.

"I don't know," he answered.

I recognized the millions of people trapped in Kampala. With the lack of resources, and the scarcity of money, especially in the informal sector, many will soon turn to crime. As they say, "Necessity is the mother of invention, but also the father of crime."

Escape and the Road to Gulu

Then, I got a call from Odong, who promised me a lift to Gulu. I found him parked near Gayaza roundabout. The road was nearly empty—no traffic jam. If it weren't for the lockdown, it would have been impossible to park here.

The journey had started late. It was 2:00 pm, and we were supposed to have left by 10:00 am. Odong was struggling to get clearance from his boss for his "essential" job. The country could not do without these workers during the lockdown.

Once we set off, we were talking to the trader. Odong listened, and we agreed: we were all trapped by this lockdown.

As we continued our journey, we met Zed, a young man waiting at the petrol station. His face lit up upon seeing us—he was desperate to get home, too. The virus had trapped him with relatives who complained of not having enough food. It was a painful story shared by many others.

A Long, Winding Journey

By 4:00 pm, we had left Kampala, but the road had little traffic, and as night fell, the fear of the unknown began to settle in. We kept pushing forward, listening to music and talking about how many were stuck in the city with no way to leave.

The road was becoming more deserted, and the night was cold. Eventually, the car began to strain under the pressure. We pulled over at a petrol station. The mechanic, after an hour of fixing the car, managed to get us back on the road, though our pace was slow. By the time we reached Gulu around midnight, everything had changed. The lively nightlife of Gulu, once full of activity, was now silent and abandoned. The streets were patrolled by soldiers and police officers enforcing the curfew. The pandemic had destroyed business and nightlife, leaving Gulu dark and lifeless.

The Price of Survival

As we made our way through an empty Gulu, I reflected on the struggles we all shared. The pandemic had reshaped everything, from our cities to our relationships. We were all prisoners of our circumstances, trapped in a cage with no clear way out, except for the uncertain road ahead.

Home is still home, even when it feels like a shadow of itself. We are all just trying to survive, holding onto whatever hope and strength we can find in this new world.

May 5, 2020 – San Diego, USA – "Beach Crazy, Nail Crazy, 50 States of COVID Crazy" (Kait Marcelle)

A new "normal" begins as we witness our disjointed US states start to open back up. Still, with no widespread testing. I don't understand how this reopening is possible without mass testing, but hey, I'm not in charge. And honestly, I wouldn't want to be. I've seen reports of clusters reigniting already, and cities going back into relative lockdown soon after. The US form of lockdown, however, seems to be a free-for-all—no one on the same page. Friends and family disagree. You can mostly go anywhere and get anything you need or want. The virus spread is left entirely up to our individual tenacity, willingness, and persistence at this point.

With such a diverse and large population, we must consider the unique circumstances of every area. In my state, we are still in a continuation of our original shelter-in-place orders. I don't necessarily blame those fighting back against restrictions in more spread-out communities. These areas can and should be treated differently. But where I live, we're still under "essential items only," shelter-in-place, until further notice.

As other states begin opening up non-essentials, with hair and nails being tended to, my state is increasing public mandates. Now, not having a face covering in public spaces like grocery stores imposes a misdemeanor charge from the state to anyone who doesn't comply. With these new face-covering mandates, we also saw the first weekend of beach restrictions lifting in nearly seven weeks. Different rules apply depending on whether the area is managed by the state or national parks system, or if it's a city-maintained area. But with sunny beach days in abundance, many beaches saw increased use by those who are stir-crazy after seven weeks of lockdown. In Southern California, the beach economy is a powerhouse. Our beach culture is so pervasive, it's recognized around the world with the mere utterance of "Hey Dude!" Most people understand the sun-drenched, chill vibe.

This weekend, while heading to my parents to be their tech support, grocery delivery, and take a little walk, I saw something peculiar. A cyclist was cruising down the middle of a slow road, oblivious to the cars around him. I thought, maybe the quarantine had rubbed off on him. With fewer cars on the road these past two months, he probably forgot about the usual traffic. I patiently waited until I could pass. It's not often you see cyclists and pedestrians reclaiming the roads from cars. To help people get fresh air, ease cabin fever, and stay healthy through movement, we've seen a "slow streets" initiative in some local areas. Certain streets are marked off to be pedestrian-friendly and shared with cyclists. The idea is to ease the physical tension families have been feeling, cooped up in their houses for nearly two months now. The opening of full streets helps maintain our six-foot rule while allowing for more foot traffic.

What's our new normal? Can we make this a beginning of something greater, or will we go back to the way things were? Do we rush back to normal and keep ravaging the natural world, or can we emerge with more respect for the planet? I, for one, don't want to go back to the old normal. As devastating as this has been for humanity, it's been a blessing for Earth. Globally, emissions have dropped drastically, and animals are returning to places once uninhabited. Is there denying that some beauty has emerged from this tragedy? As we watch the Earth heal, we watch more people die. Perhaps we were the problem all along.

May 7, 2020 – Chicago, USA – "COVID Confusion: A Compelling Case for Continual Quarantine" (MC ZULU)

COVID Confusion: A Compelling Case for Continual Quarantine. Try saying that fast three times! After you've met that challenge, ask yourself: Do you actually agree with the phrase above? Or have you simply been conditioned to accept it? That's the power of a catchphrase. If you hear it everywhere, you'll eventually take it as truth—no matter how valid it is.

New catchphrases are popping up daily:

STAY HOME! WEAR A MASK! SOCIAL DISTANCE! SHELTER IN PLACE!

The universal precautions regarding quarantine should be followed, but we can't let these catchphrases dominate our thoughts and actions. There's more at stake than just the words being thrown around.

Present-day America finds us in a world of self-serving citizens making daily, recreational trips to the grocery store, blissfully unaware of the societal collapse awaiting them. Many have received their stimulus checks, and they're feeling good about the day. You've wiped down your shopping cart, applied hand sanitizer, worn your gloves, and stocked up on masks before they sold out. Now you're about to post your dinner on social media and launch into a self-righteous tirade about the woman at the store without a mask. She endangered your life! GOD DAMN HER.

... And GOD DAMN YOU too, for leaving your discarded latex gloves, surgical mask, sanitation wipes, and empty kombucha bottle in the parking lot. You'll never realize what an absolute stain you are to the universe until the supply chain breaks down, and you're left eating dog food.

Can that really happen? As of April 27, 2020, Business Insider reports that farmers are destroying millions of pounds of crops because they can't get them to consumers. Millions of chickens are being destroyed due to lack of feed or staffing shortages. This is happening worldwide. If farms can't care for chickens, imagine what happens to cows and, even worse, pigs! Look up how long it takes for a pig to go feral. Imagine what happens when a human being goes feral. Some are already doing it.

Ahmaud Arbery had the audacity to be Black while jogging through a Georgia neighborhood. Gregory McMichael and his son Travis jumped in their pickup truck, hunted him down, and shot him dead. They called a retired cop buddy to help clean up the scene and fabricate a narrative of "break-ins." The district attorney recused himself because the retired cop was his friend. Before doing so, he declined to press charges against the McMichaels, citing a variation of the "Stand Your Ground" law. Now there's an interesting catchphrase.

Litehouse Whole Food Grill in Chicago's Hyde Park, known for giving away meals to those in need, was robbed at gunpoint by two frequent beneficiaries of that same policy. Robbers cited "The Coronavirus" as the reason for their crime. Rico Nance, the owner of Litehouse, did not retaliate or seek vengeance. He didn't go hunting down the robbers.

Nance said to local media: "In a world full of hatred, depression, and need, we want to be the light to shine, and I'm going to continue to do that." This isn't some catchphrase concocted by a marketing guru to influence human behavior. It's a personal mantra, stemming from a desire to help humanity.

Because of Nance's generosity, donations have poured in from across the country.

We must recognize and reward those with a humanitarian mindset. It's the only thing that will save us in the event of societal collapse. Prior to the lockdown, the most degenerate views—racism, self-hate, and apathy towards others—were glorified. We lived by manufactured catchphrases, never questioning their validity. That lack of thought makes us no better than the chickens in the factory farms. They too were on lockdown... until they were deemed expendable.

May 8, 2020 – Jeddah, Saudi Arabia – "Ramadan, Hot Pot & The Mother's Day Wish" (Sarah Rollinson)

I've been in Saudi almost four months now—two of those in lockdown. Locked away in a world I'm still trying to understand.

When you're shut in a house with people, you learn a lot about them. But more than that, you learn about yourself. I've discovered that I'm more patient than I thought... but also, that patience has limits. You learn who you can trust, and who you can't. You learn what really matters. For me, it's family and true friends—the ones who've proven their worth, not just claimed it.

I've reached a point in my life where I'm done dancing around bullshit. Life feels very black and white now. We live, or we die. I don't have time for grey areas anymore. I'm too old for this shit.

Ramadan in a Pandemic

Ramadan began here on April 23. It's the ninth month of the Islamic year, a time of fasting from dawn to sunset, followed by shared meals and prayer. It's meant to be a season of spiritual reflection, self-control, and generosity—especially toward the less fortunate.

But this year is different. Shopping sprees and nightly social gatherings aren't possible. Instead, there's an eerie quiet. I'm trying to understand more about the faith and culture around me. I'm a guest in this country, and the least I can do is learn.

Mother's Day, Miles Away

Yesterday, I Skyped with my son Liam—as I do twice a week. I told him I might finally be able to come home to Canada once my permanent residency paperwork goes through. I'm British by citizenship, but Canada has been my home most of my life.

His response? That me coming home would be the best birthday gift ever. And the best Mother's Day present, too. I couldn't agree more.

Hot Days & Hot Pot

The weather here is brutal—hot and humid, hitting nearly 50°C some days. I'd love nothing more than to go to the beach, maybe bike by the coast, but with a strict 5 p.m. curfew, even catching the sunset is out of reach.

Still, there are moments of levity. Last time my husband and I were stopped by the coast guard, they joked with him after learning he was Russian—"Bottle, bottle!" they laughed, referencing the Russian love of vodka. World Cup memories, maybe. Even in desert camo and stern uniforms, people find ways to be human.

But as I stare out my window at the sand and palm trees, all I can think of is home—maple trees, robins, blue jays, cardinals, and squirrels. It might look like a dream here, but for me, it's a hazy one. So I made "Hot Pot." A humble comfort food my mom used to throw together when the grocery store was far and she was too tired after work. Whatever root veggies you've got—potatoes, carrots, garlic, onion—simmered in stock with Worcestershire, tomatoes, and canned corned beef. I added a bit of paprika and hot spice for kick. It wasn't fancy, but it tasted like home. And for a moment, I felt safe.

Please, Just Be Kind

I'm closer to 'ground zero' than most of you. Saudi is trying very hard to keep its people safe, but this virus is everywhere. So I beg you—wear a mask. Wear gloves. Everything you touch, everything you breathe, could hurt someone. Maybe not you. But maybe your grandfather. Someone's grandmother. A kid with asthma. A chronic smoker. Someone you don't even know.

Please, think about others. Not just yourself.

Love to all,

—Sarah

May 8, 2020 – Buenos Aires, Argentina – "A Very Quarantine Birthday" (Josette)

Well, I did it. I celebrated my birthday in quarantine.

Now, I'm one of those "over-the-top" birthday people. I make sure you know about it far in advance, and I shamelessly remind you that I like presents. What can I say? It's the one day of the year—*the* whole year—that everything is supposed to go my way (or at least, that's the idea).

This year, I wasn't quite sure how I felt about it. Part of me was holding out hope that the quarantine might be lifted in time for my usual royal celebration. A week of festivities, loved ones, laughter. (I promise I'm not *that* conceited—it's just for emphasis.) But I knew better. It was going to be me, here, with my cat. Physically, at least. I worried I might feel deflated, or even depressed. But when the day arrived—my first day off in weeks—I surprised myself. I felt genuinely excited. That was the best possible way to be.

"We have to learn to coexist with the coronavirus."

A New Kind of Celebration

The messages, calls, emails, and video chats poured in. From all over the world. I felt honored that despite everything we're going through, people still took the time to wish me well. Someone sent presents. Someone sent a delicious dinner. Someone played a DJ set online—dedicated to me. It absolutely felt like a birthday party, just... different.

I even baked a carrot cake.

And during one of my Zoom calls, a few friends surprised me: they had baked cakes too, lit candles, and sang to me from their homes across the world. It was beautiful. Moving, even.

It's not impossible to celebrate like we used to—we just have to do it differently. Creatively.

By the end of the day, I was exhausted. It was the most social I'd been in two months. I'd even put on makeup (which I still remember how to do, surprisingly).

So here's a big, heartfelt THANK YOU to everyone who made this birthday just as special as any other.

Quarantine Life Continues

Now, on to other news: more quarantine. What's one more month? Here in Buenos Aires, autumn has settled in and the weather's getting colder. Authorities say May and June will be our peak COVID months. Schools remain online, and most people continue to work from home. Reliable internet is more essential than ever—though it's always been a bit of an issue here.

We're all trying to find creative, sustainable ways to keep living and stay well.

So, how are you doing? Are you working out? Sleeping properly? Separating weekdays from weekends? Dividing up your days?

Here's one thing I *do* recommend: POPSUGAR Fitness on YouTube[1]. These workouts are great.

Lessons in Awareness

This time in quarantine has helped me become more self-aware. Not just of myself, but of others. It's taught me to let go, to balance the positive and the negative. I still stand by what I said in my last post: *Both the light and the dark have their place. Finding balance between the two is key to being well.*

When you put your energy into being productive, creative, healthy—it doesn't leave much room for wasted energy. And that's a good thing. It's helping me focus where I need to, and it's reshaping my outlook.

Someone told me today that what I'm describing is called "being mature."

...I think the jury's still out on that one. (Ha!)

---

1. https://www.youtube.com/user/popsugartvfit

One Final Word

The big keyword I'm leaning into right now is:
ACCEPTANCE

Accept what was.

Accept what is.

Accept what will be.

Everything has changed. And yes, it's a hard pill to swallow. But maybe that's where it all begins—realizing that acceptance is the first step.

Some food for thought.

Stay safe. Stay healthy.

—Josette

Buenos Aires

May 8, 2020 – Chongqing, China – "Love, Patience & The Aye of the Tiger" – Part I: The Monitor Falls, the Publisher Fumbles

Day 106.

We all have good days and bad days in a pandemic. With "The Reopening" looming, we're gonna have some bad days. Yesterday was my worst, but today's looking like it might be okay.

About 80 days ago, I moved my 32" curved 4K gaming monitor from my office to the bedroom so I could spend more time with my wife. I hoped she wouldn't abandon me to go shelter with her family and leave me stranded alone in a foreign country—where even ordering a sandwich can feel like brain surgery. I mean, have you ever squinted at a slew of Chinese characters until your eyeballs throbbed?

It was a good move—until it wasn't. A week ago, I had a gut feeling it was time to move the monitor back. But it seemed like a big job, and I'm a busy guy. Then, a few days ago, in a whirlwind of coffee and chaos, double-fisting a swooshing mug and a screeching cellphone, the butterfly effect of my breeze set off a cataclysm: the precariously balanced tech-furniture stack in our bedroom met gravity. I heard the smash from the living room. My 4K screen lay askew, the PlayStation 4 on top of it, pinning the larger opponent with Judo-like precision. The HDMI cable was hopelessly bent, but the port itself seemed to have survived the assault.

Sheepish, I moved all the gear back to the office. Found a new HDMI cable. Booted it up. The monitor displayed a two-inch-wide black bar down the right side, cracked but functional. The PS4 defragged and rebooted, like a champ. I use it to hang with my dad these days. When we're too tired for actual conversations, we play hockey. Sometimes I win, sometimes he does. It's not the outcome that matters—it's the connection.

Then came another blow. A day or two later, I tried to game, but the PS4 wouldn't connect to the network. No game. No dad time. I was gutted. Something important to both of us had been quietly severed.

Meanwhile, the chaos was swirling around my book deal with the Beijing publisher. When Stephen King started out, he tacked rejection letters onto a nail on his wall until the weight of them snapped it. I just wrote a daily blog for two months, and somehow had *two* publishers in two countries wanting my book. Lightning in a bottle. Maybe I was too eager. Maybe it was love at first sight, or maybe just a convenient setup that wasn't meant to last.

One offer came from an old friend in Vancouver. She loved the strange cyberpunk realism of it all—called it "relatable dystopian sci-fi." That sounded like she got it. But I felt it was a China story. I live here. We lived through this. Shouldn't a Chinese publisher get first crack?

Back in January, I'd done a live TV interview with CTV about how Canadian expats felt stranded and unsupported. The segment aired several times. I shared screenshots online. So did my wife. Her friend in Germany called her in a panic—said reporting for Western news on sensitive topics could be dangerous in China. Some people, he warned, had gone to jail. Shaolin was rattled. We took the photos down.

Still, I wanted to tell the story—for China, with China. So I approached a local publisher. To my surprise, a major one in Beijing was interested. They said I'd have creative control. They'd only tweak grammar and logic, help fact-check, and mark their edits in a Word doc. Sounded good.

I signed, and got to work on *The Invisible War*. I kept writing the next one, *The Lighthouse*, while collaborating globally. Then things

went sideways. The chief English editor turned toxic. Condescending. Accusatory. Exhausted. I told her: just stop replying when you need rest. She didn't. Eventually, I insisted on no more contact.
The Chinese-side editor stepped in as a mediator. Things improved. I received small edits by doc—grammar stuff. I'd forgotten they promised in-line suggestions. It slipped my mind completely. Meanwhile, press conferences were being set up. Local media. My school. Principals. Officials. Everyone clapped. They were proud. I was too. This is what happens when you do the work and get a little lucky, I figured. More interviews followed. But I was burning out. So I stepped back.
I focused on the Revel Alliance and keeping our research circle going. Then Beijing tried to change the cover. *Again*. After we'd promoted it. After I'd printed T-shirts. I blew up. Threatened lawyers. The works. We hit pause.
Then came the title change suggestion. *The Invisible Enemy. The Invisible Threat*. I snapped. "What's next?" I said. "*The Invisible Fart?*" Dash wrote a theme song for the current title. We had a brand. You don't just change that. I told them if they tried, I'd walk—and we'd spend the next five years in court. They thought I was dramatic. I gathered clips of Xi, Trump, Trudeau, Johnson, and Macron all calling this a *war*. They worried the word might delay an ISBN in China. I stood my ground.
Eventually, my newspaper boss called theirs and smoothed it out. "Let the guy have his title," they said. I'd won. I was tired, but I'd won.
Then they changed the back cover copy. Instead of "a feverish fear," they wrote "a feverish period." I told them in no uncertain terms I did *not* want to sound like I'd caught a case of the metaphorical menstruation.
And the saga wasn't over yet...

Part II – Rocky Balboa, Righteous Fury, and the Lemonade Epiphany

Once she'd gone, all I had left was my anger, my rage, my internet, people I was mad at on the internet in China, outside China, cable TV, and a tuna fish sandwich. It was a long, sad, desperate night. I felt like shit. The lowest I'd been in 106 days.

I told the publisher and my agent that under no circumstances were they to publish this tone-deaf heap of garbage that was this version of the book. We had big problems ahead. Either I got my version back—or they took my name off it, my pictures out of it, and I'd walk away from the whole monstrosity.

I sat in a ball of suck, thinking: I want this.

I want that.

I wa. I wa. I wa wrawawawa.

I am a baby. Crying. Burp me and put me to bed.

Shaolin came home, late. I kept a straight face. I wasn't a baby anymore. I avoided the thin-skinned need for consolation she hated—my little pretty-faced Yoda momma—and we functioned. We even watched a movie. Slept. And then—

In a whirling eruption of chaos, I found myself at the bottom of a volcano.

I fell in and out of love at least twice. I wandered through house parties—some real, some legendary, some clearly fictional. I was buzzed. I bumped into a silver screen icon, waiting for the bathroom. Fela Kuti blasted unabashedly horny jazz down the hallway. Hoodie up, shoulders against the wall, he noticed me and jabbed a thick thumb at the off-white bathroom door. In a gravelly Italian-American accent, he muttered, "They've been in there ten minutes. Geez. The party's out here. My girl's gotta pee."

I looked around. No girl. I looked back. Really?

I smiled. Quirked a brow. "Sly?"

"Naw," he said. "You got the wrong guy."

But I knew him. Younger, impossible.

"Rock?" I asked.

He smiled. "You gotta problem with fictional characters?"

There was fire in his eyes. I was all out of love.

"No, you do you, brother," I said. "I'll call you Sly—for legal purposes." I glanced around. No lawyers lurking. "My battery's drained. They mopped the floor with me." He waited. Something in his eyes softened, so I kept rambling. "I feel like the whole world is closing in. Everybody's taking a piece. When they're done, I'll be a stain. Nothing left."

He crossed his arms and frowned. "Every champion," he said, "was once a contender who just refused to give up."

"Sure," I replied. "You're the champ, the inspiration. In Philly, they still play your theme song when the Flyers score. You're not even real, and you've got a statue. That's wild. I'm just some gu—"

He grabbed my shirt. Pulled me close. "Not real? I'm not real to you? Do I feel real?" He waved a meaty fist in my face. "Does this look real enough to you?"

I gulped. "Sure, Rock. You're real. At least in this place. And this is the place...we're still waiting for the bathroom. Right?"

"So my advice is no good to you? 'Cause you live in a different universe?"

"No, man. You're inspiring. Don't hit me. I get it. You're the champ. I'm just fed up. This giant behemoth, the state publisher—China's printing company is part of the state. I'm just some guy, trying to win the fight of my life."

"A giant?" He mirrored. "When I fought Mr. T or the Hulk, those guys felt like giants. Ivan was a giant."

I laughed, nervous. "Yeah, Mr. T was pretty impressive. You got a big heart, Rock. This is a different kind of fight. Half my friends think I'm a fool for loving Chongqing. They don't believe me. They say the positive things I write are propaganda. Like I have no credibility. Like if they change my book's name, or strip out the artistry, it'll be a mutilated Quasimodo. I won't even want my name on it."

"So is the fight over?" he asked.

"What?"

"Did you lose?"

"No. It's just not looking good."

"So the fight's not over—and you're already acting like the loser."

He shook his head and knocked on the bathroom door. "Hey, open up, man!" he shouted. Laughter echoed inside.

"Sly, I'm tired of getting beat up. Knocked down. How many times can I take it? I feel like hamburger helpless."

He turned back to me. Shrugged. "Well, let me tell you something you already know. The world ain't all sunshine and rainbows."

"Did you make a lot of money...making the movie?"

"I would've done the whole thing for a donut and a tuna fish sandwich," he said. "The money meant nothing. It was the opportunity to prove to myself that I wasn't a liar. That I wasn't living a life of disillusionment. When you think you're a creative person, and then you turn around and realize you've been living a lie..."

I nodded, dizzy. The door opened. A couple of giggling girls danced out. Sly was gone. I was alone, surrounded by the crowd and my thoughts.

And something clicked.

No one wants this to work more than me. They clock out. They go home. They sleep. But this? This is my life.

Everything spun. A chaotic kaleidoscope.

With a jolt, I woke up. The weird little house was gone. I was back in China. My arm was vibrating. The dogs were dreaming, feet twitching. Benben was running in a field of yellow daisies. Shaolin slept beside me. My family.

It's a new day. And I'm ready for a new fight.

My dad sent me a picture: all eight HEPA filter masks had arrived after all. We got confused, turned around for nothing. I checked my phone: that damn PayPal transfer still pending. I refunded it. We were good. Nobody had to feel sorry. We just needed to do our best. He had his masks. I'd find mine. I'd be okay.

A few hours passed. I taught three packed classes—like doing standup in a small room. Good jokes. Good lessons. Applause. Shaolin made me lunch: tomato and egg over rice with soup. I made coffee. When I turned around, she had cut up some of the fresh lemons her dad had given us, added rock sugar, and handed me a glass of lemonade.

"Here," she said with a smile. "Don't drink it all at once. You can fill it back up for later and enjoy it for a while."

May 10, 2020 – Turin, Italy – "Phase 2 Exciting Perks" (Alessia Martino)

Exercising outside isn't illegal anymore—nor is grabbing a bar-made coffee or ordering takeaway from a restaurant. Phase 2 in Italy has officially begun, and people can now visit parents, fiancés, girlfriends, and boyfriends. The streets are filling again, and dogs can finally take a break from the constant "walks." It feels like people are happy just to be outside again—but personally, I haven't taken full advantage of the new perks just yet.

Mostly, I've just gone up and down to throw out the garbage. Even that's become an adventure. I've avoided the river—it's been packed with cars, bikes, families; it looks like a festival. The dog doesn't stop barking. One trip, I stopped at the gate to let two unmasked boys pass with their bikes before safely heading to the trash bins. I held the door with one hand, tossed the trash with the other. That hand wouldn't touch anything else until the full wash-down ritual was complete. At the same time, a neighbor came out with her garbage. She patiently gave me space to move, waiting before she approached. That tiny act of thoughtfulness restored a bit of my faith in humanity.

I still drink my coffee at home, solo with my Chinese-made Staresso portable machine, or with my family using the Moka. Sure, cafés are open now—but under Phase 2 rules, even ordering a simple espresso requires a text-in reservation to stagger pickup times. The texts double as proof of a legal, contactless transaction in case the police ask. Do I miss café coffee? Absolutely. Am I willing to jump through all these hoops? Honestly, no. Besides, having coffee out was always a shared experience—sitting down, talking over a cup for ten minutes or four hours. That part, the soul of the café, still feels like a distant memory.

YEAR OF THE RAT

I haven't seen my mom yet. The last time was a week before lockdown. Oddly, I'm used to not seeing her for long stretches—I've lived abroad—but now we're just a car ride apart. The problem is, I don't own a car. I'd need one of my siblings to drive me, and even then, I'd have to sit in the back seat, mask on, regardless of whether we share living space. Only two people per car are allowed unless there's a child involved. But even more than that, I didn't spend two months away from her just to show up and hug her because the law suddenly says I can. I *want* to hug my mom—but when I see her, we'll be masked and distanced. That's the new reality.

One perk I *have* enjoyed: sushi. We'd missed it so much. It took me longer than expected to decide what to order—partly because, for the same price, you get much less than the pre-pandemic all-you-can-eat deals. In the end, I went for beef yaki udon to satisfy my noodle craving and a mixed sushi box. It was over an hour late, but worth the wait. When it finally arrived, each bite sent fireworks through my taste buds.

May 10, 2020 – Chongqing, China – "Wanting Nothing Is Having Everything"

Day 108. Today I feel peaceful, lighthearted, and free. It's a wonderful change. If you found my last blog entry a steaming pile of emotional horseshit, then I guess I'm an excellent communicator—because that's exactly how I felt. But today is different. I woke up curious, open, ready to explore.

The problems that had weighed me down? They didn't matter anymore.

Broken gear? No problem.

Lost PPE? No problem.

Cranky wife? No problem.

Everybody hates me? No problem.

Fucked book? No problem.

"The greatest portion of peace of mind is doing nothing wrong. Those who lack self-control live disoriented and disturbed lives."
—Seneca

I read that and thought, in what world could this ever apply to me? Well, maybe this one. Today, I'll strive to be at peace—with my actions and reactions, my conditions, my reality. Just let what is... be. It's the wishing for something else that twists us up. (It is.)

Yesterday, I woke feeling decent and taught two solid classes over four hours. Aside from yelling at a bratty boy who wouldn't stop sipping soda, misusing his mask, and manhandling my dog like a plush toy, things went fine. I explained, firmly, that studying in a teacher's home is a privilege. If they couldn't show respect, lessons would end—and either way, I'd be fine.

That night we hosted a small Mother's Day dinner for Shaolin, Jinn, and his girlfriend Cici. Korean BBQ, Japanese sushi, and

American donuts—all in honor of my mom, thousands of miles away. I video-called her so she could see the spread. It was meaningful. It made my heart full.

Earlier that day I'd read that falling tourism investment was freeing up apartments in Europe. Fewer Airbnb listings meant more locals could afford beautiful places again. That's a silver lining. But I remember our own dreamy travels—our flat in Marseille above a bakery, our cliffside studio in Santorini, the sun-washed nook in Florence. Each one a whole lifetime compressed into a week. I know now: the luxuries of the rich often cost the common man. The best we can do is enjoy them fleetingly and leave something beautiful behind.

Later that evening, I called my 90-year-old grandmother. Despite a bug infestation and months in isolation, she was still smiling. "Your grandma loves two things," my mom said, "a clean house and a good conversation." Losing both at once is tough—but she's finding her way. If she can smile, I can, too.

Even our recent inconveniences—no water one day, no electricity the next—couldn't break me. We managed. Life continues. And if I had to go without the internet for a week? I'd finally tackle my bookshelf. Every problem carries a hidden blessing.

If we want nothing, we truly have everything.

I ignored messages from my publisher for a few days, but after some negotiation via my agent, it seems they want to make the book better, not just neuter it. The trippy dream sequence? Still there—but they're asking if I might revise it. (Maybe they mean, trim it. Maybe I'll make it longer.) Either way, my favorite parts are back. Things are going to be okay. Eye of the tiger, heart of the lion. I've got this.

At 10 a.m., I prepped for my 11:20 class. Black NASA-engineered shirt, red Haida Raven Power tie, jeans, handmade belt, suede wheat AF1s. I packed my air purifier with a new HEPA filter, knowing it would scrub the air clean of any one-micron droplets floating through the room. Science is good for peace of mind.

This was technically week three with my new Monday class, but our first real meeting. Week one I was out getting tested for COVID. Week two was Labor Day. So today was showtime. I walked in: just me, the masked foreigner, and a sea of bare-faced Chinese students. I introduced myself with some Shakespeare: "To mask or not to mask." It landed well. We watched a video about sneezes and the power of the elbow block. One boy at the back wore a mask, like me. That felt... good. A win.

At lunch, I played hockey with my dad online while finishing leftover sushi. Shaolin was at her sister's place for Meimei's birthday. I'd call later to send my love.

After lunch, I taught three more classes. And I did something big: I took off my mask.

Standing inside my dome of purification, I trusted the protocols, the science, and the city. I kept my distance. I washed my hands. But for those few moments, I felt free. When a student at the back sneezed, I bolted out, put my mask back on, and finished the class properly. Still—a leap of faith.

Today, I needed nothing—and so I had everything.

Broken gear? Adapted. I have my family. I'm okay.

Lost PPE? Turns out it was a mix-up. Nothing lost.

Cranky wife? Water under the bridge. We're fine today.

Everybody hates me? Just a loud minority, mad at the world. I've got my people. Even if I didn't, I'd be fine on my own.

Fucked book? I'm fixing it. If people hate it, that's okay. I've got another one coming. And then another.

It's easy to think your job, your marriage, your life are broken. Easy to dream of a new one, where everything goes your way. But that's fantasy. The truth is, the best partners, friends, and opportunities *challenge* us. We grow under resistance. Like building muscle, we build character through adversity.

"I don't wish for an easy life," Bruce Lee said, "but the strength to endure a difficult one."

Me too, Bruce. And today? I think I've found it.

May 11, 2020 – PEI, Canada – "Happy Mother's Day" (Dara Mac)

More than half of the victims in the recent brutal Nova Scotia massacre were women—many of them mothers. In the past two months, nine women in Canada have been murdered by their partners in their homes, including one mother of six just last week in New Brunswick. I send love and light to their children; may they be guided, loved, and protected. These have indeed been challenging times.

My 90-year-old mom's life typically revolves around her social activities, which help keep her motivated and energized. She plays bridge a few times a week, goes to church with a friend on weekends, takes the bus to her local shopping mall and library, and eats out regularly with family and friends. She's known as the Ambassador of her Ottawa high-rise, always the first to greet new tenants as they move in. My heart aches for the challenges she's had to endure during this lockdown. But as a "senior senior," as she calls herself, she's been a real trouper. She's the last surviving member of her immediate family and the oldest living grandparent of my son.

Not many make it to such a ripe old age. Just this past week, we lost one of PEI's most colourful characters—Bill McFadden—at age 72. Bill was an actor, preacher, town crier, and had a role as a narc in the island film *Pogey Beach*. He had an incredible memory, able to recite lengthy texts at the drop of a hat. I remember one sunny summer evening sitting on a patio on Queen Street in Charlottetown, watching Bill peddle past on his bicycle—waistcoat and scarf flapping, top hat perched like Willy Wonka. He will be dearly missed by his twelve children and all who appreciated the uniqueness he brought to our little island.

YEAR OF THE RAT

There's more heartbreaking news from Nova Scotia with the disappearance of a three-year-old boy visiting his grandmother. Search crews worked through the night but found only his tiny rubber boots floating in the Salmon River. It's now become a recovery effort. My heart goes out to his family and their community.

To honour the East Coast's recent tragedies, the Snowbirds flew over New Brunswick, Nova Scotia, and PEI. My dad loved them—he loved flying—and used to take us to air shows when we were kids. I remember sitting on blankets atop the car, waiting for the sky to explode with sound. He was also a veteran of World War II, and this past week we marked the 75th anniversary of Victory in Europe Day: "Protected in our darkest hours."

Meanwhile, the town of Souris, PEI, faced its own moment of tension when residents were told by the RCMP to stay indoors. A 25-year-old man barricaded himself in a friend's apartment with a long gun, threatening police. After eight hours of negotiation, he surrendered. His motive remains unclear.

Also in Souris, a beloved local landmark, The Blue Fin, burned to the ground. It had been a classic spot to grab a meal while attending the Rollo Bay Fiddle Festival, which has also been canceled this year for the first time in 44 years. In its place, the Chaisson family will host a 24-hour livestream concert—a digital echo of community and tradition.

Cancellations continue to roll in, including the Charlottetown Festival's long-running musical *Anne*, which will not take the stage this summer for the first time in over fifty years. Thankfully, all cruise ship visits have been cancelled too, sparing the North Atlantic Right Whales as they return to the Gulf of St. Lawrence. Our Chief Medical Officer says we never really had a curve to flatten here, likely thanks to the firm restrictions put in place early on. Non-residents are still not welcome. Just this week, seven travelers were turned back at the airport and sent away on the next flight.

To date, all 27 COVID-19 cases on PEI have recovered, with no community transmission reported. So, restrictions are loosening slightly: five people can now gather indoors, ten outdoors. If my son and mom were here, that would've made a world of difference. Instead, I celebrated Mother's Day with my son, daughter-in-law, grandson, and his girlfriend in China via video chat. Shaolin prepared a beautiful sushi and Korean BBQ dinner in my honour. Happy to have shared that virtual moment together. Three years ago, I was there in person and enjoyed many fine meals and incredible kindness, generosity, and hospitality.

Despite the May snowfall, spring's signs are everywhere: recreational fishing has resumed, two North Atlantic Right Whales have returned, and the air is filled with birdsong—including the haunting "Who cooks for you?" call of the local Barred Owl.

The war in 2020 is an invisible one, and each of us fights it in isolation, seeking light through our own darkness. Mine comes in the form of growing microgreens, planning a greenhouse, and practicing the drum daily. All my life, I've asked: *Where would I be without music?* That question has never felt more relevant.

"Common suffering builds strong bonds," says Dr. Bonnie Henry, PEI-born and raised. More than ever, I appreciate the deep connections I have with family, friends, and my tribe of musicians. I pray you, too, have found that connection with your own love, your own passion.

Stay safe and well,
Dara

May 11, 2020 – Toronto, Canada – "We're Not in the Same Boat (Some of Us Aren't Even in the Same Sea)" (Rhett Morita)

We are not all in the same boat. We are all out at sea in the middle of a raging storm, tossed by three-meter waves, each of us in wildly different vessels. Some cling to overloaded rubber zodiacs. Some shelter below deck in ten-meter catamarans. A few of the 'lucky' ones ride out the storm 200 meters beneath the surface in nuclear submarines. Others plow forward in 250-meter-long Bismarck battleships. And many—too many—paddle alone, exposed, on planks and makeshift rafts stitched together from plastic bottles. The diversity of pandemic experience is as vast and varied as the number of cereal brands on supermarket shelves.

Yes, we are all human. We are born, we breathe, eat, drink, love, suffer, grow old (sometimes), and die. But our realities are shaped by a matrix of social, economic, geographical, psychological, spiritual, and circumstantial factors. To say "we're all in the same boat" is ignorant, even insulting.

I've never been shot, but I've been shot at—by five police officers, unloading entire clips at me from ten meters away, behind plexiglass. For a movie. I volunteered for the take, overruled my operator, and positioned myself with my assistant under a blanket atop a cube van 45 meters away. We used real guns, firing half-load blanks. It wasn't real, but my heart didn't know that. It pounded for minutes. That's the difference between knowing a fact and *living* it.

Facts take on a different weight when you've lived them. People toss around phrases, statistics, and slogans, but lived experience engraves truth into the bone. That's why so many facts, even when true, ring hollow to those untouched by them. If you've lost your home, been bankrupt, buried a loved one—then no one needs to tell you the truth of those moments. You carry it with you.

Truth and fact diverge here. There are facts with a capital F—undeniable, universal—and then there are experiential truths, backed by memory, pain, fear, and resilience. If you've never lived through it, you can't fully understand it. And yet, we're bombarded by people repeating truths they've never experienced. It's not their fault. But the impact differs. You can't equate a teenager's talk about sex to a 46-year-old on his third marriage, raising kids. One has theory. The other has life.

Today, that difference is everywhere. Politicians speak of aid for artists, for single moms, for baristas. But how many have *lived* those lives? How many of them have ever waited in line at a food bank or watched their job disappear in a puff of viral smoke?

This isn't about blaming leaders. It's about the absurdity of sweeping platitudes like "we're all in this together." We're not. We may be in the same storm, but we are absolutely not in the same boat. Even within a single family, our boats may differ wildly.

We are now adrift in a moment of uneasy stillness in North America—a pause, maybe, before the tide turns again. We could use this time to realign our governments, our societies, our futures. We have a chance to evolve into something better.

Yes, I'm still a dreamer. I'd rather surf the waves than smash through them.

—Rhett "the JETT" Morita

May 18, 2020 – Chongqing, China – ◇◇◇, "A Wide Net and the Lonely Road"
Part I: Harbinger Days and Harsh Contrasts

Day 116.

I began this blog on a lonely road, racing down a misty mountain, digitally traversing thousands of miles to share what I saw coming from my solitary perch. There was no mistaking the roiling, nasty, virulent global pandemic with the power to kill millions and grind the global economy to a halt. From lockdown, I watched it spread. Some listened. Some argued. Some laughed. Some bullied me for sounding the alarm and disrupting their chill.

For a while, we walked together, my latter days of lockdown shared by many who realized my strange and early journey would soon be theirs. And for a while, I felt less alone. Mavor called me the canary in the coal mine. Ryan called me the Harbinger. These strange names gave me strength. They reminded me I had a higher purpose than just surviving. They kept the anxiety and panic at bay. But now, the road feels quiet and dark again. At least for the moment, I walk alone.

This week has affected us all differently. In some places—Italy, for instance—there's a bubbling joy as they prepare to reopen to tourism. Sicily is even offering to pay visitors to come, to get things rolling again. (Things, not COVID.) Most aren't openly planning for a second wave, but they're not exactly planning to stop one either. A detailed CDC guide to reopening the USA was shelved as "impractical." The White House requested a "softer" version—easier to manage, or to mismanage.

The kind of widespread testing, contact tracing, and quarantine apps used in China and South Korea are bogged down elsewhere by the same privacy debates that hamper mask use—and will likely rear their heads again when a vaccine is available.

I don't understand it.

In my opinion, you don't have the right to infect the people around you. You just don't.

Cover your damn face. Install the app. Get cleared. Be part of the solution.

Otherwise, you're on Team Virus.

Part II: Vigilance in the City of Bridges

Local CQTV did a deep-dive feature on me, my writing, and my book. Shaolin said it was nice. I didn't watch it. My school offered me a new contract. And while I'm overworked and miss those hundred days of writing and stillness, I know I'm lucky. I'm grateful for the work, for the life I have.

Some dance in the streets, believing the worst is over. Others return to work or school. Still others remain in lockdown, facing the even graver threat of starvation. In India and parts of Africa, malnutrition is now a bigger threat than COVID. UNICEF estimates one million children could starve to death this year. Another source suggests 250 million people globally are at risk. Yet in places where healthcare systems are minimal—no ECMOs, no ventilators, no medicine—a pandemic with a CFR of 1–3% could rise to 10–15%. How do you weigh these things?

These are not easy times.

In Chongqing, we're forging ahead. Our last COVID case was discharged two months ago. We've had a few imported cases—eight asymptomatic from Hubei, one from France—all caught in our quarantine net. No outbreaks. No community transmission.

Three weeks ago, I returned to school. I've been tutoring students at home, too. Last week, in some classrooms, students removed their masks. I still haul around my HEPA-filter air purifier and wear my mask most of the time. I've trained my students to cough into their elbows and not sneeze unless absolutely necessary—and even then, elbows only. Sometimes I remove my mask to speak clearly if the filter bubble around me is strong, but I always put it back on. I'm still the weird astronaut among civilians, though in fleeting moments, I'm just a teacher again.

Sometimes headteachers walk around mid-class, pointing thermometers at foreheads. It's just part of life now. In Harbin and Heilongjiang province, new cases still emerge from the border with Russia. Wuhan is undertaking full-scale testing of all 11 million residents after a small cluster reappeared. A woman interviewed by CNA expressed concern: "The safety measures inside are really bad. People are too close. I didn't see the tester wash his hands."

Meanwhile, we lost power during a class last weekend. Two hours without electricity in the heat. We ran a battery fan on the students, let them remove their masks, and I stood three meters away wearing mine. It was another risk. Another compromise.

I currently teach 1,500 students a week. Assuming five people per household, that's 7,500 vectors. Factor in secondhand contact—parents, grandparents, office workers, club members, restaurant staff—and we're easily talking 75,000 weekly connections, all feeding back into my classrooms.

That's a wide net.

And I'm the catch.

Part III: Salsa, Stocks, and 520

Despite it all, Chongqing is one of the safest places on Earth right now. But I remain vigilant, alert, a sentinel for the return of the virus. So far, the silence holds.

My friends are quiet too—many returning to work, many fatigued. Parks in Toronto are packed. Beaches in Florida are full. People are tired. It's spring. They want to move on. But a week after reopening, Texas reported thousands of new cases.

This lockdown is the pause. What comes next won't be what came before. We used to borrow from the future, hoping one day to pay it back. But now, we must live within our means—economically, ecologically, emotionally.

We'll need masks. Distance. Discipline.

We'll need to protect each other. And mean it.

The stock market is high on borrowed serotonin. It can't grind its teeth in blissful denial forever while real people and real companies teeter on collapse. If you're still holding your fortune in stocks, this may be your last chance to divest. Buy land. Grow a garden. That's the advice.

How can we brace for a second wave when most are still battling the first? I expect late May and June to be hard. But I've been wrong before, and I hope I'm wrong now.

To stay grounded, I made salsa. My first one. Mozzarella. Refried beans. Nachos. The little things.

I made a new playlist for the Freakeasy crew in Chicago—channeling my 20-year-old self to lift up my friends. We have to remember to laugh and smile and sing. "Always look on the bright side of life," and all that jazz.

Tomorrow is May 20, Chinese Valentine's Day—520—because the numbers sound like "◇◇◇." I love you. Shaolin and I will celebrate by wandering a mall, buying snacks and souvenirs. Another little adventure in this strange astronaut life.

And just like that, I get a ping—Alessia's back, writing from Italy. Then another—Dara, from PEI.

After a stressful week holding my torch high, I'm not alone anymore.

Not today.

May 19, 2020 – PEI, Canada – "Death, Isolation, Fear, Uncertainty, and Despair" (Dara Mac)

How's your mental health? How's your day to day? I overheard two younger women chatting six feet apart along the Charlottetown boardwalk. "It's hard to get up and get going," one of them said. "I mean, what's the point?"

What's the point? The point of what—living each day? It sounded conditional, like: *If I have somewhere I need to be—work, school—then I have a purpose. Otherwise, left to my own devices, what's the point?* I can understand that mindset, especially in younger people. When you're a teen, rewards need to be immediate. The important things—friends, clothes, dating, sports, dances, socials—have all gone underground during this pandemic. It's a rare artistic teen who thrives in solitude, creating or gaming online. We live in an extroverted world, where, as my mother would say, "solitude is for the birds."

I've met people who can't stand being in nature because it's just too quiet—or maybe their thoughts are too loud. I've long believed that children should be taught how to manage their thoughts from a young age. I meet so many adults whose minds behave like wild horses—no rider in sight. Given that scenario, I can see how difficult isolation may be, and how many turn to self-medication. Our Chief Medical Officer has commented on the rise in alcohol consumption on PEI since lockdown began in mid-March. Accidental opioid overdoses are also on the rise. Fentanyl is now being found in cocaine.

Yesterday, Captain Jenn Casey of Halifax died in the crash of a Snowbird jet during a cross-country tour intended to offer hope and inspiration in a time of fear and grief. The aircraft burst into flames shortly after takeoff and crashed into a home—one occupant was in the backyard, the other in the basement. A neighbor across the street watched in horror as the jet came within fifteen feet of his house. Unforeseeable risks. We cannot let them govern our every move and decision.

Some of my own riskiest behavior happened years ago when I was training with the Ottawa Bicycle Club to ride in the Vermont mountains. One clinic in the Gatineau Hills had us practicing aerodynamic descents—I hit 77 km/hr on my skinny, high-pressure tires. During our actual descent down Smuggler's Notch in Vermont, my teammate's bike frame suddenly split. He crashed right in front of me. Miraculously, no one was injured. But it reminded me how quickly risk can find you, even when you're prepared.

These days, even leaving the house can trigger overwhelming anxiety. I've felt it myself at the grocery store. It starts with a single thought: *This isn't safe.* My body responds—freeze, flight, fight—and off we go.

And yet, here on PEI, all 27 reported COVID-19 cases have recovered. There has been no community transmission, no hospitalizations, and no deaths. So, I've decided to keep some precautions and slowly ease up on others. I remind myself: *No one has died of COVID-19 here. Certainly not while grocery shopping.* The lobster boats are back out. "Nice to see something normal, isn't it?" said a fellow walker on the Rustico boardwalk.

This Friday, PEI will enter Phase 2 of reopening. Retail outlets, greenhouses, car washes, and hairstylists will be allowed to open their doors. (More than ever, I'm grateful I gave up hair dye over a year ago!)

Through the years, I've learned that true joy comes from reconnecting with our own gracious gratitude. I begin my daily drumming practice with mindfulness and prayer—thankful for the passion instilled in me for music, the desire to improve my skills, and the means to play each day, uninterrupted.

What are you grateful for? Sometimes, it's as simple as one breath. Smile. Be kind. Know that the spirit is strong, and love will overcome.

May 19, 2020 – Turin, Italy – "Masked and Exercised" (Alessia Martino)

Now that outdoor walks aren't illegal anymore, and I finally got a free washable mask from my region, I'm all set. Actually, I have two masks that I can alternate. So on Tuesday, I went for the longest and farthest masked walk of this lockdown.

I started with a walk to the same 200-meter spot by the river. I didn't wear my mask the whole time, as there was no one on my way there. It didn't feel necessary to strain my breathing when there were no people around. Wearing a mask in the sun while walking can be pretty challenging as the CO_2 gradually takes over, and the O_2 starts to run low. I am, of course, an advocate for mask use—within reason.

However, as soon as I saw an unmasked man coming toward me, shoveling sand, I masked up and kept my distance. After that, I ventured a bit farther, making a loop that took me across a blueberry field and back home. I don't even remember the last time I did that walk—30 minutes of pure joy.

Soon after, I invited my sister and the dog to join me on a different path in the opposite direction. It was so nice to see different surroundings and admire the wildflowers in full bloom. There were more people on this path, but we kept our distance. Some said hi, almost grasping for months of missing human interaction. It felt weird, as though other humans were aliens on a planet we had decided to explore. By the end of the 2-hour walk, I was both happy and exercised—maybe a bit tired from the effort of keeping my breathing steady. I sat down to relax and just breathe, unmasked, after washing my hands. As someone once said, "Life isn't measured by how many breaths we take, but by the moments that take our breath away." Those walks were literally breathtaking in every sense.

The next morning, I found myself having walked an additional 10,000 steps before lunch, just by moving things around in the greenhouse. Pretty sweet and revitalizing. In the afternoon, feeling energized, I decided to make homemade ragù. It was so delicious and lasted for several meals throughout the week. Now I'm trying to mix things up in the kitchen, though as I'm writing, a craving for Burger King has begun to surge. I see some BK in my future… though not right now. According to Italian Coldiretti, the average Italian has gained at least 2kg since the start of quarantine. I may have gained some too, but as a Facebook meme humorously points out, "Unless I'm sitting on your face, it's not your business." This applies whether it's a pandemic or not, and it's hilarious.

The rest of the week has been pretty quiet and uneventful, as it's been raining pretty much nonstop. I watched a lot of TV and YouTube and did some indoor physical exercise. I'm looking forward to the clothing store reopening next week. I've been facing a trousers shortage, and two months of quarantine might be starting to show.

May 21, 2020 – Gulu, Uganda – "Prostitutes Press for Aid in Food Blackmail (and Win)" (Aliker P' Ocitti)

Part 1: Shadows on the Street, Voices on the Air

It is the sixth week of the lockdown. The streets are empty at night, and all lodges and hotels are closed. The government of Uganda is running a curfew that begins at 7:00 pm till 6:30 am leaving no room for the oldest trade in the history of humankind, prostitution, to thrive in Gulu, a small town in Uganda.

On Wednesday, May 13, I received a call from Gulu's greatest talk show host Stephen Balmoi to attend Teyat, a program on Radio Mega (102 FM), the most popular Saturday radio Talkshow in the district.

"David, I would be grateful to have you as a panelist in my show on Saturday. Do you have time?" asked Stephen, whose giggle could be heard from my side of the call.

"Sure, what are we discussing?" I politely asked, flashing the phone a concerned look.

"Gulu prostitutes have promised to release a name and shame list and photos of district leaders who are their clients if they are not given food aid." It was a chilling and clear response from an enthusiastic Talk Show host ready to rock his show the next day.

"Why me?" I wondered. I was curious to know his thoughts on my previous articles in defense of the rights of prostitutes.

"You speak for them. Since I can not have any of them for my show, I thought I would offer you a platform to represent their views," Stephen cajoled me to be the face of prostitutes in my town on the biggest radio platform ever in the district.

Initially, my instincts preferred flight, but eventually, my mind guided me to use the district's biggest radio platform as an activist.

"It's Ok. I will be there," I said.

"Thanks," he responded as he signed off.

Prostitution is illegal in Uganda, and when caught in the act, one is liable to imprisonment in jail.

However, the law also protects the rights of every citizen. For prostitution to happen, it takes two people, but why are men never arrested? Why can't they benefit from freedom of expression? I asked myself. It's these conversations in my mind that forced me to accept the task of representing them.

Here, they earn their living by lining up on streets in strategic places within metropolitan Gulu waiting for customers.

So what drives them into this business? Many people think they are looking for an easier way to get money.

But prostitution is not easy too. Have you imagined what they face in the experience of meeting every stranger in the dark? I wondered.

Most of them hire lodges to host their clients for a short time or the whole night.

They charge ranging from $2 to $10 per session or per night, depending on your negotiation.

But who benefits when these lodges are hired? The complex nature of the business is that while they permanently live in hiding because of the illegal nature of the business, the very same people to get them out of the business are benefiting as owners of the lodges and buying their services.

Part 2: Broadcasts, Backlash, and Breaking Taboos

Like prostitution anywhere else, it has its push factor. Most of these girls are uneducated and unemployed, with no clear source of livelihood for themselves and their families.

With these ideas, I was convinced to represent them on the radio to speak of uncomfortable realities for the leaders to know that unless we look at them as victims of our broken society that doesn't care for the poor, we will continue to have more girls and single mothers fending for their families by selling the only God-given product they have, even when it's illegal. There is no difference between illegal prostitution and the corruption of the same people who have been in prison as both are illegal.

During this lockdown, most businesses are closed, and everyone except for those working in designated essential areas is in quarantine. Gulu's streets are abandoned in the night, supervised by the military and police who are deployed to observe curfew.

The presidential directive is to have all hotels and lodges closed, including bars and saloons, which are all potential sources of livelihood for the prostitutes.

In an effort to fend for their families, prostitutes have warned through emissaries and social media that they will publish a list of district leaders who are their clients if they are not given food aid like any to their vulnerable groups.

In view of the fact that most Western countries, who formed the bulk of countries and nationals who donate to Uganda but have been grossly affected by the coronavirus (COVID-19), it was prudent that Uganda relied on its own citizens and their businesses for survival.

It marked the new normal for Uganda in terms of sourcing food aid to replace what they would have received from World Food Programs (WFP).

Gulu District Covid19 Taskforce is a decentralized branch of the Uganda National Covid19 Task-force mandated to mobilize resources, food aid, and distribute it to vulnerable members of its community.

The District Covid19 Taskforce is headed by the Resident District Commissioners (RDC), who represent the President in the district. The Chairman of Local Council 5 of the District is in charge of fundraising, and the District Police Commander (DPC) is in charge of security in the district.

May 22, 2020 – San Diego, USA – "Taking Time to Mourn" (Kait Marcelle)

If you're looking for hope or positive news, please stay far away from this home.

A few days before Mother's Day, I found out something I never wanted to know. In an instant, my entire foundation cracked. There was no air left in the room. I collapsed to the floor and tried my hardest not to let the person on the other end of the phone hear me weeping over the loved one I had just lost.

Not a moment has gone by in over a week when this information hasn't been searing through my brain. From the moment I wake, I beg for the sweet relief of unconsciousness that never seems to come soon enough. Even small rituals—like making tea or coffee, two things I usually love—have become joyless. "Just choose one," I tell myself. But my body stumbles, my mind spirals, my senses burn. I forget what I was doing. The weight of it is all-consuming.

And that's all before the coffee is made.

I've been home completing finals. I only cross the threshold to toss in laundry (shared in my building) or to fetch a package. If it weren't for the constant flow of projects to work on, I fear I'd be in a far worse state, left alone too long with my own thoughts. I work from home as well. No contact with the outside world. For the first time, I'm grateful for the mandated reclusiveness—no plans to cancel, no friends to disappoint.

My usual coping mechanisms involve friends, trees, and long meandering walks through the wet wilderness. I fell in love with a boy from the Pacific Northwest over a decade ago, and I must admit—my love for the land up there and my love for him are about equal. He's okay with that. We all agree: how could you not love it? The vast, ancient forests are the most magical place I've ever known.

But now? Walking down the hot, busy street sounds like torture. Heading to the sunny beach feels like a nightmare. I'm clearly not a "typical" California girl—despite being born here.

San Diego is doing relatively well. Our cases are declining. Local restrictions are starting to lift. Retail is reopening. More will follow throughout the summer. I just hope social distancing remains in place—especially on the coasts. Crowded beaches seem like a recipe for disaster.

Most businesses have stepped up cleaning measures, and masks are required for entry. That's fantastic. But I think there's still more to be done before we can claim anything close to a "new normal."

Speaking of that new normal, what *can* we look forward to this summer? I vote 10/10 for bringing back drive-ins—for everything. Movies, concerts, performances. Even restaurant dining—pull up in your car and order like it's your table. Okay, maybe I'm dreaming too far. Still, it would allow us a way to get out of the house safely.

My bachelorette party was supposed to happen this summer, but with everything so uncertain, I've canceled it until further notice.

On the practical front, my partner reports that the stores are staying stocked. Panic buying has eased up a bit, although item limits are still common. From my apartment, I hear more cars on the road now. More sirens, too. First responders. I imagine the worst. I hope for the best.

And here's the thing—I'm of the firm belief that if I can endure *this* moment, in the middle of a pandemic, I can handle just about anything life throws at me from here on out.

As the world begins to return to some version of normal, I know that my life—and the lives of my family—will never be the same. Coping with grief and loss is something we're all likely feeling in

some form. Whether it's the life we had before this, or someone we've loved and lost—it's paramount.
Take the time to mourn.

May 22, 2020 – Melbourne, Australia – "Surrender to the Deep Wisdom of the Universe (One Day at a Time)" (Skye Lazure)
Part I: Tea, Breath, and the Space Between

I wake up to my alarm at 8:45 a.m. and allow myself to come slowly back into the world after my adventures in dreamland. My dreams have become vivid lately—more alive somehow. Sometimes I start the day with breathing exercises. Other times, I scroll my messages, easing in gently.

I have chronic allergic rhinitis—think hay fever on crack—so my first hour is usually a fog of nose-blowing and sluggishness. I feel sorry for anyone who sleeps next to me. My sneeze might be cute, but the morning foghorn? Not so much.

Still, I've learned how to care for myself through this transition. I make a nice cup of tea and start the day slowly. If the sun's out, I sip it in a patch of warmth. If not, I curl up on the couch in a fluffy dressing gown with Felix, my big chocolate Lab, snuggled beside me.

I don't watch mainstream news anymore—or scroll conspiracy theories online. I focus on my intentions: building sustainable communities, living self-sufficiently, expanding my mind, questioning the status quo, healing, and lifting others up. These are my anchors now.

Even before lockdown, I worked mostly from home. I write, mentor people online and over the phone, make art, and spend time in self-study. I've moved some of my workshops online and offer them by donation to help out during this unsettling time. So while the world has changed drastically, my own life hasn't changed all that much. I'm an extroverted introvert—I love people, but I also thrive alone, working on my own projects and learning new things.

I've been diving deep: nutrition, detox, martial arts, death philosophies, van-life, solar power, hunting, plant medicine, shamanism, and earth magick. That's just the shortlist.

Part II: Learning to Trust the Slow Path

Here in Melbourne, the restrictions have started to ease. We're now allowed five guests in our homes and gatherings of up to ten outdoors. Parks and walking trails are full again. The roads, once silent, buzz with sudden activity.

While I'm glad we're emerging from lockdown, I'm moving carefully. I trust that what will be, will be—and I don't worry too much about what others do. I just do what feels right for me. Living with a chronic illness (CFS) has taught me to be discerning about how I spend my time and energy. It's made me slow down, and put things into perspective. That's why my detox studies and health practices mean so much to me now.

People are finding creative ways to adapt: drive-in movies, concerts—even drive-through strip clubs in the States. I say, do what feels right for you. I support women being sexually empowered, but personally, I prefer picnics, hikes, and stargazing over neon lights and windshields.

Fortunately, food and supplies have caught up. No more empty shelves. Even the toilet paper's back.

What's kept me sane is maintaining virtual connections with loved ones, reminding each other what really matters. I avoid social media drama. I've adopted more of a non-reactive Zen approach—focusing on nature, good food, sleep, stillness, and compassion. And if I feel "lazy" or "unproductive" for a day? That's okay too.

I just keep chipping away at my work, following the path of least resistance, taking daily steps toward building the life I want to live. A future I believe in.

My dreams have been more vivid than ever. Sometimes even lucid. I haven't had an out-of-body experience—yet—but I feel like I'm close. Before bed, my partner and I debrief, process the day, hold each other, and sometimes cry. Other nights, we watch web series or movies and just zone out.

Whatever the day holds, I try to give it permission to *be what it is*. I surrender to the deep wisdom of the universe, and wake again, ready to take it one more day at a time.

May 23, 2020 – Buenos Aires, Argentina – "Icing on the Cake" (Josette)
Part I: Buzzkills and Borderlines

Hello, out there world. It's been a couple of weeks. Sorry about that, but the times—they be a challengin'.

It's now been over two months of pure quarantine. The only real face-to-face interaction I've had is with the neighbors downstairs, after I had to help them deal with another neighbor who decided he didn't like any of us foreigners in the building. Among a string of obscenities, he made sure to let both the building and the police outside know that we immigrants should all "go back to our countries."

The icing on the cake? He not only assaulted my neighbor but basically assaulted the police officer, and the cops did... nothing. Instead, they asked for *our* ID numbers so they could check our immigration status. Did they arrest the non-foreigner guy from the nice neighborhood who was actually attacking people? Of course not.

That whole mess left me gutted. I didn't want it to, but it's made it hard to deal with anything else. And it's *not* the time for aggressive behavior. Still, I'm proud I didn't let it break me—aside from the very real fear of seeing that guy again.

Then, just as things were calming down, a new neighbor moved in next door—with a three-year-old. She's a loud talker. I can hear *everything*, as if they're living in my apartment. I don't believe the first thing you hear when you wake up should be someone else's noise. But here we are. Earplugs don't help. Thankfully, I'm a DJ—so, hello, music.

Still, the proximity is wearing me down. These walls are thin. The world feels thinner.

Part II: Masked Up, Caked Up, and Still Here

We have more quarantine. More restrictions. If China took six months to fully reopen, I'm hoping that means August for us?

It's getting colder now. Case numbers are rising. Inflation is wild. I've been trying to move—but as always, moving here is about as easy as cutting off a limb.

The warm week we had? Gone. It's officially autumn: chilly, windy, grey. People are getting fed up with quarantine. A lot of people I know are breaking the rules—and yet, the numbers keep climbing.

I want to break quarantine. Can I?

Going outside is still stressful. Too many people wear masks wrong—or not at all. Too many ignore distancing. I often end up walking in the street with the cars just to avoid them.

And don't even get me started on the ones standing in doorways, glued to their phones.

"Excuse me, I'd like to pass by you."

"Go ahead."

"Actually, could you step back a bit?"

"Oh, I'm not going to give you the virus."

"I'm asthmatic, so I'd prefer some space."

I shouldn't *have* to ask. Isn't it my right to feel safe?

(For the record, studies say asthma might not be such a big risk factor. Still—80% of Argentina's cases are asymptomatic. Hello.)

Between my neighbors, a tooth issue, cockroaches (yup, plural), failing internet, and economic stress, everything is just... not coming up Jojo. But I'll get through it. I don't really have a choice.

Some Recoleta DJ played music in his apartment (who knows how loud), and the cops got called. Other neighbors came out in support. I mean—DJs gotta play. If we're broadcasting online from our homes, as long as it's within quiet hours, just "cerra el orto" and enjoy.

On a brighter note—there's cake.

Chocolate zucchini cake. Carrot cake. There's cake in my freezer. I sent some to a friend via motorcycle delivery, but there's still a surplus. Anyone want cake?

Or a cockroach?

I'm kidding. Kind of.

Don't worry—I'll keep on keeping on, if you promise to do the same.

One love,

Jojo

May 25, 2020 – Turin, Italy – "Out of Body Shopping Experience" (Alessia Martino)

Part I: Welcome to the New Mall

I've been inside for 71 days. I counted them, out of curiosity, until March 19—when I finally gathered the courage to venture beyond the house. That makes it ten weeks and one day.

My sisters and I decided to go to the mall. I needed new clothes, and I suspect my sister just wanted me to finally do my own grocery shopping. We masked up, grabbed a cart, and entered. The mall had been restructured to allow for one-way foot traffic, with free sanitizer at the entrance.

First stop: H&M, a brand I trust for sizes and prices no matter where I am in the world. I was pleased to see another hand gel dispenser at their door, along with a kind man—masked, of course—greeting customers with a thermometer gun to the forehead and what I think was a smile behind his mask. Inside, the staff were friendly and conscious of all safety protocols. Fitting rooms had been reduced and were cleaned after each use. Clothes that weren't purchased were set aside for sanitization before returning to the racks.

I tried on three items and ended up buying... two pairs of socks. The store was nearly empty, half the merchandise was on sale, and even the new collection was discounted—20% off, 30% with a membership card. It was tempting to buy more, but I stuck to what I needed. I knew they were trying to recover from months of closure, as so many shops are.

Still, I left the store feeling satisfied—and slightly shocked. The whole thing felt like an out-of-body experience.

Part II: Grapes, Gloves, and a Glimpse of the Past

On a separate trip, we went grocery shopping. This time, I put on gloves before entering, planning to dispose of them afterward. I had a list, but once I was inside, the sheer number of choices overwhelmed me. The list became obsolete. Suddenly, everything was a *yes*. I see it, I like it, I take it.

Because I'd spent so little on clothes, I gave myself permission to enjoy food. I found the noodle aisle and grabbed one of each type—not the fresh ones, but still, they made me happy. I picked up cereals (finally found a brand that didn't demand a kidney), stocked up on pasta and sauces, and even splurged on out-of-season grapes imported from Chile.

My small cart filled quickly—almost four bags in total—which made checkout a bit tricky. The person behind me had to wait. I struggled to open the bags (always an art form), but the sweet cashier helped me out.

Afterward, I sat on a bench outside the mall, near the parking lot, watching people as I waited for my sisters. Some removed their masks, others fidgeted with gloves, some stopped to chat. It was comforting to see most people respecting the rules. Then I heard my name.

I turned and, after a beat, recognized an old friend. I've known her since childhood. Even though she looked different, I recognized her voice immediately. We chatted briefly—it was a lovely surprise. Then, time to go home.

The next day, I had lunch with my mom—for the first time in 80 days. I wore a mask in the car and kept my distance inside. I washed and sanitized my hands often. We sat at opposite ends of the table and enjoyed the meal: pasta with pesto, buffalo mozzarella, broccoli, and homegrown strawberries.

I saw her again the next day when she gave my younger sister a lift. We had coffee outside together. It doesn't get more Italian than that.

The rest of the week, I took as a chance to keep putting my life in order. Reconnecting. Not getting eaten alive by mosquitoes, thanks to my new diffuser. I'm still mostly inside, but every now and then, I step out—just to remember that the world is still there.

May 25, 2020 – Chongqing, China – "Pansplaining the Uncomfortable"

Day 126.

Part I: The Dream of Sanity and the Idiots Among Us

There are two kinds of people in this world: those who read my blog—and idiots.

No, no. Too controversial. Can't say that. Not if you want to be commercially viable. You can't just call people idiots, even when they are. Too narrow a focus.

Fine. Better than "you're all a bunch of careless fools," I suppose.

I had a dream last night—one of those lucid, high-frequency ones where I vibrated sideways through the Metaverse and landed in New York City, but not ours. This was one of the many timelines where Bernie Sanders became President. I sat in a cozy café eating the most delicious sesame bagels with lox, listening to competent leaders listen to scientists, calmly managing a small epidemic because they'd funded their pandemic prevention office instead of pouring billions into a border wall.

It was beautiful. It made sense. Waking up felt like crashing through glass.

In our world, Canada's top doc Theresa Tam is still tentatively admitting that masks "may offer some protection." May? It's been 126 days since we locked down in China. People here knew that on Day 1. The West's political dithering is more about optics than epidemiology. A U.S. congressional testimony even revealed that the White House pressured the CDC to downplay masks to hide their lack of preparedness. That lie rolled downhill and contaminated the whole western response.

It's hard to be inspiring when you're furious. Mother's Day saw well-meaning family gatherings. We warned them. But people said, "Come on, it's Mom." A week later, Ontario reported its highest daily case count yet—over 400—while beaches and parks in Toronto overflowed with sunburned optimism.

Are they all Trumps in disguise? Or just white people feeling exempt from consequence? Not all, of course, but if you had to bet on which demographic treats public health laws as gentle suggestions, you know the odds.

But I'm not here to rage against the obvious. Today is Towel Day—a tribute to Douglas Adams. A good towel is essential in any intergalactic crisis. Signal distress. Ward off noxious fumes. Wield it in hand-to-hand combat. Dry yourself off.

And in a pinch, it's a pandemic mask.

Part II: Channeling the Sun, Avoiding the Microwaves

Rats in some cities are reportedly turning cannibalistic now that restaurants are closed. Cute metaphor. Creepy reality.

Still—don't panic.

There's always going to be a mix of COVIDIOTS and the cautious. Some reckless people will get lucky, infect no one. Others will kill a loved one without realizing it. We can't control that. We *can* control who we let into our homes, who we stand beside, what risks we take. Build agency. Create your own safety net.

I've been channeling the RZA lately, trying to find my Zen flow. I imagine all the distractions as little asteroids sizzling in the heat of my focused momentum. I am the sun. Burn, baby, burn.

Austria made mask use mandatory and saw a 90% drop in cases. Clear line. Masks work. Countries that embrace science are managing this better. Countries that don't—well, Sweden's disastrous flirtation with herd immunity has led to a death rate eight times higher than its Nordic neighbors.

Even Sweden can't stay neutral when the virus comes knocking.

Meanwhile, in China, foreign-owned companies like Star Rapid have released videos showing how they implement local safety protocols to great success. It's simple stuff. The West could do it too—if it wanted to. But many still act like the virus can be ignored, shushed away, or solved by political spin.

Even in my own home, absurdity persists. Shaolin and I got into a heated argument over microwave safety. She took the food out and closed the door, letting the microwave run empty for a few moments. I panicked. She rolled her eyes. To me, that's a violation of physics. To her, I'm a lunatic. I suspect she just doesn't respect microwave technology like I do.

Later that night, we had friends over—like old times. Beer, video games, birthday laughs. Orlando told me about a graphic novel he's writing, where MIB-style agents investigate the paranormal but show extreme fear around... microwaves. They'll even unplug them before entering a room. My kind of people.

Part III: Elbow Coughing and KaiCore Comebacks

Life in Chongqing is slowly normalizing. I now teach with my mask off—sometimes. I've told students outright: if you cough in the open air, you fail my class. Hand coughers get a B+. Only elbow coughers make the A-list.

The new primary rule in my classroom? Don't kill your teacher.

It's been over two months since we've had a single hospitalized COVID-19 case in this city. That's incredible. Still, I wear my mask on the street. I haul my HEPA purifier to every class. I stand in my little bubble of purified air and knock on wood every chance I get. Shaolin and I even rode the subway. Two stops. Just to go to the mall for sushi and lobster. We're letting students remove their masks during weekend tutoring classes—*if* they wash their hands at the door, sneeze into their elbows, and accept that I run the air purifiers on full blast. It's a risk. But we manage it.

My first COVID diary, *The Invisible War*, is almost done. The Chinese edition is nearly ready. The English editor is still snarky, the translator has questions, but it's moving. Hopefully, we'll have it out in time for the second wave. If it helps a few people, it'll be worth it.

Meanwhile, I made a DJ mix—*KaiCore 2020*. COVID raps. Health PSAs. Hardcore beats. It's educational. It's ridiculous. It's very me. Maybe if I killed the '90s rave scene with KaiCore, I can kill COVID-19 with it too.

Dr. Sachdev Sidhu at the University of Toronto says his team may have found a cure—a synthetic antibody. We'll see. I'm watching closely.

If you're in a city still battling waves of stupidity and infection, don't lose heart. The response may not be national, rational, or

united—but you can still make smart personal choices. Limit your exposure. Wear the mask. Avoid the party people.
You'll be okay.
I'm on the other side now. Not forever, not invincible. But hopeful. I wish you the same—soon.
Stay safe. Stay smart. Stay uncomfortably aware.

May 26, 2020 – PEI, Canada – "Drumming, Bonfires & Ospreys" (Dara Mac)

Prince Edward Island, like much of the world, is slowly emerging from lockdown. We've just entered Phase 2, which now includes shopping malls, car washes, pet grooming, and hairstylists. Nursing homes remain off-limits to visitors, and gyms are set to reopen on June 1.

To the dismay of many, the Premier announced that applications for seasonal residents would reopen June 1. This includes roughly 3,500 part-time islanders who, according to Dennis King, contribute between $50 and $80 million to the local economy. The backlash was swift: the RCMP were called to the Premier's home after an angry constituent approached his wife and 13-year-old daughter while he was away. The discontent was also palpable in the trembling voice of our Chief Medical Officer, Dr. Heather Morrison, who nearly broke down during her latest address, pleading with Islanders to be kind and patient.

Thus far, we have been blessed. All 27 COVID-19 cases on PEI have recovered. No hospitalizations. No deaths. That's in no small part thanks to Dr. Morrison, whose emotion and exhaustion brought tears to my own eyes. I feel such compassion for her in this impossible moment—caught between health, politics, and public fatigue.

We're currently governed by a Conservative mandate that tends to favor business and economic reopening. But I wonder whether this quiet return to "normal" is any more sustainable than the demands made under the previous Liberal government—whose pressures on front-line mental health workers forced many excellent staff to resign, and pushed me into early retirement.

The sobering reality hits again: I haven't seen my son and his wife in nearly two years. Their plans to visit PEI this summer—first for a month, then onward to Ottawa to visit his 90-year-old Gramma and the rest of the family—are fading faster than the day's light. For now, I hold onto the fact that they're doing well. And I keep preparing for the day we'll meet again.

Still, life finds a way.

I'm enjoying the rhythm of growing microgreens—a hobby sparked by a friend's daughter. I learned how to buff out scratches on my car with soap, water, and paper towel after a friend insisted it wasn't as hard as I thought. The shed is painted and ready for trim. That same friend offered some great ideas on how to organize my garden tools. There's nothing like a pandemic to show you who your real friends are.

Each day, I drum. I'm blessed to be connected to a passionate drumming community here on PEI, meeting weekly through Zoom. What a joy to have something to return to—a craft, a discipline, a heartbeat.

My daily beach walks remind me of the sheer beauty of this place I call home. The sound of the waves. The ospreys in flight. Fresh seafood from our local fishers. Of all the places I've lived, this little island is where my roots are. Where my soul exhales.

Wherever you are in the world, remember to pause—and enjoy the moment twice.

May 28, 2020 – Melbourne, Australia – "We Are Open, Curious, Playful, and Flowing" (Skye Lazure)

An American guy living in Australia once told me there's a "tall poppy" culture here that he found deeply self-destructive. At the time, I wasn't quite sure what he meant.

But after traveling extensively, I began to understand. I realized how deeply embedded this mindset is in our culture—especially among those who've been victimized or carry distorted self-worth. Yet it touches everyone, to some degree.

It's that subtle self-deprecation. The quiet instinct to dismiss our own achievements. We downplay our brilliance so we don't outshine others. Rather than celebrating one another's wins, we cut the poppies down so we can all feel "equal." But this is a toxic social norm. It creates a culture where people feel they can't truly express their beauty or power without being called vain or arrogant.

And here's the kicker: when we cut others down, we also sever the flow of our own gifts and creative energy. We shrink from our own magic. We deny our value.

It's a strange cycle: *If you're special, then I must be a piece of shit—so I attack!*

But that's immature. It's undeveloped.

What if, instead, we were open? Curious? Playful? Flowing?

In that space, new and awesome expressions can emerge—things that benefit not only ourselves but the whole collective. This isn't about swinging to the other extreme, where we believe the sun shines out of our asses and we're all superior, all-knowing messiahs. There's a middle ground.

I'm working on claiming that middle ground. Celebrating myself more. Not by rubbing my accomplishments in anyone's face—but by not dimming my light either. Not diminishing how hard I've worked or how far I've come just to make others comfortable.

Humility is a quality I hold dear. But there's a difference between *humility*—as in "we are all special"—and *self-erasure*: "I'm not special at all."

So in the name of rewriting the rules, I invite you:

◈ Share something you've accomplished recently that you're proud of.

◈ Share one thing you love about yourself.

◈ Share a gift you've nurtured—whether it comes naturally or through effort.

And let's celebrate our wins, together.

May 29, 2020 – Buenos Aires, Argentina – "Do Not Pass Go" (Josette)

Dear Diary,

Do not pass GO. Do not collect $200.
I've decided to move in the middle of quarantine.
I thought I could manage, but I can't. No, I really can't. And by that, I mean I can't keep living in a place that just isn't cutting it. So please cross your fingers that something better comes along—it's time. Another chance for a space that's just mine (and the cat's, of course). Just the two of us.
I'm not sure how the logistics are going to work, but somehow, they will. Maybe cross your toes too while you're at it.
Now, for a little story from last week that people have asked me about...
We've all probably wondered what it would be like if we needed a doctor or dentist during lockdown. That moment came for me. A dental issue flared up and all I could think was, "Crap."
Luckily, I have a fantastic contact—a periodontist, technically (they deal with the structures of your mouth more than cavities), but he agreed to see me as an "emergency" and assured me it would be okay.
Step one was getting across the city. I hired a friend who's been doing deliveries and private rides during the pandemic. We agreed on a price, and I made the appointment. Cue mild panic.
After two and a half months of isolation, suddenly I was out in the world again—and *this* is what I saw on Santa Fe Avenue:
Traffic. Foot traffic. Like, *a lot* of it.
"Oh, but isn't there a quarantine?" you might ask.
Yeah... you could've fooled me.

I was nervous, but Doc's office was as strict as could be. I was the only patient (as usual), and when he opened the door, this is what went down:

1. Sanitize hands.
2. Sit down, place jacket and bag in a plastic bag.
3. Temperature check.
4. Sign a waiver confirming I had no symptoms and understood the risk.
5. Sanitize hands again.
6. Doc put surgical booties on my shoes.
7. A surgical cap went on my head.
8. Wash hands for 20 seconds.
9. Put on a full surgical gown over my clothes.
10. Finally, sit in the chair and rinse my mouth with "agua oxigenada" (hydrogen peroxide—yep, it was as gross and strong as it sounds).

In the end, the issue wasn't serious. Doc resolved it, and I was genuinely impressed and grateful for his level of care and precaution. We have to find ways to coexist with this virus—and this felt like a model of how it can be done.

Now, back at home, I've been leaning into hobbies and self-care. I'd forgotten how much I love cooking. Lately, I've been obsessed with what I call *cheater pho*—a shortcut version using store-bought broth. (Look, I know real pho is better, but this still hits the spot.) What I wouldn't give to be in a place like Toronto where you can order real ethnic food on a whim. But until then, I'll keep trying new recipes, chasing that taste of being somewhere else.

I know everyone's been baking, but what new, delicious thing have you tried making lately? And if you haven't—why not start?

It's been two and a half months in quarantine.

Don't give up.

Be okay.
—Josette
Buenos Aires, Argentina

June 1, 2020 – Chicago, USA – "Coronavirus—What's the Deal with These Numbers?" (MC ZULU)

Most people don't know this about me, but I've been a nurse since the 1990s. I started out as an Army medic.

Last Thursday, a colleague of mine—someone I've known for years—messaged me: "In the ICU with COVID." By Tuesday, her son had taken over her social media accounts to post memorial pictures and goodbye messages. It was that fast. Another friend of mine was found unresponsive in bed by his wife. Both deaths, no doubt, will be chalked up to COVID-19.

It's heartbreaking. Surreal. And to be honest? Scary.

I haven't been active on social media lately, but I've been watching. The distrust of official narratives has reached epic proportions. People are turning on each other. Between the conspiracy theorists on one side and the frightened "sheeple" on the other, it feels like nobody is truly listening.

Somewhere in the noise, I started to form my own theory.

What if everyone is a little bit right?

What if many of these recent deaths *are* COVID-related—but at the same time, what if certain interests have something to gain from overreporting or underreporting numbers?

What if it's not always malice—what if it's just… mistakes? Honest ones, made under pressure, in the middle of a crisis no one's ever seen before?

This whole thing sounds a lot like life: messy, complicated, and filled with competing interests and human error.

The only thing that's made sense to me, consistently, throughout this saga?

Treat everyone like they could be infected.

That's it.
That's the only solid advice I've trusted.
Take universal precautions. Stay clean. Keep your distance. Protect your people.
What we don't talk about enough is how COVID takes advantage of the body's pre-existing weaknesses. Circulatory, respiratory—even integumentary systems (that's your skin, y'all). It all matters. My fellow medical workers will catch that pun—and understand the gallows humor behind it. It's a dark little coping mechanism we carry to survive long shifts filled with grief.
Even if you're questioning the official version of events—even if you're joking about the absurdity of it all—remember this: **People are dying.**
If you're immunocompromised, you're at risk. Full stop.
So while we're all hunkered down, fearful of each other, this is also the time to evaluate your own routine. Take stock. What habits are helping? What's hurting? How can you live a little healthier, a little wiser?
One day, we'll have the benefit of hindsight. One day, the root causes and politics and failures will be clearer. But for now, we're still deep in the chaos. And in chaos, only one position makes sense:
A defensive one.
Keep your physical distance from danger—but also take this time to look inward.
In a world full of conflicting truths, now's the moment to be *truly* honest with yourself.

June 1, 2020 – Turin, Italy – "Newly Found Freedom" (Alessia Martino)

A New Kind of Normal

Italians are technically not under quarantine anymore, although still bound to regional movements. Even that is supposed to change soon, making interregional movement possible again. This is welcomed news, especially for those that have family elsewhere in the country. Since May 23, bars and restaurants can operate with physical distancing measures in place, allowing for seated service once again. Hairdressers and beauty salons have also opened, answering to those in need of a familiar image, or perhaps a reinvention.

It's a new week, with new rules, and new adventures. I still spend a lot of time around the house, but I do want to take advantage of the newly found freedom while applying safe common sense—because slowly dies one who becomes a slave to routines and never changes paths.

Cafe Adventure: A Quiet Resurgence

I sat at a café with my sister on a hot Tuesday afternoon, waiting for the other one to join us. It was surreal, and perhaps a bit sad. We entered to ask for ice cream but settled for iced tea when they didn't have what we desired. The place was completely empty, save for the waitstaff, who greeted us with a nice smile and a squirt of hand gel at the door. We sat outside in a large outdoor area that now held only three tables, and the others were stacked and chained to the poles—almost as if they were there just for display.

It was nice to have the place to ourselves, but we couldn't help but notice how grim things felt for small businesses. The ice tea was expensive, but we were happy to contribute to the local economy. Afterward, we dined at Burger King, sitting at one of the outdoor tables. Only one person per family was allowed inside, masked up, and maintaining a meter distance. It was peaceful, with only two or three other groups scattered around. It felt like a temporary glimpse of normalcy, but I knew these small businesses were struggling to get by.

A Hike Into the Mountains

The greatest adventure of the week came on Sunday. My siblings and I decided to take a hiking trip to the mountains and enjoy some food at our usual spot. We got off to a late start, and though we were exhausted at the beginning of the hike, we made it to our destination. Our love for the mountains goes way back—since childhood, we'd been taking hikes with Dad. We'd called ahead to reserve a table, and thankfully, we were seated outside with good coverage, adhering to safety protocols.

We had a traditional mountain lunch—cutlets, mountain cheeses, polenta with sausages, and mashed potatoes—followed by apricot jam pie, espresso, and a shot of mountain liquor. That's tradition; no lunch in the mountains is complete without a shot. Afterward, I took a quick nap at the table before we hiked down and made our way home.

It was great to be together, though it doesn't happen often. We managed to end the day watching *Avengers: Infinity War* as part of our ongoing Marvel movie marathon.

Looking Forward

Another month has passed, and I feel excited for what's ahead. The sun is shining more often now, and I see more mountain trips in my future. As life slowly returns to normal, I'll keep making the most of these small, precious moments.

June 1, 2020 – London, UK – "We Do Not Get to Tell Someone How to Process Their Pain" (Aliya Lily)

Hi friends, please hear me out on something important.

Especially to those saying, "Focus on love and unity—this is only creating more separation"—I understand that you mean well, but the **energetics of that response are weak and flawed**. There are far stronger, more effective ways your energy can be of service right now.

Maybe it's confusing. That's okay. Let me try to break it down.

I have some questions for you:

- If a friend came to you and told you they'd been raped, and they needed a shoulder to cry on—needed to scream, to rage, to process—what would you do?
- If you were in a plant medicine ceremony, and the person next to you started purging—crying, vomiting, shaking—what would you do?
- If your sister, your brother, your mother or father came to you in the aftermath of trauma, asking for space, what would you do?

Would you honor their process? Would you hold space for them to feel it all?

Or would you interrupt them with your discomfort—your version of how they should heal?

We do not get to tell someone how to process their pain. That is the bottom line. We can support them. We can hold space. We can offer words—if asked. But we do not get to decide how healing should look.

Imagine someone doing that to you while you were in the midst of your own pain.

Imagine being told that what you're feeling is not valid.

What's happening now—through the lens of Spirit—is the **largest collective trauma-healing ceremony Earth has ever seen.** And more groups will go through this. We're lifting the veil, slowly and painfully, to look at our wounds. The feminine has been going through it. Now the deep racial pain is rising to the surface.

And we have a choice: **to hold space for that healing—or to continue to oppress it.** There is no neutral ground. That's the illusion. You either make space, or you contribute to the silence.

This isn't about white people being evil or inherently bad. It's not even about guilt. It's about **acknowledging who's hurting most, and listening.**

Right now, it's time to listen to Black and Brown communities.

Not to center yourself.

Not to argue.

Not to spiritual bypass with "it's all love and light."

Imagine you're in a ceremony. The shaman has been helping you, but now they turn to help someone else, someone in acute crisis. You feel left out. You feel like healing attention should stay on you. That's not how it works. Now is their time.

Look at our human history.

Hundreds of years of **control, slavery, rape, systemic violence.** That pain is rising now. It's ancestral. It's sacred. It demands space. What we're witnessing is grief. Exhaustion. Sacred rage. And all we need to do is **hold space.**

Cry with it.

Meditate with it.

Make art with it.

Listen.

This is not a race war. That's fear talking.

This is an ancient trauma ceremony. A purge. A grief that has finally been given permission to rise. And from that pain—if we let it move—will come **exquisite wisdom**, and a deep, Earth-rooted healing.

White people have pain too. Of course. And oppressive systems hurt all but a very select few. But in this moment, having lighter skin means you sit closer to safety. And that is **not something everyone has**.

Let that sink in.

This is the time to **listen more than we speak**, to **amplify the voices that have gone unheard**. To sit with the discomfort instead of trying to spiritually gloss over it.

Because saying "focus on love and light" while people are crying out in pain?

That's not mature spirituality.

That's avoidance.

It's time we grow out of that.

I see us in a global ceremony, stomping and shaking, as our collective wounds rise to be witnessed. And I believe, from this place, we will **birth new systems, new wisdom**, and **a more humble humanity**.

Hands, ears, hearts to the ground.

And just remember:

Right now, we hold space for those hurting the most.

It's not about you.

—Aliya Lily

June 1, 2020 – Philadelphia, USA – "Keep Standing Tall, My Brothers, My Sisters" (Stephen Williams)

I'm tired.
I'm beaten.
I'm saddened.
I am exhausted.
Another one of us—beaten, killed.
Another Black life taken.
And somehow, this has become the social norm.
I'm tired of us dying at their hands.
I'm exhausted by prayers, hand-holding, hashtags, peaceful protests, and the constant refrain:
"Oh, if he/she had just complied."
I hate that my brown skin is a target.
It disgusts me that no matter how intelligent I am, they see trash.
No matter how successful I am, they see an animal.
No matter how civilized I am, they see a "super predator" that needs to be controlled.
In case you forgot:
My people built your country.
We picked your cotton.
We birthed your babies when you raped our women.
We made your homes shine for your guests.
And still, you tell us we don't belong here.
Not in *Amerikkka*.
I'm tired of being on the news.
I'm tired of driving while Black.
Walking while Black.
Working while Black.

Jogging while Black.
Being born Black.
Our children are taken from us by the police—and we pray.
Our women are taken from us—and we hashtag.
Our men are taken from us—and we march.
We scream.
We yell.
We demand to be seen.
We demand to be heard.
But isn't it time—when we fight back—they finally listen?
Isn't it time the streets understand our pain—feel it in the blood, in the pavement, in the air?
Keep standing tall,
My brothers.
My sisters.
We will be appreciated.
We will be valued.
We will be seen.
We will be loved.
Because we refuse to DiE.

June 2, 2020 – Washington, DC – "Swann Street Siege (The People United)" ('Aaron Nonymous')

If you're not following the Swann Street siege story this morning—stop what you're doing. It's incredible.
Last night in Washington, D.C., police corralled a large group of peaceful demonstrators into a residential neighborhood using a tactic known as **"kettling."**
Kettling is a military maneuver. You encircle a group on all sides, forcing them into tighter and tighter space until there's no retreat. In protest contexts, it's not a method of dispersal—it's a method of punishment. Once kettled, people can't escape. They're often subjected to **tear gas, batons, pepper spray**, and **brutal arrests**. It's designed not just to incapacitate but to cut off access to **medics, aid, water, and safety.**
That's exactly what D.C. police attempted last night.
But the community was watching.
Residents on Swann Street, seeing what was happening, **threw open their doors**—sheltering protestors from the violence unfolding outside. One of them, **Rahul Dubey**, a first-generation Indian-American, welcomed more than **100 demonstrators** into his home and stood firm as the police tried **multiple times** to enter.
They were **repelled each time.**
Tear gas seeped through the streets. Police tried different ways to breach the private property. But Rahul and his neighbors held the line, offering **sanctuary, food, water, first aid**, and eventually **lawyers and safe morning escorts** for those they protected.
It was a **spontaneous miracle of solidarity** in the face of state aggression.
Want to know what community looks like? This is it.

June 4, 2020 – Orchard Road, Singapore – "Hip Hop, Deep Thoughts & Black Lives Matter" (Masia One)

I want to address and deconstruct a perspective I've seen surface again and again among my Asian friends—namely, the hashtag: **#AllLivesMatter.**

Yes, all lives matter. And yes, it's not just about "Black vs. White"—it's about **everyone vs. racism.** These words often come from my most open-hearted friends—people who embrace all cultures, who cried when they watched videos of police brutality, who speak out against discrimination in their communities. I see you. I love you. I *was* you.

Not long ago, I got into a Facebook argument on Rosina Kazi's page after an open critique of Lilly Singh (IISuperwomanII) for appropriating Black culture without giving back to the communities she borrowed from. I defended her. I said she grew up in Brampton, Ontario—where Black slang and style are a part of everyday life. Surely that's not appropriation? I argued it was a natural progression, and that people should teach her, not cancel her.

I was met with a wall of criticism. Accused of being "anti-Black," "a problem," "a culture vulture."

I was stunned. I thought my intent was clear. I thought I was standing up for understanding and dialogue. What I've realized since is this: **my intent does not matter more than the pain** of those who have suffered. If I am really listening, then I must accept that it's **not about me.**

Sometimes, the best way to learn is to **shut up, listen, understand,** and be willing to unlearn.

Black Lives Matter is not a confrontation. It is not exclusionary. It is aspirational.

Saying "Black Lives Matter" does not mean others don't. It is a rallying cry, a call to correct the statistical imbalance that proves—without a shadow of doubt—that Black people are more than twice as likely to be killed by police while unarmed. That's not opinion. That's fact. **Systemic racism is real**, and whiteness—and proximity to whiteness—offers safety that people of color do not enjoy equally.

You want proof? Look at the systems meant to "protect": the police, the courts, healthcare, the media, even public space. Those same systems disproportionately harm Black communities. Take a scroll through Instagram. You'll see Black and brown people marching for their right to live while influencers post quarantine makeup tutorials. That's the contrast. That's the dissonance.

I was an immigrant who moved to an all-white neighborhood in Canada. I've been called "chink," told to "speak English" (though I always have), and worse—especially when I entered the music industry as a **female Asian rapper**. But I've never had a gun to my head for the color of my skin. I've never had family imprisoned for their melanin. Whether we like it or not, **our skin gives us privilege**. It's time to acknowledge it.

I haven't even touched on the generational trauma from slavery, segregation, or the KKK. Let's be real—I have the longest-running career of any Singaporean hip-hop artist. This culture is my life, but I am still a **guest in a house Black lives built**.

That's why I call myself the **#FarEastEmpress**—to reclaim my crown, to stand with other Southeast Asians and say: We are royalty too. And royalty means **accountability**.

Part of reclaiming the throne means sitting with discomfort. It means acknowledging that we may have spoken from privilege. That we may have been wrong. That we can do better.

Maybe it's the geographical distance. Maybe it's cultural disconnect. But I'm asking my people—brown, yellow, Black, rojak: **Go**

deeper. Imagine what it means to be **killed** for your skin color. Not teased. Not mocked. **Killed.**

As a Singaporean, as an artist, as a person of color in a global hip-hop community, I support **Black Lives Matter**.

—Masia One

June 7, 2020 – Toronto, Canada – "The Start of a Great New Journey" (Rhett Morita)

We are at the start of a great new journey—one that promises new standards, perceptions, and values worthy of the human condition. It's bold, untested, both inspiring and daunting.

But let's be real: this won't be achieved in a year. In fact, I'd consider it miraculous if it were fully incorporated, adopted, and integrated in 20 years. Thirty would still be fantastic. Forty? That would be just fine, all things considered.

True change—deep, meaningful, sustainable change—requires constant, focused, guided work. It doesn't happen haphazardly just because we *want* it to. That's a naïve, arrogant notion. Especially if we're talking about rewriting deeply ingrained biases that have been carved into us our entire lives, often without our conscious awareness. These systems—our media, our education, our conditioning—must be reprogrammed for something better to emerge. That's no small task.

I know this from personal experience. At 27, I was fed up with who I was. By some grace, I found a school that helped me "rewire" my thinking and rebalance my emotional processes. I dove in. Three concentrated meetings a week. Studying 35 to 40 books. I gave up most of my outside pursuits—including clubbing (a big deal for someone who once went 14 nights in a row)—and instead worked side by side with 60 others, each on their own unique path of growth.

For three years, I didn't set foot in a club, and didn't miss it. After that intense period, I might have gone out two or three times a year. And I love clubs. I *love* dancing.

After seven years of focused self-work, I'd estimate I was 60% of the way to my personal goal. That's how hard rewiring is, even with skilled instructors, the right environment, and my total commitment. I spent 50% of my waking hours training, studying, and absorbing audiotapes—learning about the world, and about myself.

Now compare that to the sweeping change being asked of the world right now. Change that millions *want*, but many don't yet understand—or fear. Even those who *do* want it may underestimate what it takes. Are we really ready for 24/7 commitment to growth, to uncovering our blind spots, to falling down and getting up again—500 times if needed? Are we willing to be wrong, to be called out gently, again and again, and still return to the work?

Because the battle is real. The moment you try to change, your programming pushes back. Doubt creeps in. The world around you resists. You'll need community. Mentors. Guides. A higher perspective. And most of all: endurance.

This is not a one-year sprint. This is a **25-year marathon**.

I don't expect most people to drop everything for seven years of intensive work. So realistically, I believe it will take 30 to 40 years to truly implement this kind of massive shift—especially without a shared roadmap or unified teaching. So many mixed messages are out there, and many will fall off the path in six weeks, six months, six years. I've seen it happen. That's just how it is.

But still, **let's do it**. This is the tipping point into a better world.

A quick note: if you don't see me screaming at the front of a protest, even though I'm just as enraged, it's because I'm older now—and, I hope, wiser. I've witnessed people give the most impassioned speeches of their lives, moved to tears by new insight, pledging to dedicate their lives to the cause. And then two weeks later, they're gone. A month later, forgotten.

After you've seen that five or six times, you realize the trap. So I choose to be the guy **still standing there 20 years from now**, fist raised, *ready for the next 20.*

Let's start this journey—together.

June 8, 2020 – Turin, Italy – "Just Breathe" (Alessia Martino)

We are still here, in a COVID world, in a locked country. The situation is, however, changing, always in motion, on every front. According to the official website of the Italian Health Ministry (Ministero della salute), where I got the information from, as a reliable source, lockdown measures effectively helped to control the virus transmission in the country, although there are differences per region. We have COVID-free areas and others going towards the same goal. Others might be further from reaching it, but the situation is generally under control. There are more cases, but the rate is declining. More tests are carried out as the country decided to randomly select a sample of 150 thousand people (diversified by gender, six levels of age and occupation) to inquire further about the current situation and the development of antibodies (working to understand herd immunity). This will also permit scientists to uncover some data about asymptomatic cases. The selected are not forced to take the test, so they can opt-out, however getting tested is seen as a civic duty, other than the fact that said **TURIN, ITALY: JUST BREATHE**

June 8, 2020

By Alessia Martino

We're still here—living in a COVID world, in a country slowly unlocking. The situation is always shifting, in motion on every front. According to Italy's Ministry of Health, lockdown measures have successfully helped control the virus's transmission, though regional differences remain. Some areas are already COVID-free, while others are working toward that goal. The overall trajectory, however, is promising.

More testing is underway. The government has launched a randomized study of 150,000 people across six age brackets, occupations, and gender groups to understand the development of antibodies and track asymptomatic cases. Participation is voluntary, but the public is encouraged to treat testing as a civic duty. (Privately, the test would cost 30–60 euros.)

To move toward a truly COVID-free Italy, strict safety measures remain. Life is resuming, though in a new form. Not everything is open. Not every problem is solved. But hopefully, we're getting there.

June 2 marked the Italian National Day—our Festa della Repubblica. It commemorates the founding of the Republic in 1948: a vision of equality, democracy, and renewal. Italian flags colored the skies in cities across the country. The gesture was both celebratory and commemorative, paying tribute to those who died from or are still recovering from COVID-19.

It was a beautiful gesture, though perhaps a little counterproductive, as many people still gathered to watch. Some probably used the day off to barbeque and socialize. My region even requested broader mask use for the occasion. I kept it simple—resting, reorganizing, and reflecting.

Later that week, I escaped to the mountains to breathe. The weather was temperamental—rainy, windy, finally sunny—but the air was fresh, the space needed. It reminded me I need better trekking shoes; my old hiking boots are too heavy now. So, I went out and bought some new gear. I'm eager to break it in.

On the downside, my phone died. Buying a new one during a pandemic is tricky, as long, distanced lines and occupancy limits make stores hard to access. I've now been without a phone for a week. It's not the end of the world, but I miss being able to video call. Hopefully, I'll get a replacement soon.

Saturday night, I went out. I honestly can't remember the last time I did. We met at a friend's café for aperitivo—cocktails and snacks—sitting outdoors with all safety measures in place. Masks when moving, hand gel at the entrance, and at least a meter between tables. I had a peach-based cocktail (delicious) and nibbled on pizza, breadsticks, and salami. I used two wooden cocktail sticks—mine and my sister's—to pluck peanuts from a bowl, chopstick-style. My little sister tried too. She nailed it. I was so proud.

I went home smiling, and as I settled into bed, I looked out the window and caught distant fireworks lighting up the night. A simple joy, just before sleep.

June 12, 2020 – Buenos Aires, Argentina – "Hoping for Change" (Josette)

Dear World,
Well—it's been almost three months of "strict" quarantine... and counting.

They say it might last until September (yep, you heard that right—**six months** of lockdown) in an effort to "skip" winter. Sadly, it makes sense. The arrival of chillier weather has brought a spike in cases. Yet somehow, at the same time, some restrictions are being relaxed? How does that work?

This past week, the government decided to allow running and walking in local parks between 8 p.m. and 8 a.m. (supposedly within five blocks of home... not that anyone checks). So what does that look like?

This.

Thousands of people flooded the parks, stretching the rules to escape home confinement and get some fresh air—if not exactly "exercise." Honestly, I've thought about going for a walk, but the idea of navigating all those people to do something *relaxing* stresses me out. If a four-block trip to the ATM fills me with dread, I can't imagine doing laps in a packed park.

Also: **dengue.**

Yes, dengue has now reached nearby neighborhoods. The mosquitoes are vicious, and I have sweet blood—like, *target-acquired* kind of sweet. I stepped outside my building for ten minutes and got bitten three times. Everyone's talking about coronavirus, but dengue is quietly carrying its own death toll. There's not enough mosquito repellant in the world—unless someone's selling hazmat suits?

Another joy of quarantine: **dog poop.**

Buenos Aires has always had a bit of a sidewalk minefield issue, but it seems quarantine has amplified people's laziness. Walking outside feels like a high-stakes obstacle course, especially in autumn. Your challenge: **is it just a leaf? Or is it a leaf with a surprise underneath?** Heads up so you don't bump into people—but also, heads down so you don't step in... surprises. Complicated.

The president is now considering taking us back to Phase 1—**full lockdown**—after a record 1,200 new cases yesterday, the highest daily count so far. And yet, I'm seeing more activity: clothing stores open, shoe shops, casual strolls through the city. "Quarantine?" people joke. "What quarantine?"

I've also seen a lot of violence on the news lately—here and abroad. Beyond the global anti-racism movement, there are more local concerns. Petty crimes are turning violent. Everyone's home, which increases the risk of being targeted as you arrive at your front door. Car batteries are being stolen because cars aren't in use. Grocery shoppers are being mugged. One woman was dragged by her hair on a motorcycle because the thief didn't let go. Horrible.

So yes, I'm looking to move. While moving house during a pandemic isn't *ideal* for my anxiety, I don't think I can make it until September in my current apartment. My new neighbor has been torturing me with 7:30 a.m. blender marathons on Sunday mornings, and midnight screamfests with her child. I've been organizing (purging ten and a half years of stuff), working, and cooking. This week I made chickpea curry for the first time. It was **delicious**.

It's hard knowing the rest of the world is slowly easing into its "new normal," while here, despite an early and strict lockdown, we might have the **longest** one. It's not even about seeing friends. For me, it's just the freedom to change the air I breathe—to take my laptop to a café and work. I never realized how much that change of atmosphere affected my productivity. Some days, anything can set me off and shut me down.

A friend in Spain told me that getting back out there is hard at first—you get used to being home, being alone. She described the anxiety, but promised me it gets better.

I'm still scared to go out, really. But today, for the first time in three months, I'm going to walk to see an apartment. It'll be about 4 km round trip. I'm excited and nervous. The bright side is I can stick to residential streets, which feels safer.

I worry about my friends and family around the world. But maybe... I need to start worrying about myself a little more, too.

Be okay.
—Josette

June 16, 2020 – Chongqing, China – "In the Eye of the Storm (Fracturing Reality)"

Part I – The Eye of the Storm

Day 146. I'm in the eye of a storm, looking out with awe, shock, and profound respect. I live in one of the few countries that clamped down on the COVID-19 pandemic with ferocious determination and rooted it out—more or less. Along with my current home base in China, Vietnam, Mongolia, and New Zealand have also claimed relative freedom from the virus. But even here, as we reopen, welcome back expats, and resume trade, new cases trickle in.

In Singapore, the second wave came from crowded migrant worker dorms. In South Korea, it was nightlife, clubs, and dancing. Both countries are back on their feet now, but they can't call themselves virus-free. Just as I sit down to write this, Beijing—after 56 days with zero reported cases—has confirmed roughly 100 new infections. Thousands are quarantined and tested. How did this happen? Two theories: first, that asymptomatic cases had been quietly spreading in corners until symptoms finally emerged. Second, that someone lied about travel history and brought the virus back. Both are under investigation.

It's unsettling. Investigators traced the outbreak to a wholesale food market and even detected the virus on salmon imported from Norway. Now, Beijing fish markets are under strict surveillance, and we're swearing off sushi for a while. Better safe than sorry.

Meanwhile in Chongqing, three imported cases have been detected—two from Bangladesh, one from Sudan. All asymptomatic at departure but flagged by PCR testing upon arrival. Everyone on their flights is now in 14-day quarantine. The system, so far, is holding.

Outside of China, however, things are a mess. Globally, we are now repeating patterns from the Spanish Flu of 1918: initial outbreaks followed by fatigue, complacency, and ultimately, a deadlier second wave. History told us this would happen. We know better. Yet, around the world, people are tearing off their masks, gathering in large groups, ignoring all precautions. The cognitive dissonance is profound.

At first, I felt like the smartest person in the room—relaying vital information months before the CDC or WHO caught up. But now? It's chaos. Overwhelming. And honestly, I don't always know what to say anymore.

So, I go swimming. I dive into the pool every day until it hurts. The water is cool, cleansing. In the blistering 38-degree heat, it grounds me. My anxiety? Almost gone. For a month or two now, life has been normal again. I almost killed my dog with a bone (he's fine). My book *The Invisible War* is stalled unless I agree to rename it *Kai's Diary*—a government-friendly nod to Wuhan's "Fang Fang's Diary." The artist in me is gutted. But I can always push for my real title later, once the gears are moving again. Humility may not be my strength, but it's something I've been working on.

Life in Chongqing continues. I teach. I get haircuts. I go to restaurants with friends. I am, by all accounts, in the eye of the storm.

Part II – Fracturing Reality

Beyond our borders, the world is on fire. Quite literally, in some places. This is a complete reversal from the winter, when China was locked down and the rest of the world seemed blissfully intact. Now, chaos unfurls across continents.

In India, a massive storm triggered emergency evacuations during lockdown, and countless migrant workers are dying as they trek hundreds of kilometers on foot—cities having no work left to offer.

Across Africa, both pro- and anti-lockdown protests are paralyzing already-fragile systems. And in America? The country is convulsing.

George Floyd's murder, caught on video, was the breaking point. His repeated cries—"I can't breathe"—ignored by the police officer who knelt on his neck for almost ten minutes. The world watched in horror. This wasn't new. It followed a long, familiar lineage: a man selling loose cigarettes, a boy in a hoodie, a jogger out for exercise—all murdered for the crime of being Black in America. After Amy Cooper's now-infamous "Karen" call in Central Park, we saw just how weaponized whiteness can be. Systemic racism isn't just American. It's embedded in Canada, the U.K., and all the echoes of colonial power.

Cities around the world began to march. Statues of slave owners and genocidal leaders were toppled. And still, we argue over whether they should be preserved as history. My answer? If they're of historical value, move them to museums. Public squares shouldn't glorify oppression. We have a chance—right now—to reimagine our cities, our symbols, our social contracts.

Trevor Noah said it best: society is a contract, and when those in power break their side—abandoning their duty to protect and serve—don't ask why people are looting Target. Ask why they shouldn't. That kind of raw logic cuts through centuries of denial.

This moment feels like a convergence of collapses: social, economic, environmental, ideological. A burning point of no return. And yet—there's hope. A fragile, furious hope. A hope that capitalism's failures will no longer be swept under the rug. That colonial hierarchies can finally be dismantled. That we can end the burning of fossil fuels before 2030 melts the Earth. That we can survive the storm of overlapping catastrophes: hurricanes, floods, fires, pandemics, blackouts. The climate chaos we feared has begun to knock—five crises at once in some places—and we have no more time to waste.

Social media, once a force for connection, is becoming a battlefield. I've seen callouts where collaborators threaten to leak unfiltered vocals if their white colleagues stay silent. I've seen anger, encouragement, division, and desperate attempts to speak up without speaking over. But it's getting noisy. It's getting hard to breathe.

I joined in at first—blocking racists, sharing memes, flipping off trolls alongside Seth Rogen in solidarity. But then I posted about Canada's brutal history with its First Nations people—highlighting that we, too, have a reckoning to face. A First Nations acquaintance told me to "step off, honky," that he didn't want my support. I respected his view, but I also reminded myself: I don't need his permission to speak out against injustice. I speak not to win likes or approval. I speak because silence is complicity.

Part III – The Center Must Hold

To this, I turn to a guide for me—the ancient sage Seneca—and his seventh letter to Lucilius, on the subject of crowds: "For I never bring back home the same character that I took abroad with me. Something of that which I have forced to be calm within me is disturbed; some of the foes that I have routed return again" (VII.1). What is he warning against? What is the peril of going with the popular crowd?

"To consort with the crowd is harmful; there is no person who does not make some vice attractive to us, or stamp it upon us, or taint us unconsciously therewith. Certainly, the greater the mob with which we mingle, the greater the danger... I mean that I come home more greedy, more ambitious, more voluptuous, and even more cruel and inhuman because I have been among human beings" (VII.2–3).

Even well-meaning crowds can become unruly. I think we must follow our hearts rather than the whims of the mob. In Seneca's time, a period of great injustice, he might witness this on a walk through the square: "In the morning they throw men to the lions and the bears; at noon, they throw them to the spectators... And when the games stop for the intermission, they announce: 'A little throat-cutting in the meantime, so that there may still be something going on!'" (VII.4–5).

Ultimately, it's a futile path to try to please the crowd. If we see eye to eye on an issue—whether it's being pro-mask, anti-virus, anti-racist, pro-equality, pro-virtue, or pro-environment—then let us rejoice in our shared cause. But I will not moderate my internal work, my thoughts, or my voice based on the whims of others. They blow in every direction, asking me to speak or to stay silent, to engage or to back away. If I tie myself in knots trying to appease everyone, I'll only find myself the next target for daring to exist at all.

After a few weeks of blocking and calling out overt racists, I fear social media is now turning on itself—seeking any misstep or poorly phrased comment as a chance to cancel, isolate, or destroy. Just today, an acquaintance questioned why I'd advocate mask use, sharing a doctor's opinion that anyone arguing against masks in the U.S. right now is a fool. I've worn a mask every day since January. But instead of engaging in a meaningful conversation, he decided to debate in bad faith, asking about obscure exemptions and then accusing me of... agreeing with myself?

Some people are simply looking for a fight. They don't spark joy. So I banish them from my thoughts and my digital space with a click. That's all it takes.

In the end, crowds can create powerful change—but we must remain centered. Public approval is fleeting. Popularity is fickle. Doing the right thing, digging deep, and discovering who you are—that's the real journey. Virtue is the compass, and this life is ours to navigate.

So I continue forward—quietly, steadily—through the eye of the storm.

May the center hold.

June 17, 2020 – Turin, Italy – "The Sun Shines Again" (Alessia Martino)

This week, like the last, has been unusually cold. It's poured rain, we had a fifteen-minute hailstorm, and summer still feels like a rumor. But on Saturday night, I sat by the same window I always do, gazing out at the same mountains, only this time they looked different. The sky had cleared after a full day of grey. Birds were chirping, the dog barked at the occasional passing car, and music drifted softly from the distance. I heard peace—and I felt peace.

Then came Sunday, living up to its name. The sun was shining again.

Naturally, I grabbed the sunscreen. I had just bought it the week before but hadn't yet had a reason to use it. Good sunscreen is expensive, so I chose the spray-gun version—it was cheaper and came with more product than its competitors. Practicality matters. I got to shoot and save my skin.

It was the perfect day to eat outdoors, so we splurged on a barbecue, some drinks, and a full day under the open sky. We even took the dog for a long walk along the river. It felt good. The day ended with a hearty dinner and smiles all around.

Midweek brought more good news: I finally got a new phone. It was my first time ordering one online, and I was completely lost in the ocean of options. In the end, I got the same model as my friend. When it arrived, it was bigger than I remembered—definitely not pocket-friendly—but it's great for watching movies. I used to insist on small phones for my small hands, but I'm learning to adapt. I've already adapted to so many changes; what's one more?

Most importantly, I'm happy to be able to connect again. One friend, in particular, uses only one messaging app, and I couldn't access it without my new phone. It took me days to set it up, but

I finally reached him. We caught up on our last trips, current challenges, and life in general. I laughed when he said people in his country describe Italy like it's some zombie apocalypse. Meanwhile, life here is steadily improving. Things are getting better.

I even had my first video call of the pandemic. On Saturday afternoon, I connected with my little sister. We tried every filter and background we could find. I turned into a pizza, floated through space with cats, and took a pretend vacation to a desert and a lake. All things considered, life is improving on most fronts. Let's buckle up for the rest of the ride.

June 20, 2020 – Tokyo, Japan – "Revolutionary Stoicism: Liberty" (Charmika Monet)

Part I – Stoic Foundations of Freedom

"What is freedom, you ask? It means not being a slave to any circumstance, to any constraint, to any chance; it means compelling Fortune to enter the lists on equal terms."

—Seneca, *On Baiae and Morals*

The Stoics scattered references to freedom and slavery throughout their works. For them, freedom was a **psychological state**, not a material condition: a mindset immune to external forces once trained in its practice. That mindset then finds expression in our deeds—the very manifestation of liberty. It was this universal, ever-available notion of freedom that first drew me to Stoicism, a philosophy whose power to transform mind and action still resonates today.

Part II – Rethinking the Ancients for the Twenty-First Century

My initial foray into Stoicism revealed a complete, coherent worldview—one I still cherish. Yet 2020's upheavals have forced many of us into fresh reflection on our lives and societies. Under Capitalism's relentless demands, our time is regularly stolen; forced work and consumption often become rituals of self-sacrifice.

I realized I'd been reading the ancients too literally, mapping Roman institutions directly onto modern ones. But twenty-first-century philosophy has taught me to deconstruct those texts more playfully. Roman life differed qualitatively from ours—its assumptions, its social structures. So too must our interpretations evolve, adapting Stoic tenets to our drastically changed world.

Part III – Liberty, Dignity, and Social Duty

Logically, if freedom is a state of mind available in any circumstance, then it cannot be **conferred or revoked** by the State. Yet the Stoics also urged civic participation—even governance itself informed by Stoicism has shaped Western jurisprudence. Does this mean our duty to others ends at teaching them mental fortitude? Surely not. The ancients recognized the physical suffering of slaves, the poor, the ill—inevitable, perhaps, in their era but never to be dismissed. They argued that our dignity, an inalienable gift of Nature, is bound up with freedom, which springs from Reason's proper use rather than from circumstance alone.

Part IV – A Spectrum of Freedom

Freedom, reimagined, is not a binary but a **hierarchy**—a graduated scale of dignity and human flourishing. As we ascend this scale, our capacity for self-expression and shared creativity multiplies, opening new horizons of wealth that depend on no one's deprivation. Socrates proclaimed himself "a citizen of the world" to signal an expanded liberty. What might await us once we embrace our role as "citizens of the known universe"? While each mind must secure its own freedom, society bears responsibility to furnish the material conditions—however subject to Fortune's whims—that enable collective exploration of our potential.

Part V – Heidegger's Existential Freedom

Though Heidegger never drew on Stoicism, *Being and Time* illuminates how our awareness of mortality shapes freedom's value. Every choice edges us closer to non-existence, yet in exercising our liberty—through work, curiosity, travel, art—we affirm our humanity.

Far from mere leisure, these acts are the highest expression of what it means to be human. Conversely, enforced uniformity in speech, clothing, or labor stifles our very essence, reducing life to mechanical routine and "the man...performing a few simple operations...generally becomes as stupid and ignorant as it is possible for a human creature to become."[1]

Part VI – Building a Society of Liberation

Despite unprecedented material abundance, poor distribution and economic anxiety imprison many minds. Suddenly, with enforced "free" time, we feel like liberated slaves—unfamiliar with leisure, constrained by financial fear. Marcus Aurelius reminds us, "Do what is necessary, and whatever the reason of a social animal naturally requires, and as it requires."[2]

I believe it is our collective responsibility to forge societies that maximize both individual and communal liberty—and to wield that liberty virtuously, in service of others, as we express and cultivate our shared humanity.

July 1, 2020 – Turin, Italy – "Traveling Italy in the Time of COVID" (Alessia Martino)

Part I – A Breath of Freedom

Life feels normal again. Since June 15, Italy has allowed interregional travel, and I've now experienced firsthand what that means. It was a last-minute decision: a car ride into heaven, weaving between fields and castles.

I traveled partly because I needed a breather—and partly because I knew safety measures were in place. Having spent much time abroad, this seemed like the perfect moment to explore a piece of my own country.

The trip began with a safe drive, making masked stops along the way (as required by law). Soon we were far from everything, nestled in nature. Beautiful flora and fauna surrounded us. I loved every single sunset. But the point of going somewhere new is also to explore.

Part II – Ferry Rides and Lakeside Escapes

One day, we decided to visit an island on a lake in the next region. We took the earliest ferry to maximize daylight and avoid crowds. That first ferry ride was nearly empty, peaceful and quiet—the return, nearly full but still safe. Regardless of passenger numbers, masks were required for everyone, whether seated inside or outside. Seating was arranged for physical distancing, with every second seat left unused.

As soon as we set foot on the island, I grabbed a cappuccino and the day began. We explored three old churches, wandered a charming main street, picnicked by scenic viewpoints, and admired the wildlife—especially the pheasants, which made it even more magical. Although more visitors arrived later in the day, the island had plenty of space for everyone.

Part III – Culture Without Crowds

Another day, I explored one of the region's main towns. Museums and churches had reopened—many of which normally charge for entry. Since not all exhibits were available and they couldn't justify full prices for "half" the experience, tickets were temporarily free. I took full advantage. After securing a free ticket, I masked up and entered. What surprised me most was the procedure: after greeting me, one staff member radioed another to announce, "A girl is coming in and going up the stairs." The same happened when I exited. It was simply a safety measure to manage headcounts and prevent overcrowding, but it made me feel oddly important.

Because of these measures, I got entire rooms to myself—something that's normally impossible. I may have seen fewer things overall, but I was able to savor each moment, unrushed and undistracted. Less is more.

Part IV – Beach Days and Safe Enjoyment

I also visited the beach again. The first beach had both paid and free areas. Even the free section maintained social distancing: umbrellas were spaced out, and beach beds were set about 1.5 meters apart. Masks were required only in restaurant zones.

Swimming felt wonderfully normal. That same day, 20,000 people crowded Bournemouth Beach in the UK. It's proof that rules and enforcement *do* make a difference—without demanding paranoia.

At the second beach, the free area had no umbrellas, but people were respectful and spaced out. The paid area had stricter rules: distanced sunbeds, mask requirements in shared spaces, and a new lunch system. You had to order before noon, and meals were delivered in takeaway bags—likely to minimize contact, though it raised concerns about waste.

Restaurants, in general, have reopened. Fewer tables, masked servers, and spaced-out seating seem to be working well. And the sea? That part remains blissfully unchanged.

Part V – Travel Is Still Possible

Of course, I expect places will get busier. But I believe safe travel is still possible.

Can we ever be *completely* sure of anything? Isn't that always the case? Should we stop living? I don't think so. With common sense, some research into a location's risk level, and awareness of local rules, I believe people can still enjoy a non-stressful holiday—and continue to appreciate everything this life has to offer.

July 7, 2020 – Chongqing, China – "A Very Special Gaokao"
Part I – A New Kind of Gaokao

Last year, I wrote about the last "normal" Gaokao of 2019—China's equivalent of the academic Olympics. This national exam decides university placement and, by extension, the shape of students' futures. Top scores unlock top universities. Lower scores lead to more modest institutions. For many, it is the culmination of 18 years of near-constant study.

This year, though, everything is different. Held amid a global pandemic, the Gaokao carried an extra weight of uncertainty. Senior Three students spent months at home self-studying, and many felt an added layer of stress, fearing they weren't as prepared as they should be.

Yesterday morning, my wife Shaolin and I stepped out of our apartment on the Foreign Language School campus in Shiqiaopu and witnessed the pre-Gaokao send-off. Dozens of buses lined the campus road, ready to ferry students to the testing sites. Rows of excited, anxious, and supportive parents stood in parade formation—snapping photos, waving, and even crying. As the buses rolled past, we joined the ritual of shouting "Jia you!" (Keep going!) and offered thumbs-up and clenched fists of encouragement. Some students, perhaps foreign, waved back at us shyly.

My wife is always stirred by the sight of Senior Three students preparing for the Gaokao. I suspect it brings her back to her own youth, to dreams made or dashed in those decisive days.

Part II – Rain, Family, and a Veteran's Smile

This morning, we rushed over to see our niece, Zhang Yidan—also known as Eden—after she finished her Chinese exam. It's the final week of my own classes before a very odd "staycation" summer break, one that will mostly include writing, gym sessions, and the occasional pool trip. But today, our priority was family.

We left home at 11:00 a.m. to meet Yidan as she exited her exam at 11:30. Due to recent flooding, I'd sprained my ankle on a slippery stairway days earlier, so when our cab dropped us at the wrong school, I had to hustle with a "fast limp" through the rain. I wasn't impressed—but I got there. Less Canadian than I used to be, not quite Chinese either, I like to say I'm "Kai-nese."

Outside the school, a crowd of parents buzzed with nervous anticipation. We found our gang—Yidan's mom, a family friend, and her son—and waited. Within minutes, Yidan appeared, trudging down the stairs with the quiet gravity of someone returning from the front lines.

"How was it?" I asked. She just shook her head—no words, only the haunted gaze of a Gaokao veteran. "Did you do okay?" I pressed. She nodded, slowly. That was all she could offer in the moment. We bided our time and grabbed a few photos.

Part III – A Walk, a Smile, and the Warrior's Path

The rain had picked up again, and we decided to walk to the family house for lunch. It was uphill, through winding paths and buildings. My ankle protested, but I followed like a weary missionary, trailing behind our family's chosen one.

As we walked, Yidan began to relax. She asked about my ankle. I smiled. She smiled back. I told her I was still alive. She nodded—so was she. I reminded her of the interview we did last year, where she spoke about the pressures of the Gaokao. Would she be up for talking about it again? She agreed.

"It was okay," she said. Chinese is her strong subject, and she felt confident. But the others? Nerves were high. Months of inconsistent self-study had left many classmates uneasy. Some had relaxed more than they should have. Now they faced the standardized test that would determine their college prospects. The stakes were real—and heavy.

Despite a cold, swollen glands, and a headache a few days earlier, Yidan looked bright and healthy today. She was giving it her all. Her dream is to become a psychologist or enter the medical field. I believe she'll get her chance.

Part IV – Lunch, Legacy, and an Afternoon Exam

Back at the family house, we climbed nine floors and were greeted by our in-laws and a beautifully prepared light Chinese lunch. It was fresh, grounding, and filled with chatter and encouragement. Afterward, we rested while Yidan took a short nap.

At 2:00 p.m., her mother gently woke her, and she prepared for her next exam—math. She says she's not that strong at it, despite expensive tutoring all year. She lost her father to cancer as a baby, and our extended family has spared no expense to give her every opportunity for a meaningful future. That's how important the Gaokao is here. This is not just about grades; this is legacy.

We took one last selfie, offered a few parting words of encouragement, and sent her off for her next round.

Part V – A Swim and One English Exam Tip

Back at the house with a few hours to spare, I went for a swim. My childhood Taekwondo master, Korean Grandmaster Tae E Lee, once told me, "If you're not swimming uphill, you're getting pushed back down." So I swam. My ankle appreciated the movement. My mind appreciated the stillness.

Tomorrow, Yidan will face three science-related exams in the morning, and her English exam in the afternoon. While math and physics aren't my area of expertise, English is. So here's one tip I always share with students preparing for their English reading comprehension:

Bonus – One Tip to Master Difficult English Vocabulary

A lot of students struggle with difficult words during the English exam. Here's the trick: be like **Sherlock Holmes**. Look for **clues** *inside* the reading passage.

There are four types of clues you can use:

1. **Definition Clues** – The meaning is explained in the sentence.
   Example: "Some twins are identical; they look exactly alike."
   → "They look exactly alike" defines *identical*.
2. **Synonym or Antonym Clues** – Look for words that are similar or opposite in meaning.
   Example: "The new boy was haughty, arrogant, and proud."
   → Even if you don't know *haughty*, you can guess from the synonyms.
   Or: "The new boy wasn't haughty. He was polite, humble, and kind."
   → The antonyms help you guess the meaning.
3. **Substitution Clues** – Try plugging in different words.
   Example: "The deleterious smoke wafted up from the acid spill."
   → Try "good smoke"? Doesn't make sense.
   → Try "bad smoke"? Better, but not exact.
   → What does acid do? It *damages*. So deleterious = *harmful*.
4. **Context Clues** – Think about what's happening overall. What would make sense in this situation?

The key takeaway: **Never give up** and say "Ting bu dong" (I don't understand). The answer is usually in the sentence—if you know how to look.

Good luck, Yidan. Good luck to all. May your dreams be equal to your effort.

July 8, 2020 – Chongqing, China – "Legacies and Memento Mori"

Day 168

Part I – Time, Death, and Questions That Matter

I am already dead. It is the end of my life, and I'm working backward. How old am I? Where was I? Was I rich or poor? Will anyone remember me? What mattered? Did I feel content?

No big deal, no pressure—it's just life. Just questions.

In this pandemic, many of us have been home for months, and even the endless drip of Netflix and digital distraction is starting to dry up. We're asking harder questions. These questions are fueling protests—against systemic racism, against widening inequality. We're talking about defunding police states and funding the social programs that could actually help.

I thought about writing on July 1, or July 4. (Yay—*all countries matter!*) But in the chaos and noise, even those national birthdays blur. Did Trump notice the trolling hashtags? "All birthdays matter"? Maybe. But maybe that's not what matters.

Black Lives Matter. BIPOC lives matter.

We are listening. We are changing—slowly, painfully—as a society. And that matters. Living well, making things better for those around us, *that* matters. This year has been brutal. But we've had conversations, we've broken silences. The veneer of civility cracked, and we're confronting the raw truth of an uncivil society—and a collapsing ecosystem.

We will adapt, or we will die. And in the end, I don't think it's about whether we collectively succeed—not in our lifetimes, anyway. What matters is that **we personally did our best**. That is enough.

Part II – Life After Lasers: A Quiet Mountain

For six years now, I've lived on this mountain, far from the lasers and bass. After two decades touring with our band—playing Olympic ceremonies, Burning Man, top-tier festivals in North America, and fielding calls from Europe and Asia—I walked away. I wanted nothingness. Silence. Peace. A chance to grow old writing books.

In the last six years, I've lived in more than a dozen countries across North and Central America, Europe, and Asia. I've written novels. I've chronicled a pandemic. If I died now, would I be happy?

Yes. I'm married. I've built a home. I've supported those who supported me. I've tried to give back, to leave the world a little better than I found it. I did something.

And still—I'm not done.

Part III – Plague Years and the Politics of Death

We've passed 10 million cases. Then 11. Then 12 million. Half a million dead. Now 550,000. The numbers are accelerating—*exponentially*.

I remember when 100,000 global cases felt like a lot. Now over 130,000 Americans are dead. And according to recent studies, 99% of those deaths could've been prevented—with a competent, science-based response like South Korea's.

But instead, Trump dismantled the pandemic prevention office—to fund more chain-link fencing along the southern border. To appease a base of xenophobic, frightened, white nationalists.

The global rise of far-right leadership—anti-science, anti-truth—fills me with dread. I feel numbed. I feel sick.

I put on *Zoe's Extraordinary Playlist* and cried quietly. Remembered Broadway. Remembered joy. Singing. Dancing. Love. It's all still inside us, even if New York is shuttered.

But we're not out of the woods. The virus is surging again in the U.S., the U.K., Brazil, Russia, and beyond. Mask mandates have arrived in parts of Canada and the U.S., but so have the maskholes—barreling into supermarkets and subways like clumps of viral particles bound together by fake tanner and entitlement.

Part IV – On Dying and Designing a Life

How old am I? How will I go?

A decade ago, I could've died in any number of ways—breaking up bar fights at DJ gigs, crowd-surfing accidents, dehydration in the desert, wild nights ending in arrests or near-death drives.

Now? Stroke? Blood clot? Heart attack? Early-onset dementia? Who knows.

But this much I do know:

The things we choose to matter, matter. The rest doesn't.

I'm happy. In the past few years, I dug out from under student debt. I started planning for a modest retirement. By 44, I hope to step back from full-time teaching—maybe lecture a class or two each week in creative writing, and spend my time writing books. That sounds like peace to me.

In this pandemic, security has become an illusion. We don't know what's next. Will lost jobs return? Or will AI and automation claim the spaces we vacated while sheltering from the storm? If emergency relief doesn't evolve into a real UBI, many will fall through the cracks.

So we must remain agile. We must adapt.

Part V – What Comes Next

This summer, I'll keep writing *The Lighthouse* with my global friends. I'll finish my solarpunk *Amos the Amazing* novel for the kids who need a good story. I'll rewrite *Where the Wicked Rest*, my paranormal thriller. I'll publish everything before 2021 if I can. That's a good goal.
The Invisible War may be muzzled for now, but it will be out when it's time. I've done all I can. Until then: gym, swimming, games, friends, wife, family, furry kids. This is life. And it is good.

Part VI – Broken Stairs, Quiet Classrooms, and Imagined Freedoms

Right now, I'm sitting in our Senior 2 IELTS classroom. The students are quietly finishing their grammar review and practice test. It's my second-last class before summer vacation. I'll do some tutoring, daily writing and editing, but mostly? I'll rest.

At the end of the year, I finally told my students the truth: no one can *really* teach writing. Surprise. But I hope I've helped them become self-motivated learners—students of the craft.

Last week, I slipped on a flight of wet stairs and tore the ligaments in my foot. I wear a brace. I swim slowly, favor the good foot. I won't miss teaching on the eighth floor with no elevator.

This afternoon, I walked slowly back to my apartment. A police car was parked at the gate—lights flashing, voices raised. Unusual. This place is normally tranquil. Studious.

I felt grateful: I'm not breaking rocks in Siberia. We may feel like we're in lockdown prisons—but they're mostly of our own design. We're free to breathe air, to see the sky.

Maybe life is just a series of self-made prisons. If so, we must design one we can live inside—and, ultimately, find freedom in our minds, our work, our imaginations.

Part VII – The Future We Build

Eden, our 18-year-old niece, just finished the two-day gauntlet of her college entrance exams—the Gaokao. I hope she did well. I hope she gets to live her dream of becoming a psychologist. She's bright. She's kind. She deserves a good life.

I may live to be 80 or 100. Or, by then, maybe 300. Maybe I'll live on another planet.

So I prepare: I swim, I write, I save, I eat well. I try to be happy, and kind, and not make life harder for others.

I wear a mask for me. I wear it for you.

Together, we must make the changes we need—drastic, nimble, difficult. In the next decade, we must reshape the Earth into a place that can still nurture intelligent life.

We have to. Because we still can.

July 9, 2020 – Buenos Aires, Argentina – "All I Can Do Is Live" (Josette)

Well, I'm back.

And it's done.

I can't believe it.

I moved apartments during quarantine—yes, *quarantine*: almost four months and counting.

It was quite the feat, actually.

Here's the cat, enjoying her new kingdom...

A week and a half ago, the president announced that we'd be going back to **Phase 1** in Buenos Aires. The idea was to cut off the metropolitan area from the rest of the country—it's the national epicenter. He explained that without our strict lockdown, we might have seen numbers more like Brazil's.

To paint a better picture: Canada had about 100,000 cases and 8,500 deaths. Argentina, by comparison, had about 50,000 cases and only 1,000 deaths when I last checked. That says something, doesn't it?

Today's numbers show about 83,000 cases and 1,600 deaths. Still—considering global trends—I think we're doing okay. In some developing countries, the low number of reported recoveries speaks volumes about how their healthcare systems are coping.

The Move

I thought I had time. The plan was to move the following weekend, get the necessary government permission form, hire a small moving truck, and—voilà! Done.

But after the president's June 25 speech, justifying tighter restrictions, everyone around me—between that Thursday and Friday night—started saying:

"Why don't you just move this weekend and get it over with?"

"Nah, I'm not ready. It'll be fine."

Spoiler: It was not fine.

At 6 p.m. on Friday, my real estate agent called. He was with the owner. They both suggested I move the very next day. Suddenly—boom—**it got real**.

By the next afternoon, I had a truck, everything was packed, and by 4 p.m. (two hours early), the movers arrived. An hour later, I was hauling my life—ten years of it—into a new apartment.

The cat was traumatized and didn't sleep that night. She made sure I knew it.

I moved my entire life in under 24 hours.

And then: **BAM.** Phase 1 lockdown began again.

There was no time to get my bearings. But the owner was amazing—he pointed out key places for supplies. That helped.

And I discovered a *huge* grocery store with all the products I could ever need.

(*Hello, kale!*)

The cat and I are okay. We're in a more peaceful place—no bugs, no noise, no stress (so far).

Becoming Whole Again

I realized I arrived here as a shell of a person. So I'm giving myself space to **heal**. To become whole again. Because it's so important not to lose yourself in all of this.

In just a few days, it will have been **four full months** since my quarantine began. So much has changed—relationships, routines, spaces... everything.

But here's the thing:

I'm not scared anymore.

All I can do is live.

And making this move? It was the biggest, scariest thing I've done in a long time. But it was necessary. It helped me keep going. Helped me avoid disappearing into the overwhelm.

Now, I get to be excited again—about the things I *should* be excited about. And I don't need to waste energy stressing over what doesn't serve me.

I'm grateful. I'm lucky. And I hope I can pass on that energy—good energy—not anxiety, not fear.

I hope everyone finds a way to be whole during this crazy time.

And if you can't?

What can you do to become whole again?

Signing off,

Josette – Buenos Aires, Argentine Independence Day

July 9, 2020

July 17, 2020 – Chicago, USA – "Bacon's Rebels and the Necessity of Culture" (MC ZULU)

After almost 500 years on this land...
Have you ever wondered what makes us a **color** in AmeriKKKa—
and not a **culture**?
Black. White. Yellow. Red.
What a joke.
Nathaniel Bacon's Rebellion took place in **1676**,
a full **century before the American Revolution.**
Regardless of skin color, poor indentured servants rose up—
a grassroots "purge" against the rich
and their trading partners (including Native Americans
with whom the elite traded furs and tobacco).
But unity was a threat.
To break this formidable coalition of disaffected laborers,
the ruling class conceived a new idea: **RACE.**
1681.
Intermarriage was made illegal.
Land ownership laws followed.
Indentured servitude was abolished.
And the transatlantic African slave trade
became the new economic engine.
White workers were handed the whip.
A legal tool of control.
White supremacy became law.
Not to empower the poor.
But to weaken everyone's bargaining position—
except the elite.
Some of you think it's a sweet deal—

a gift from White Jesus.
But it just keeps **us** out of the middle class
and **you** out of the upper class.
Today, as the rich grow richer,
the middle class collapses.
That's why so many White folks are on welfare.
They've been trained to rely on privilege—
not skill, not merit—
to get jobs, school placements, security.
To all the **ALLIES**
standing against all forms of oppression:
This is why we fight.
Don't let the ignorant
tell you that **Black supremacy** is coming.
That's not what this is.
We see race
for what it really is—
class warfare.
And here's the truth:
The moment we begin to **build a culture**,
is the moment
we begin to become
a family.

July 22, 2020 – Chongqing, China – "The Pandemic Chugs On & the Steep Fall of Giants"

Part I – Warnings Revisited

I'll be brief—my time and focus are stretched thin. The business of living is a full-time job. My ankle, injured in a fall, is healing slowly thanks to daily swims. Here in Chongqing, I'm grateful: we wear masks out of caution, but there hasn't been a single case of community spread in over four months.

Much of what I wrote in my first diary, *The Invisible War*, chronicled the early Chinese lockdown and laid out a simple truth: **if you take basic precautions, you can stop the spread. If you don't, your population will be ravaged.** That warning went largely ignored in many parts of the world, and now, tragically, we're seeing the consequences.

Experts predict a horrific fall and winter ahead—a mass death event. Civilians are being told to brace themselves.

Part II – Life, Humor, and Maskholes

This weekend is Shaolin's birthday. I ordered a cake, a bouquet of flowers, signed a card, bought some small gifts, and booked a party room at a clean, quiet restaurant for 15 close family members. This is what we're *still* allowed to do—because we complied early. 100% masking. Contact tracing. Quarantine without protest. That's what worked.

Meanwhile, my brain runs wild:

Me: Let's hit the gym, have lunch, and crank out 2,000 words.

Also me: You know what would be a brilliant name for bondage-style portable Bluetooth bass enhancers for people walking yappy dogs?

Sub Woofers™. (Pending.)

Online, though, I'm exhausted. I've been "undercover" in two Canadian-linked anti-mask groups.

- **MAD: Mothers Against (Social Distancing)** tries to brand COVID safety as child abuse. One of their loudest voices? A muscled, tattooed man named Chris who physically assaults frontline workers on camera. I tried to reason with them—banned within minutes.
- **MASK FREE** was my second try. I used the Socratic method, asking them to explain their arguments. The mental gymnastics required to avoid basic empathy was staggering.

Eventually, I left. That kind of ignorance is a cancer. Don't argue with them. Isolate yourself. When they get sick—or when their loved ones die—they'll change. Until then, protect your peace.

Part III – Vaccine Hopes and Global Curveballs

There's promising news in vaccine development:

- Oxford's candidate appears to train the immune system to produce and *sustain* antibodies.
- Two million members of the Chinese military are now participating in a vaccine trial.
- Other studies show antibodies may deplete quickly—suggesting a seasonal vaccine might be necessary.
- T cells and memory T cells are becoming a hot area of focus in explaining why some cases are severe and others mild.

Some early speculation even links fermented cabbage, sauerkraut, and kimchi to possible protective effects by blocking ACE2 receptor binding—but that's extremely preliminary.
As for the numbers:

- **15.3 million global cases**
- **630,000 deaths**
- The U.S. alone: 4.1 million reported cases, but likely closer to **40 million**
- **146,000 American deaths**—99% of which could have been prevented with a South Korean–style response.

Instead, Trump dismantled the pandemic response office, diverted funds to the border wall, and now parades himself in a mask as if it's an accomplishment. Meanwhile, he's deployed unmarked federal agents to snatch protesters off the streets in Portland. Critics say it's a reelection tactic, feeding his base with law-and-order spectacle while offering no pandemic plan.

Part IV – Global Flareups and Chongqing Calm

Around the world:

- **Barcelona** has locked down 1.5 million people to stop a second wave.
- **Ürümqi**, the capital of Xinjiang, has re-entered full lockdown.
- **Beijing** just dropped back to Level 3 after 14 days with no new cases.

Here in Chongqing, I took Shaolin downtown to shop for a new phone. The Apple Store was enforcing proper measures: masks, temperature checks, hand sanitizer. The same was true at the mall and bookstore.

Last week, I had Hot Pot with my colleagues from the *Chongqing Daily News* and Canadian YouTuber **Gailo60** (aka Kirk). He's a retired businessman who now travels China making videos. Ironically, he's probably seen more of China in 2020 than I have in all the years I've lived here. Fingers crossed we both remain COVID-free.

Part V – The Fall of Giants

This year has exposed corruption, predation, and abuse at every level. As Trump clings to the last threads of power, small giants tumble.

Bassnectar
I grew up in Ottawa's dance music scene, and gave early gigs to **Dylan Lane**—aka **ill Gates**. We stayed in touch over the years and worked together in Toronto. One of his close collaborators was **Lorin Ashton**, better known as **Bassnectar**.
To many, Bassnectar was a movement. A progressive, antifascist, profeminist force with psychedelic stadium shows and a $20 million empire. But power corrupts, and allegations surfaced: intimate relationships with teenage girls (16–18), documented via voice messages and emails posted to Instagram.
He issued a quick apology. He stepped down. The empire crumbled. Another fallen star.

Peter Nygård
Back in Canada, fashion mogul **Peter Nygård**—the 70th richest Canadian—is also facing a reckoning. Allegations of sexual abuse of minors, including children, trace back to his private island mansion in the Bahamas: **Nygård Quay**. Armed guards. Shark-infested waters. Seized passports. Hunted women.
It sounds cartoonishly evil. It's not.
Years ago, when I was a touring DJ, my girlfriend at the time—a model—was invited to one of Nygård's infamous parties. She offered me a seat on a chartered plane. I declined. The next day, she said **Robert De Niro** had taken my spot.
Weeks later, shaken and exhausted, she recounted the surreal horror: girls being hunted through the jungle for sport. One slipped and cracked her skull. Another hid under a bridge for hours, submerged up to her chin. Coming home was its own nightmare.

His neighbors hated him—especially when *their* children went missing.

Part VI – A World Remade

I'm glad to see these giants fall.
The pandemic chugs on. The year isn't over. But this year is **reshaping the world**—dismantling the untouchable and exposing those who built kingdoms of cruelty. It's not enough yet. But it's a start.

July 26, 2020 – Turin, Italy – "State of Emergency Extended to End of Year" (Alessia Martino)

Part I – A Prolonged Precaution

It's the middle of summer now, and while cases continue to pop up here and there, the overall situation in Italy remains stable. Still, out of concern for a possible second wave in the colder months, the government has extended the **State of Emergency until the end of the year**.

The stated reason is to allow officials to implement new measures more quickly if needed. However, some people believe this move has underlying motives beyond public health. There are many who downplay the virus's severity—or believe it has disappeared entirely. Still, the virus is active, and the precautions remain in place.

For example, **masks are mandatory in enclosed spaces**, and violations carry steep fines: a customer without a mask can be fined €400, while shops face even higher penalties, including **temporary forced closure**. That may seem harsh, but it works as a deterrent. And nobody wants to deal with that.

Part II – The "New Normal" in Public Life

Life continues, adapting to a new rhythm. **Summer camps** are running with modified protocols:

- Each morning, parents must declare that their children are symptom-free, and temperatures are checked.
- Kids are divided into small groups, each assigned to a single teacher to minimize exposure.
- Children over six and all teachers wear masks when distancing isn't possible.
- Everyone brings their own lunch, and sharing food is not allowed.
- Emphasis is placed on **outdoor activities** and frequent cleaning.

Meanwhile, **clubs are open**, a decision many see as economically driven, if not entirely safe. **Sports continue**, but games are played behind closed doors. **Cinemas and theaters remain closed**, with exceptions only for **open-air screenings** and **drive-ins**.

Part III – Movies, Markets, and Mountains

My sister invited me to an **improvised drive-in cinema** in a gas station parking lot. A screen and speakers were set up, and while the sound was great, a larger car partially blocked the lower half of the screen.

Still, the experience was enjoyable. Inside the car, we had a **private space** where we could move freely and talk without disturbing anyone. We brought our own snacks but also ordered food from the on-site bar. The setup wasn't perfect—and prices were a little high—but the concept was solid. With better organization, I hope more places catch on. A big parking lot, a raised screen, and a warm summer night could make a great evening.

I also went to a more traditional **open-air screening**—a beloved Italian summer tradition. This year, they simply started ticket sales earlier to control the flow. Masks were worn, and empty seats left between groups to ensure proper distancing.

In the mountains, I visited some **farmers' markets**. Hiking trails offer plenty of space, so masks aren't necessary there. The markets themselves are carefully regulated: vendors wear masks, and customers are asked—or required, depending on the town—to do the same. Being outdoors helps. Stalls are spaced far apart, and people tend not to linger.

Part IV – Looking Ahead

Overall, I'm pleased with my country's current safety measures. I'm especially glad to see Italy preparing in advance for **school reopenings** and potential **imported cases**.
Right now:

- Travelers arriving from **outside the EU** must undergo a **14-day quarantine**.
- People coming from **blacklisted high-risk countries** are barred from entry—regardless of citizenship.

I hope the government implements **rapid testing at airports** soon. It would make everything easier and more secure.

July 28, 2020 – Chongqing, China – "Through the Bullsh!t, I Endure (A Meditation)"

Part I – Eat Sh!t With a Spoon

"Sometimes even to live is an act of courage."
—Lucius Annaeus Seneca

Day 184.

The Stoics knew something that all of us should be practicing this year: *he who knows how to suffer, suffers less.* Pain lightens when we view it without emotional magnification—when we stop drawing circles around it, layering on despair. Or to put it more bluntly: **if you have to eat sh!t for breakfast, at least use a spoon.**

I swim every morning. Monday is shoulders, Tuesday arms, Wednesday chest and back, Thursday legs. My torn ankle is slowly healing. Here, I must walk carefully—my feet are freakishly large for Chinese stairwells. I now descend the stairs at an angle, like a skier, to avoid another summer crash.

The **floods continue**—millions displaced. **Thirty percent of Bangladesh is underwater.** If you haven't gotten the memo yet: move to high ground. Sea levels are rising. It's not going to get easier.

Part II – Staying Put and Staying Sane

We were offered a trip to **Tibet** for my birthday. Top of the world? Maybe wait for 42.
We thought about it—it would've been amazing. But right now? Too risky. We just paid off the house. Liquid cash is tight. If we got hit with a pair of quarantine bills, we'd be scrambling.
So we're staying put. Here in Chongqing, we're lucky. We can eat out, visit family, go to the gym. That's more than most. And so, I focus on building strength for what's ahead. I keep writing. I endure 40°C days and try not to get cranky. That's something.

Part III – Collapse Has Layers: MASC and the End of Supremacy

Some writers have been resonating with me lately—clear voices shining through the chaos.
One idea gaining traction is **MASC**: *Mother of All Social Collapses.* The premise? This isn't just a pandemic or recession. It's a **multi-pronged collapse**:

- Economic systems work only for the ultra-rich.
- Protesters battle police while children rot in cages.
- Society fractures along every fault line.
- Global leadership is absent.
- "Normal life" isn't coming back—and maybe it shouldn't.

I often blame the Western Enlightenment's **worst slogan**: *Cogito ergo sum.*
I think, therefore I am.
The unspoken inverse: *You don't think—therefore, you are not.* That brutal logic justified centuries of violence—against women, BIPOC, animals, nature itself. It helped pave the road to **climate collapse** and the brink of ecosystem failure.
It's time to **end human supremacy** (#endhumansupremacy).
There is no "top of the food chain." There's only a fragile web of life, and we've trashed it.

Part IV – From DJ to Discipline: Tools for the Storm Ahead

Over the last decade, I've transformed—
From **hedonistic superstar DJ** to something more sustainable.
I trained in **CBT (cognitive behavioral therapy)** to face hardship without medication or escape.
I studied **Rumi**, embraced **mindfulness meditation**, and adopted **Stoic philosophy**.
These became my toolkit. They helped me find **happiness without illusion**, and made me okay with discomfort, grief, and imperfection.
Many of you are suffering. I hope some of these tools help you too.
We may be heading into **decades of chaos**:

- The '20s: pandemics and economic upheaval.
- The '30s: mass environmental displacement.
- The '40s: food shortages.
- The '50s: ecosystem collapse.
- And maybe... by the '60s?
  A **Solarpunk renaissance**.
  A smaller, more humble humanity, rising from the rubble of failed capitalism, colonialism, and white imperialism.

Part V – Seeds for the Next Civilization

It's our responsibility to **preserve Indigenous knowledge**, natural wisdom, and sustainable traditions—so that when the time comes, we can **plant again**.

We shouldn't be clinging to a life that was **killing us**.

If anything, we should be accelerating the entropy of this doomed world order—so we can reach the reset faster. The deeper the collapse of 2020, the sooner the potential for renewal.

Madness? Perhaps. But remember:

"Anyone who tells the truth sounds crazy... because hardly anyone ever tells the truth."

(Anonymous?)

Part VI – Stoic Tools for Surviving the Bullsh!t

In parting, here are **four Stoic techniques** that may help you survive the dumpster fire we call modern civilization:

Tip #1: Distinguish What You Can Control

"Make the best of what is in our power, and take the rest as it naturally happens." —Epictetus

Sound familiar? It's the basis of the Serenity Prayer:

"Grant me the serenity to accept the things I cannot change..."

Identify which parts of your suffering are in your control—your reactions, your thoughts—and which aren't.

Tip #2: Acceptance Beats Resistance

What happens when you stop fighting pain you can't avoid?

Often, it's not the pain—but the **fear of pain**—that breaks us.

The Stoics teach us to **face discomfort rationally**, without amplifying it.

Tip #3: Let Go of the Inner Struggle

Imagine life as a cart. You're the dog tied to it.

Struggle, and you'll get dragged.

Match its pace, and you'll move more smoothly.

Acceptance isn't weakness—it's wisdom.

Tip #4: Zoom Out

The "View from Above" technique helps us regain perspective.

Picture your life from the sky—or better yet, from space.

Most problems shrink under that kind of cosmic lens.

August 1, 2020 – Chicago, USA – "Babylon in Turmoil... (But the Irony Is Poetic)" (MC ZULU)

Once authorities finally decided to implement precautions for COVID-19, many people were caught off guard by the sudden shift in the social climate.

In late April, I walked into a local grocery store looking to *buy* a mask—and was immediately intercepted by a man who informed me that **face coverings were now required**. I tried to sidestep him with a polite, "I'm actually going to buy a mask."

He wasn't having it.

He explained that the store could now be **heavily fined** for letting anyone inside unmasked—it was the law. What I didn't realize at the time was that **he was The Law**: an official **compliance officer**, placed there to enforce it.

He suggested I head back to my car and use a shirt to cover my face. By the time I returned, the masks were sold out. He pointed me toward some **bandannas**. I finally caught a glimpse of his badge and realized—**Chicago is not playing.**

Babylon is burning.

The next day, I walked into a gas station, bandanna in place, compliance-ready.

The poor clerk jumped out of his skin.

He relaxed only after realizing I was just following guidelines. This is what I looked like.

So I have to ask:

Is it my fault my appearance makes you want to hit the silent alarm?

I even bought a **white** bandanna to avoid any gang-related confusion.

YEAR OF THE RAT

A month later, the country would erupt in flames.

A police officer knelt on a man's neck, killing him over an alleged **counterfeit $20 bill**. The same officer, it turns out, was a **tax evader**—to the tune of **hundreds of thousands of dollars**.

Once again, bandanna-wearing "Negroes" struck fear in the hearts of shop owners—

But this time, it turned out most of the so-called "looters" were **White Supremacists**.

The disparity is what sickens us:

- In **perception**
- In the **application of the law**
- In the **presumption of guilt**

This is AmeriKKKa.

The deindustrialization of Black communities.

The flooding of drugs and guns into those same areas.

It **created** the character you're so afraid of.

And now?

Now, you **reap what you sow**.

The very children you meant to inherit your system of corruption... **are the ones chanting #BlackLivesMatter even louder than we do**.

The irony is poetic.

August 6, 2020 – Chongqing, China – "Close the Schools, Save the Children"

Day 199

Part I – Herman Cain Is Dead, and So Might Be Our Sense

Herman Cain is dead. Long live Herman Cain.

His life was large—but his death from COVID-19, just weeks after mocking masks at a Trump rally, was a dark mic drop. A tragic warning ignored.

Masks are not political. They are critical. And as we brace for a brutal fall and winter, crowded classrooms may be the worst place to send our kids.

I don't expect this letter alone to grind the machine to a halt. But I want to be on the record—as a **conscientious objector**. If enough of us speak up, maybe we can steer our leaders in the right direction.

Part II – The Reckless Reopening

Teachers spent the summer writing their wills. Others scoured online stores for friendlier-looking gas masks and HEPA filters, trying to make their classrooms slightly less dangerous.

Meanwhile, parents nervously debated school or homeschool, weighing the mental cost of isolation against the mortal cost of exposure.

To them I say: **safe time with loving family is not a loss—it's salvation.**

If children get infected, many will go on to infect their families. Some won't show symptoms. But many will suffer long-term effects: **lung scarring, strokes, organ damage, neurological issues** we don't yet understand.

What's the cost of opening schools?

Have we really thought it through?

Part III – Leadership in Absentia

Governments know the truth—but they fear the voters. Rather than lead with data, they **cling to popularity polls**, acting as if they're as uninformed as the mob. But the science is clear.

- **One-third to one-half** of COVID cases are asymptomatic.
- **Children** may not suffer severe symptoms—but they are excellent spreaders.
- In **Israel**, weeks after reopening schools, they lost months of lockdown gains.
- Across **Canada and the U.S.**, summer camps became new cruise ships.
- And still, we haven't fully embraced **masking**, let alone **goggles**, even though experts say the virus can hang in the air **for hours** and enters the body **100x more effectively** through mucus membranes—**eyes included**.

Dr. Fauci and the CDC backed this in June. I warned of it in February. We're still behind.

Part IV – Strike for the Living

It's also the fault of **school boards and teachers' unions** who haven't drawn a hard line.

If teachers can strike for benefits, why can't they strike for their lives?

Where is the moral leadership?

Mexico canceled in-person classes, broadcasting school over public television to reach even the most remote households. That's bold leadership. That's responsibility.

What do we do? Reopen—and hope.

Hope our kids don't come home with something deadly. Hope our teachers don't become martyrs. Hope doesn't build safety. **Planning does.**

Part V – What Real Alternatives Look Like

Here are a few options better than wishful thinking:

- **Outdoor classes**—as they did during the 1918–1920 flu pandemic. Let children study April–November outdoors, then stay home in winter, doing homework and spending time with family.
- **The NHL bubble model**—test everyone before they enter a school "bubble." Retest regularly. Is it costly? Yes. But it's better than funerals.

And if that fails? At least **postpone the school year** and **build a real online education platform**, not a rushed patchwork. Because here's what happens if we don't:

- Schools reopen in September.
- A few weeks later: outbreaks.
- Hundreds of families quarantined.
- Hospitals overwhelmed.
- Teachers sick.
- Kids traumatized.
- Some don't make it.
- Schools close. Again.

Or we could lead now. Before the suffering begins.

Part VI – Camus, VR, and Birthday Gifts from the Future

So I wrote this letter. Sent it to the media. Not because I expect it to change the world, but because I need to be able to say: *I did what I could.*

I'm still swimming daily, listening to *The Tao of Seneca* and **Albert Camus'** *The Plague* on audiobook. I'm still healing my ankle. Still writing. Still trying to stay in shape. My fantasy novel's coming along—and though it feels like a digression, maybe it's one of the few things that still brings hope.

"They fancied themselves free, and no one will ever be free so long as there are pestilences."
—Albert Camus, *The Plague*

Yesterday, I played VR with friends. It was surprisingly immersive. At one point, Dan tried to pass through a door and punched Orlando in the face. Another time, he launched a grenade and tossed his controller across the room. I floated, flew, got dizzy. It felt **real**. Then we ordered pizza. That reminded me which world I lived in.

Part VII – Real Monsters and Real Gifts

Ethan loves **Ultraman**. He's never seen a movie, so to him, Ultraman might be **real**—our planet's great hero. This weekend, we're taking him to a live Ultraman fight. I'm pretty excited. It's also my birthday on Sunday.

Shaolin got me gifts. One was a **golden necklace** engraved with the Tibetan mantra:

Om mani padme hum
Praise to the jewel in the lotus.
It's said to contain the essence of enlightenment—the secret of how to uproot suffering.

She also got me a pair of **Bose Frames**—smart sunglasses I've nicknamed **Chairman Meow**. Stylish. Great sound. If you're going to live through a century plague, it helps to have **shades and a soundtrack**.

"There have been as many plagues as wars in history...
Yet always, plagues and wars take people equally by surprise."
—Camus

August 8, 2020 – Chongqing, China – "How Sweet It Is"

Tomorrow, I turn 41.

It's the little birthday between the cartoon milestone of *turning 40* and the mythical, Adamsian profundity of turning **42**. I handled 40 well—somehow managing to gracefully transition out of the absurd spectacle that was "Doctor Danish" (complete with Chaplin mustache, dreadlocks, and a trilby hat wall) and into... something more human.

I spent my 40th wandering Florence on a 40-day walkabout through old-world Europe, just before everything changed. I don't know how I knew, but I felt it in my bones—and I was just in time. For 42? Maybe Tibet. Maybe a trip back to Canada to see the people I love.

But this year? This one I'm spending at home.

Part I – Quiet Blessings

Luckily, *home* in Chongqing means:

- We wear masks in public, but we don't really worry.
- There hasn't been a single case in four months.
- Everything is open. Life is normal(ish).

We've skipped the big pool parties, music festivals, and nightclubs. Mentally, I'm not there yet. Instead, I swim every morning, work out, eat healthy lunches, crank the AC to beat the 40°C heat, and write.

Book II of my nonfiction pandemic diary, *The Lighthouse*, is getting long. My new fantasy novel about a boy on a magical journey is pure joy to write—I want to get it out before winter, so I'm staying focused.

Today, though, I was sore—leg day had me hobbling like a baby deer. I made coffee, skipped the gym, and played **NHL 2020** on PS4 with my dad. He won one, I won one. Then we logged off and headed to the family house for lunch.

Part II – Heroes, Burgers & Birthday Phones

Montreal eliminated Crosby's Penguins—on his 33rd birthday, no less. A good omen? I hope Canada beats the odds, too.

Baby Ethan was thrilled to see me. We had a light lunch and a nap, then I took him to the mall to meet **Ultraman**, his hero. He was absolutely riveted.

Afterward, Shaolin and I bought Eden a **new Huawei phone**—her graduation gift. She's headed to college this fall.

I'm grateful. My family—both in China and Canada—are safe and well. I can enjoy the day without worry, and that's no small thing.

Part III – Politics, Phones, and Pandemics

Speaking of phones...
We'll wait to upgrade our iPhones. Trump's executive order banning TikTok and WeChat from U.S. devices will basically **cripple iPhones in China**, where those apps are essential. The result? **A massive boost for Huawei**—the very company Trump is trying to destroy.
Did you catch that?
He's hurting American companies and helping Chinese ones.
The man is truly a marvel.
Globally, we're now at **19.5 million cases** of COVID-19. By weekend's end, we'll hit 20 million. Some believe a vaccine is coming soon. Others say the virus is here to stay—and we'll simply adapt. No one knows.
So we keep going. **Chin up. Heart open. Every day is a gift.**

Part IV – Chairmen, Cheeseburgers & Carrot Cake

I managed to hack a pair of blue-light transparent lenses into my **Bose Frames smart glasses**—so now I can wear them while teaching or working indoors, streaming Fela Kuti or meditation tracks straight into my ears. Honestly? That's a vibe.

After buying Eden's phone, Shaolin and I went to **Light Burger**. I had a salad and a blue cheese "Frenchie." She had the classic American cheeseburger. It's the only place in Chongqing with **really good, healthy veggie burgers**, made in-house with fresh ingredients.

Afterward, we took a walk. I'm thrilled that my ankle is healing.

On the way home, the skies opened up—**torrential rain**. We flagged a little motorcycle taxi (a tuk-tuk, or *dien-san*) and zipped home just in time.

Then we started prepping the birthday cake.

Part V – Chaos, Carrots & the Nature of Joy

I'd ordered a kilo of Anchor cream cheese and a big bag of carrots. It was time to bake my **grandmother's famous carrot cake**, complete with cream cheese frosting.

Halfway through, as I poured the eggs and flour into the bowl, Shaolin worked the hand mixer—when suddenly, **the batter sprayed everywhere**. Her pajamas. The table. The wall. The chairs. She looked ready to cry.

She likes things neat. I, on the other hand, **howled with laughter**.

"Is it going to be okay?" she asked.

"Yeah," I said, still laughing. "It's going to be great."

An hour later, I was frosting the cake.

And yeah—it *was* great.

Part VI – A Soft Tomorrow

Tomorrow, I'll swim in fresh water, relax, and make **tacos and fajitas** for Shaolin, Jinn, and Cici. We'll watch a movie. Maybe have a drink. Laugh.
Be grateful.
For the breath in our lungs. For the cake in our fridge. For another day to love and be loved.
For the gift that is the present.

August 18, 2020 – Chongqing, China – "Spark Joy or Die"

Day 211

Part I – Welcome to the Furnace

Another scorcher in China's historic furnace. Forty degrees Celsius is average in Chongqing, and it often climbs to blistering highs in the mid-40s. Climate patterns—possibly affected by the Three Gorges Dam—have brought us more rain in recent years, offering a reprieve from the relentless sun. But this year? **A "millennial flood."**

Roads washed away. Entire villages submerged. Millions displaced. This morning, I made coffee for myself and raw honey water for Shaolin. We packed our duffle bags—hers a tiny blue cube to my hulking black Nike—and headed to the gym.

Part II – Pixies, Protein, and Pain

From 11 a.m. to 2 p.m., I shared space with the usual midday gym crowd: an almost cartoonish parade of satyrs and nymphs—trainers, models, genetic anomalies with iron abs and sculpted glutes, dressed in futuristic gymwear that would make Marvel costume designers weep.
They struck poses and snapped mirror selfies between deadlifts.
I grinned and did my thing.
Today was arms. Barbell curls until the pain pushed the world's worries out of my head. At least for a little while.
Obesity and poor health are major COVID comorbidities. In the West, I rarely hear talk of "improving the terrain"—but here, with daily cardio, weights, swimming, and sunlight, I feel like I'm doing everything I can to stay alive to finish telling this tale.
That, too, **sparks joy**.

Part III – Shrimp Viruses and Strip Club Superspreaders

In Canada, headlines broke about a COVID superspreader event at the *Brass Rail* gentlemen's club in Toronto—550 exposures in one night. In the Americas, Canada is still the darling, but that's a low bar with the U.S. surging toward six million cases.

In China, the worry is outbreaks from **frozen fish and shrimp**. In Guangdong near Hong Kong, a major one's underway—over 30,000 infections. China will lock it down and clean it up.

The West? They'd rather **defend "freedom" and order more body bags**.

The seafood scare has tanked demand. Maybe, just maybe, we'll give the ocean a break—let the fish spawn and recover while we sort ourselves out.

Part IV – A Soft Interview and a Red Stamp Surprise

I got an interview request from *Beijing Review*, China's top English-language magazine, about my book deal for *The Invisible War*—known domestically as *Kai's Diary*. It had cleared translation, passed inspection, and then... shelved. Awaiting a CIP red stamp. A bureaucratic purgatory.

I almost declined. Then I saw it was from **Li Nan**, the brilliant translator who'd worked tirelessly to bring my words into Chinese. I owed her.

Also, a feature in *Beijing Review* might just nudge the publishing office to *move*.

After a sweaty gym session and a race around the computer mall to fix a busted projector screen—essential for the interview backdrop—I got home just in time to meet Li Nan with a socially distanced elbow bump and foot shake.

The interview? Friendly. Flattering. Pro-China. Focused on science, not politics. It'll hit the stands on **September 9**.

That night, I got a call: **My CIP number was approved. The book is coming out.**

A coincidence? Maybe. But a good one.

Part V – Hate Mail and Hilarious Cowards

The next day, I opened Facebook to a new message request: "Your book sucks. Your grammar is awful. You're only getting published because you're a foreigner. We look forward to your next disaster—*if you even manage one.*"

Wow. Happy Tuesday.

Shaolin shrugged. "If you want to be famous, you need thick skin." She's right. But it still stung.

I traced the message to **Alex**, a local expat, journalist, and alleged editor. He'd sent similar hate messages to my **agent and publisher**, despite the book not even being out. Something smelled off.

A few quiet inquiries and one not-so-subtle meme later, I realized this wasn't just Alex—it was probably part of a long-running smear campaign by an old frenemy I'll call **Hian Hameson** (a name only the most micro-endowed men would dare claim). He'd raged about my diary from the beginning, calling me arrogant, fear-mongering, and "wrong about everything."

Of course, **everything I predicted came true.**

And somehow, he got angrier.

But here's the thing:

Haters are a gift.

They save you time. They reveal who's jealous. And they give you fuel to write the next book, while they stew in last year's gossip. I cut them all out.

Did it spark joy?

Absolutely.

Part VI – A Love That Sparks Joy

Shaolin and I just celebrated **our fourth anniversary.**
Friday held a cranky fight. Monday, potholes. But the weekend?
We stayed cool.
We laughed.
We remembered that we're still here, together, and mostly sane. That's worth celebrating.
I'm grateful to live in a city that handled the pandemic well—swift, science-based, effective. In the West, even masks are seen as tyranny. But as far as I'm concerned, **mandatory seatbelts and sober drivers don't infringe on anyone's freedom.**
In Chongqing, we trust.

Part VII – The Kondo Method for Life

Now, with a few weeks before the school year begins, I'm doing what I can to **improve the terrain**. Hitting the gym. Getting strong. Preparing for whatever this next chapter brings.

At home, I'm on a Marie Kondo mission—clearing out anything that doesn't **spark joy**. Books, clutter, people. They've gotta go.

Every hour I "lose" at the gym or in meditation, I gain back in stamina, discipline, and emotional clarity. That's how I plan to keep writing for decades.

Three books in development:

- *The Lighthouse* (Book II)
- *Amos the Amazing*
- A rewrite of *Where the Wicked Rest*

All of them spark joy.
So I'll keep going. And I'll keep writing.

August 19, 2020 – Chongqing, China – "Chongqing Floods Grow Daily"

Day 212

Chongqing is flooding.
The Jialing and Yangtze Rivers have risen to historic levels, and the government has officially declared this a millennium flood year. The famous Hongyadong tourist district is closed. The Sheraton Hotel on Nanbin Lu has more than a foot of water inside its marble lobby. Water creeps up the steps of riverfront cafés and bursts through the manholes in sudden geysers. The air is heavy, humid, watching.
And still the river rises.
We wait with bated breath. The entire city—**the world's largest municipal metropolis**—holds its breath too.
I've never seen the rivers like this. The brown, churning water feels alive, massive, patient. Not angry—just inevitable. Flood sirens echo in the distance. Emergency text alerts hit my phone. I stay indoors, watching the water swallow the shoreline one streetlight at a time.
It's hard not to see it as a metaphor: the tide rising, slow but unstoppable, and all we can do is prepare, wait, and hope the high ground holds.

August 21, 2020 – Kazan, Russia – "Returning to China Will Be the Happiest Moment in My Life" (Alina)

I get up most days around 9 or 10, depending on what I need to do. I drink my coffee and eat a typical Russian breakfast—bread and butter, a slice of cheese or salami. And every morning, the same thought hits me: *Where am I?*

Am I in my bed in Chongqing, and all of this has just been a bad dream?

But no. It's real. I'm not in China. I'm not home. I'm back in Russia, and the life I love feels far away.

When I first left for a two-week visit to see my family, I never imagined I wouldn't be able to return. First, I thought maybe I'd go back by May. Then August. Now it's August, and I'm still here—and scared.

A few months ago, I started teaching English online—first with a Chinese school, then a Russian one. But the salaries don't even compare, so I left the Russian job. I video call my boyfriend in Chongqing every day. I miss him. I miss everything.

When the virus began to spread in Russia, the government pretended to take things seriously—declaring lockdown measures, but forcing half the population to keep working. There was no real support. The virus spread quickly, and it's still bad here. The borders are closed—maybe for a year, they've said.

Every month, I have a breakdown. I even had to see a doctor.

I go to sleep thinking, *I never would've gone back to Russia if I'd known I wouldn't be able to return.* My two biggest mistakes were leaving in February and obeying the order to cancel my return ticket—just to avoid losing my scholarship.

The government here has done almost nothing to stop the virus. They fine people for not wearing gloves or masks, even in the streets, while police walk around with cotton masks on their chins. It's all just so stupid and frustrating.
During lockdown, everything was closed—no cinemas, no restaurants, no escape. We survived, but it was hard. It still is.
I can't sleep unless I listen to audiobooks—I'm finishing my fourth one. You should try it if you're struggling to sleep. It helps a little. But I'm emotionally exhausted. I'm tired of hoping that tomorrow—or the next day—China will announce we can return.
I know this for sure: **when that day comes, it will be the happiest moment of my life so far.**
Editor's Note:
Alina never made it back to China. Life had other plans. Last we heard, she was living in Dubai—and happy.

August 26, 2020 – Buenos Aires, Argentina – "Good People Respect Others' Decisions" (Josette)

Quarantine Fatigue

Dear quarantined world,

It's been a minute.

But I'm grateful—because I've been *busy*. So busy, I almost need a vacation *from* quarantine. Can you believe it's been over five months? Even now, social gatherings indoors are prohibited, even with family. The workaround? People meet outside in parks and plazas—no more than four at a time. But let's be honest, the virus is in the air, and nothing feels guaranteed anymore.

Argentina keeps climbing in the global case rankings—we're now sitting at number 13. Sure, our death rate is relatively low compared to some countries with fewer cases, but that doesn't really make me feel any better.

Strange New Normals

I'm not sure what the government's plan is moving forward. Hair salons are open. People can walk or run between 6 p.m. and 10 a.m., with or without masks—but how do you social distance when the parks are packed?

Still, I've been making the most of it. Music has been taking off. I played at one of Buenos Aires' most well-known clubs a couple of weeks ago. No crowd, of course—just a few DJs, a sound guy, and maybe one of the owners. The club was empty. Cold. The "audience" was a handful of dancing mannequins (which I *really* wish had been fully clothed, by the way).

But the nerves? They were real. When you're being live-streamed, the pressure doesn't go away—if anything, it multiplies. Online, anyone from anywhere can tune in. The audience could be far *bigger* than a packed club.

Dating, Distancing, and Decisions

Who knows when real events will return—and even if they do, they might look very different. I've seen models in other countries: concerts where you stand in tiny platforms with just your bubble of three. That might work elsewhere. But here? In a country where rules are seen more as *suggestions*? I doubt it.

People still struggle with the basics of distancing. Masks have been mandatory for over five months now. Most people wear them—though some still wear them on their chins, or in their hands like magic amulets. There's been a big push to normalize masks and handwashing, but almost no public messaging around social distancing. I don't know why.

The new mentality seems to be: "If I'm wearing a mask, I can stand as close as I want." That's... not how it works.

I've tried dating during quarantine. Let me tell you—it's not going well. Some people want to break quarantine right away. Some don't believe in talking. Sorry, buddy—no. *Good people respect other people's decisions.* If someone wants to meet for a walk, great. If someone wants to stay inside, that's great too.

I've broken quarantine a few times—but tried to stay masked, distanced, and kept to a two-week self-isolation after any in-person interaction. Is it responsible? I don't know. I hope so.

Acceptance, Astrology, and All the Feels

Five months and counting. Will it end? Maybe. Maybe in a few months. Maybe in a few years. Maybe not in our lifetime. Who knows.

But this is our life now. And we still have to live it.

One thing that's helped: a friend of mine studying astrology and spirituality has taken it upon herself to be a kind of healer. She's helped her friends (and herself) through this massive life shift.

That doesn't mean I don't still feel a lot of emotions. I do.

Acceptance is hard. But nobody wrote the manual for this.

They really should.

Be well,

Josette

August 27, 2020 – Ottawa, Canada – "The Unusual Has Become The Norm" (Cook (Not Mimsey Demon))

Trying to describe what an "average day" looks like now is a challenge. And not just because I've got the howls of the neighborhood drunks bleeding in through one ear and the screeches of a cockatiel demanding snacks through the other. It's hard because *normal* doesn't really exist anymore. The unusual *has* become the norm.

Any outing now requires a mental flowchart. Do I risk the bus? If I do, has a driver on that route tested positive recently? Will anyone on board even be wearing a mask? Would taking the long way help avoid crowds, even if it adds half an hour to the trip? Will the grocery store have a lineup? Will I melt in the sun while waiting? Did I remember my mask? And above it all: *Is this errand worth the stress and the risk?*

The Landscape Has Shifted

My neighborhood's always had some rough edges, but post-lockdown, there's a new edge of desperation. Gangs on e-scooters scout delivery trucks, hoping to snag packages off porches or rip open mailboxes. Doesn't matter if it's medical equipment or comic books—it's either usable or sellable.

Bike theft is rampant. People are losing lawn ornaments, fencing, flower pots, kayaks. A *kayak*. One week there was a full-on bike chop shop operating out of a parking lot across from my balcony. It sat right next to a police building. Nobody batted an eye.

And it's not just theft. Public intoxication, overdoses—walk a few blocks in any direction, and you'll see it. One morning at 4 a.m., I took the dog out and found a woman passed out in the middle of the street. A needle lay next to her. No mask. I didn't have mine either—didn't think I'd run into anyone on a dog walk at that hour. The dog was freaked and pulled me away, so I kept my distance and called 911. I sat nearby to keep an eye on her.

The police showed up first, five minutes later—no masks, no distancing, digging through her purse and questioning me. Then the paramedics arrived—suited up in full PPE. I stayed long enough to see her safely loaded into the ambulance. Before leaving, the cops told me to give my name and number "in case she says you assaulted her." That was... a weird way to thank someone for calling it in.

Inside the Mini-Zoo

It's not just chaos out there—it's a fire hazard too. An arsonist's been working this part of town for years. So far this year: a restaurant, a couple of houses, an apartment building, and a maple syrup shack (that one stung). The apartment fire wasn't arson, though—just some drunk geniuses doing DIY fireworks after the Canada Day celebration got canceled. Go figure.

So, I mostly stay in. I'm lucky—I live in a mini-zoo with four birds, two cats, a dog, and a roommate. Without them, I'd probably have lost my mind already. Still, the loneliness hits hard sometimes. I haven't had a hug in 2020. I've even considered hiring an escort—just to watch a movie and get a cuddle. What's the etiquette there now? Masks on the whole time, just in case? It's exhausting to even think about.

Drowning in Irony

These days, I toggle between doomscrolling the news and desperately looking for something—*anything*—to distract me from the doom I just scrolled. Pandemic spikes. Anti-mask protests. People screaming that being asked to wear a face covering is an infringement of freedom.

And then I read about Hurricane Laura.

Port Arthur, Texas. A town of 54,000 evacuated ahead of the storm. One guy stayed behind: the local liquor store owner. When asked why, he said, *"People need their vodka."* Everyone was gone. He stayed open. That's conviction. Or madness. Probably both.

If an actual hurricane barreling toward your town can't convince you to change course, what hope is there that science and compassion will change the mind of an anti-masker?

I think I've reached my quota for "outside world" thinking today. There's a decent chance we're walking into a brutal second wave. Schools reopening. Workplaces pretending everything's fine. The people with the most to lose are being asked to sacrifice again—for the profit of those who already have the privilege to stay home.

The drunks outside have either passed out or wandered off. The cockatiel's finally quiet. So, my choice now: try to sleep, or plug into VR. Either way, at least for a few hours, I can step out of whatever counts as *reality* now.

Editor's Note:

Cook—an alias for a legendary, world-class internet troll with deep roots in Ottawa's electronic music scene and a long-running (if chaotic) creative kinship with Kai—submitted this piece in the summer of 2020. Not long after, he fell down a conspiratorial rabbit hole and accused Kai of being a CPC bootlicker. He asked to be removed from the project entirely... only to later, with classic apathy, relent. We're glad he's in here. His rant still slaps.

August 28, 2020 – Toronto, Canada – "Chris Sky and the Cult of FreeDumb" (Chris Sky & Jorah Kai)

Editor's Note: In an alternate universe—one only slightly more deranged than our own—Chris Sky might've been a nightclub bouncer or a professional wrestling heel. Instead, in the pandemic year of 2020, he emerged as a sweaty, shirtless warlord of the anti-mask fringe. This surreal interview captures a collision of ideologies: science vs. spectacle, civic duty vs. toxic individualism. I couldn't help but wonder, if I had never left Canada, how much would I have doubted? But no—this path was never mine.

The science was clear. By mid-2020, countries like China, New Zealand, and South Korea had demonstrated that masks, distancing, and early lockdowns could suppress COVID-19. But in Canada, a land of polite skepticism and hockey-fueled bravado, something strange was stirring.

Enter: Chris Sky—a self-styled freedom fighter with pecs, paranoia, and a parade of viral meltdowns.

I was fascinated. Who was this guy, really? Could I, a mild-mannered expat living safely in China, find common ground with a man who believed masks were oppression and cherry-picked his science from YouTube comments?

So I reached out.

ACT I: The DM Slide

July 15, 2020, 4:24 PM

Me: Hey, I heard you were looking for mask data. Want to chat about it?

[Crickets. Two days later.]

Me (again): If you'd like to contribute your side to my global COVID diary, I have some questions. Let me know.

YEAR OF THE RAT

[The silence deepens. Then, on August 19—days after he was allegedly involved in a Cherry Beach rave-cum-weaponized mannequin orgy—Chris Sky slid into my DMs.]

Chris: Lockdown is. It requires. Mandatory masks are not about safety. Blind compliance removes your rights. Beyond ignorant.

Me: Want to explain that in a piece for my readers? I'll publish it honestly.

Chris: Give me more info and I'll consider it.

Me: I'm at the gym. Chest day. Let's talk after.

Chris: It's 4AM here. I may be sleeping.

<Narrator [increasingly bewildered, like an ornithologist who just discovered a dodo running for school board]: Here, we witness the Alpha Mask Hole asserting dominance in his native time zone. Despite the planet-wide crisis, he is primarily concerned with what hour it is for him personally, as if time zones were a conspiracy imposed by Bill Gates.*>

ACT II: Clang and Bang

Me: Just warming up. Cardio and chest, then a swim. Same routine since the Wuhan lockdown. In China, masks and lockdowns worked. Our cities are open again.

Chris: Lol. We have no emergency. Zero people age 0-20. Less than 250 age 0-59 have died in Canada.

<Narrator [circling a chalkboard like a deranged substitute teacher]: This, dear reader, is what experts refer to as "statistical cherry-picking." It's like declaring your basement flood irrelevant because the upstairs bathroom is still dry. Also, he's wrong.*>

Me: What about the 6 million U.S. cases?

Chris: That's all bullshit. They count everything as COVID.

<Narrator [deep sigh, papers ruffling]: Ah yes, the ancient art of "Everything-Is-Fake-Except-My-Abs."

Let us not forget: This is a man whose understanding of virology comes from protein powder labels and libertarian memes.*>

ACT III: The Japan Gambit
Chris: Sweden and Japan. No lockdown. No masks. Better results.
Me: Actually, Japanese culture has voluntary mask use and social distance. They didn't need mandates because they cooperated. Also: sushi.
Chris: Irrelevant. They had no lockdown. I win.
Me: What about China? Mandates, masks, and now we're back to normal.
Chris: Nope. Japan. Sweden.
<Narrator [sprawled on a fainting couch with smelling salts]: Watch closely as he clings to two outlier case studies like they're protein bars at a gluten-free libertarian picnic. Ignoring 200 countries and focusing only on his two magical unicorns: classic Skyology.*>
ACT IV: The Philosophy of FreeDumb
Chris: Mandatory masks are oppression. Mandatory vaccines? Worse. Freedom, bro.
Me: But what about your grandma? Or mine? Or anyone with cancer?
Chris: Their problem. Personal responsibility.
Me: So... your freedom includes the right to kill other people by accident?
Chris: Yes. Wait, no. That's not what I said. You're being ridiculous.
Me: Sir, this is a Cinnabon.
<Narrator [head in hands]: It is at this point that our subject reveals his core belief: that society is a cage, masks are muzzles, and kindness is a communist plot. The irony? He wants the freedom to cough on strangers, but not the responsibility to explain why.*>
ACT V: The Unraveling
Chris: You haven't addressed Japan. You haven't addressed Sweden. You haven't said ONE fact. You're emotional. You're a sheep. You're... blocked.

Me: You win, Chris. Let me know if you want to talk later. We can meet halfway.
Chris: I'm already at the finish line. (sic. possibly literal.)
<*Narrator [lighting a pipe and staring into the abyss]*: And so, dear reader, concludes our expedition into the sweaty subconscious of the Cult of FreeDumb. We set out to understand. We emerged... confused, slightly amused, and grateful for our masks.*>

If satire is the scalpel of civil discourse, this exchange was an entire operating theater of absurdity. I wanted to reach across the digital divide, to connect. But sometimes, the mask stays on.
And thank God for that.

August 29, 2020 – Chicago, USA – "The Roof Is On Fire" (MC ZULU)

OK... stop me if you've heard this one.

An armed gang of white supremacists shows up in a small town already burning with unrest—riots sparked by yet another act of racist police brutality. The police in that town don't confront them. No, they hand them water bottles. They thank them for their support.

Moments later, one of these "militia" men opens fire on the crowd. Two people die. He runs—not from justice, but toward it. Toward the police.

They let him go.

Safe haven. Into the night.

Meanwhile, the protesters—the very people being targeted—are on the ground, trying to save the wounded. And through the chaos, someone yells, instinctively, heartbreakingly:

"Call the police!"

The moral of the story? We still need public officials who will not violate the public trust. But the system doesn't just fail us—it protects the very criminals and bigots it claims to oppose. It isn't a flaw. It's the design.

The whole damn building is on fire.

And what are we doing?

Lighting candles... just to blow them out again.

That is not progress.

August 29, 2020 – Chongqing, China – "Burn Night"

We made a pyre, and we set it alight. Shaolin said her prayers to the ancestors who've passed on, and I thought about everything I've ever burned and how it brought me to this moment—on a street corner on a mountain in China during a global pandemic.

It was Saturday night, August 29. Somewhere in the multiverse, this could have been the night the Man burned in Black Rock City, where 80,000 weirdos—many of them my friends—gathered from across the globe to reforge themselves in the fire of adversity, community, and creativity.

I remembered the letters I'd written in temple burns, to those I'd lost. I thought about all the people I've loved and the many ways I've lost them. I remembered how I wept when those gorgeous, intricate temples went up in flames, and how solemn the crowd was compared to the rowdy, raucous Man burn the night before. I thought about those I still love today. I felt lucky to have family, safety, and a slice of peace in these wild times.

Chadwick Boseman died today. He was 43, and after a four-year battle with cancer, he left this world quietly, still helping children with cancer while never publicly speaking of his own. In the past few years, he played many iconic roles—but to me, none greater than T'Challa, the king of Wakanda. A hero. Strong, fit, handsome, successful—and still, mortal. It reminded me: every day is a gift. A breath. A candle's flicker. I must stay grounded in the present and not be haunted by the past or paralyzed by fears of the future.

Back in April, after the virus was contained in Chongqing, I returned to the classroom. We even took our masks off when the summer heat arrived. It had been a month without new cases, but I felt like a soldier with PTSD. A student coughing or sneezing triggered rage. My patience wore thin. Home became brittle. We'd survived the lockdown, but I was fraying at the seams.

I had planned to rewrite three books this summer: *Amos the Amazing*, this second diary volume *The Lighthouse*, and my supernatural thriller *Where the Wicked Rest*. I did some of it—but mostly, I focused on healing. My body had stored fat during lockdown, my ankle was injured, and I was vulnerable. I needed to rebuild. So I swam. Lifted weights. Meditated. I listened to music, worked on mindfulness, and let go of what I could not control.

Now, after two months of steady training, I feel like myself again. I'm not just surviving—I'm present. Grounded. Forged. I am not better than my situation; I am ready for it. I'm not buried beneath the weight of what was. I stand on strong shoulders—my own.

I am not what I lost. I am what I've rebuilt.

This summer, Shaolin stood by me—steady, supportive, and quietly fierce. We made meals together, celebrated small wins, laughed, snapped at each other, and mended. She reminded me what home feels like.

Tonight, I want to share the *Ten Principles of Burning Man*—and how I've tried to live them each day.

Radical Inclusion: Everyone is welcome. No prerequisites.
→ I try to learn from everyone, without snobbery or elitism.

Gifting: Give without expecting return.
→ I offer my time, love, writing, and energy freely when I can.

Decommodification: Resist the substitution of consumption for experience.
→ I try not to center money in my life. It's a tool, not a purpose.

Radical Self-reliance: Discover your own inner resources.
→ As an artist far from home, this one is daily bread.

Radical Self-expression: Speak your truth. Share your gift.
→ I write. I teach. I make noise. I question. I stand tall in my weirdness.

Communal Effort: Collaborate. Build the world together.
→ I support the Revel Alliance and anyone fighting the good fight—in art, activism, science, and care.
Civic Responsibility: Take responsibility for the collective good.
→ I don't pass the buck. I am the buck.
Leave No Trace: Respect the Earth. Clean up.
→ I carry my own water bottle, reusable cup, take public transit, and tread lightly.
Participation: Show up. Don't just watch—*do*.
→ I believe in action. In change. In shared effort and shared joy.
Immediacy: Be here, now.
→ We can't waste time. This is the moment. It's all we ever have.
Tonight, thousands of burners are planning unofficial events across the Black Rock Desert—masked, scattered, spaced out. Some are concerned. Some are hopeful. We'll see what happens. As for me, I carry my Burn inside me now. Every day. That's the only way it makes sense.
Tomorrow, Shaolin and I will return to the sky lounge where we celebrated our anniversary. We'll have brunch, cake, coffee, and tea. We'll sit in the sun, overlooking this crazy, concrete jungle, and I'll prepare myself to teach 2,000 students across two campuses this fall.
The last thing to burn is fear.
And when we let go of the fear of death...
Only then can we *truly* live.

August 29, 2020 – Gulu, Uganda – "Bars, Police and the COVID-19 Lockdown" (Aliker P' Ocitti)

In March 2020, the President of Uganda declared a nationwide lockdown due to COVID-19. Most businesses were shuttered. Social distancing became the new normal. A curfew was instated at 7:00 p.m., later adjusted to 9:00 p.m.

But how did addicts adjust to this new normal?

One morning, Facebook reminded me it was Becky's birthday. Becky is a childhood friend—we mind each other's business. As kids, we played in the rain and traded bottle caps. I sent her a message and teased her about a birthday without beer.

She replied: "It's beer day in my house."

A sudden thirst struck me. I needed something to take the edge off this pandemic trauma.

"What time?" I texted.

"Now," she wrote.

It was 10:00 a.m. I threw off my blanket, grabbed a towel, and hit the shower. As cold water slapped me awake, BBC News blared grim updates from Britain and America. But my craving for a cold Bell beer overpowered any fear. I needed music. I needed to numb out.

I jumped on my Bajaj motorbike, the wind tearing through my shirt as I sped toward town. A cold breeze and smoky breath reminded me I'd forgotten my mask. I bought one at the fuel station using the change from my tank.

Just before town, I passed a sluggish line of police officers patrolling for curfew breakers. They looked tired, hungry—and possibly thirsty. I wondered: if we were caught, would they seize the beer as evidence... or drink it?

Becky's house was 10 km out, past a rain-slicked, pothole-riddled road. From the tire tracks, I could tell I wasn't the first guest. For a road like that, so many tracks meant only two things: a funeral—or a party.
It was definitely a party.
The compound was packed with motorbikes and cars. Music blasted from car speakers. Young men and women wandered in and out of the house, loud and laughing, drinks in hand. No one was wearing masks.
Inside, it was a full-blown house party. I was greeted like a politician during campaign season. A crew of young women danced toward me to Mc Wang Jok's "Pe Ikwala," until Becky rescued me with a shoulder tap.
In the kitchen, she pulled four cold Bell beers from the fridge.
"How are you going to avoid the police?" I asked, suddenly sober.
Becky smiled. "That guy over there in the blue shirt? He's a police officer. Says the government has no money for fuel, so no one's chasing anyone this far out."
"What about social distancing?"
"We tried last night. But as the drinking continued... it collapsed."
"Where'd all these people come from?"
"Ran out of beer last night. Got a tip about Pato's bar staying open. It was secret—codeword entry, doors locked from the inside. We called them. They followed the beer back here. Now we've got a sleepover situation."
"Are you worried?"
"I just don't want you to get in trouble," I said.
"Rule is: no photos. No social media. That's how you get in trouble."
I grabbed my beers and wandered outside. I found Calvin—an old school friend—in his car with four slender girls and joined them. I cracked my beer using another bottle as leverage. First one down in

under three minutes. Sobriety had made me too observant. Time to catch up.

I turned to one of the girls. "I'm David," I said, offering a handshake. She declined, citing COVID.

Calvin noticed and chuckled. "David's a writer. Runs a media company."

"Oh wow," said Diana. "I'm a journalism student, final year."

We hit it off. I told her I was writing a book on infidelity.

"Why infidelity?"

"Because everyone's writing about COVID. And because nobody admits it—but everyone's haunted by it."

"Are you a character in the book?"

"Not really. But a part of me is."

"I wish I could write a book."

"Aren't you a journalism student?"

"Yes, but... I'm not sure I can."

"You will. In time."

"Hey David, that's my girl," Calvin said with a grin. "Don't get me in trouble."

"You don't have to be so protective," Diana snapped back.

We joked, drank, and gossiped. Calvin shared that at his usual bar, patrons save 1,000 shillings each night to bribe police via mobile money. The patrol routes adjust accordingly. It's part of the new ecosystem.

"I wonder why they closed bars but kept deports open," Diana mused. "If a depot is essential, so is a bar."

"The taxes," said Calvin. "They can't afford to lose that revenue."

"I think they were afraid addicts like Calvin might collapse from withdrawal," Diana said, teasing.

Everyone roared.

At 3:00 p.m., hunger hit me hard. I went looking for food. Becky apologized for the oversight and led me to the kitchen. Out of soap, I washed my hands with plain water and served up rice and stewed chicken. Delicious.

Later, Bob arrived in his sports car, packed with girls. No masks. No distancing. He whispered something to Becky. My curiosity got the better of me.

"Two friends tested positive," Bob confided. "A truck driver came to Mike's bar. He'd invited his coworkers, who brought friends. He tested positive at the border. Now they're all in quarantine."

As the party raged on, drunk guests took over bedrooms and bathrooms. I checked my watch: 7:00 p.m.—past curfew.

I wasn't staying. Too many people. Too many risks. And I wanted to write this all down while it was still fresh.

I hugged Becky goodbye. My legs buckled slightly from the alcohol. Instead of the main road, I took the railway path—no cops there. Turns out I wasn't alone. Dozens of others had the same idea. Back home, I collapsed on the couch. I meant to shower. I meant to write.

Instead, I slept hard and woke at 6:42 a.m., somehow ready for work.

August 30, 2020 – PEI, Canada – "Let Go and Count Your Blessings!" (Dara Mac)

All the violence, hatred, and negativity around us have taken their toll—and being in isolation makes it even harder to process. If I can't share something hopeful or positive that might bring some light to others, then in my mind, there's really no point. That's why it's been a few months since my last blog entry.

Pandemic. Senior. Retired. When I write those words, I think: slow down, relax, take it easy, stress less. But my reality has been anything but. New projects, steep learning curves, family separation, sleepless nights, and an inner drive that would make you think a teenager was living inside me.

When I haven't been too stressed to play, drumming has kept me grounded, focused, and feeling like my life still holds meaning and purpose. For me, playing music has always been about expression and sharing, not performance. So the tragic reality of gigs disappearing hasn't hit as hard. I've just wanted to drum like no one's listening—a near-impossible task, even in rural PEI.

So, I took the leap. I followed friends' advice and began planning a soundproof studio-slash-guest house next to my home. A neighbor agreed to build it (he was shocked to learn I was the drummer he'd been hearing a kilometre away). But after months of research, stress, and investment, I had to admit defeat. The project stalled, the lead was unfit, and I realized—this isn't the time to start something new. It's time to support what already exists.

I've also been deeply concerned about my 90-year-old mother's isolation and apartment issues. Being 1,200 kilometers away, I spent hours researching better housing options. After a stressful stint in a hotel, she decided to try a month-long stay at a retirement home.

YEAR OF THE RAT

She braved five hours of standing in 40+ degree heat over several days to get her required COVID tests. But on the very day she was meant to move in, the facility locked down with its first positive case. She dodged a bullet—since then, they've had six more cases. Thankfully, she's now settled back in her apartment with her cat. Repairs are done, and things have, mercifully, calmed down.

Here on PEI, things have opened up over the summer, though without the million-and-a-half tourists we usually see. The Atlantic Bubble has allowed travel between the Maritime provinces, which has been a blessing. My son and his wife had hoped to visit this summer—it's been two years now—but that's been postponed indefinitely. These days, I cope by staying present and practicing gratitude. We may be six feet apart from each other, but we're still connected.

(Side note: I recently learned that the tradition of burying people six feet under originated in 1655. Medical practitioners thought plague victims could still spread disease and hoped depth would help. Seems relevant.)

Despite the restrictions, people are back at cafés, and I recently met up with three fellow drummers I'd been Zooming with weekly for months. It was the first time we met in person, and we closed the patio down. Passion, music, and drumming make it hard to say goodbye. I'm so grateful for the people in my life who share that joy. One of the biggest lessons of this year has been learning who my real friends are—and who they're not. Real friends aren't self-centered, egotistical, or entitled.

This pandemic has also taught me I'm a much better indoor gardener than an outdoor one. I'm looking forward to getting back to growing microgreens. It's also taught me that love is easy. It's never far—it lives within and all around us.

I've learned how to deal with entitlement and how easy it is to walk away. I'm letting go of what no longer serves me. I want to fly high like an eagle—beyond fear, beyond greed—into a place of joy and gratitude.

Living through this pandemic has deeply impacted my life and my mental health. In the past, my colleagues might have described me as "spacey," or, if they were kind, "artistic." Now, spacey has become the new normal. I feel like a spirit having a human experience. And in a strange way, that perspective makes both permanence and impermanence easier to carry. Seeing this pandemic and the separation it brings as impermanent gives me hope.

August 30, 2020 – Verona, Italy – "Sweet Verona (Waiting for Better Days)" (Alessia Martino)

When I talk to people about 2020, I tend to call it a "weird" or "strange" year, rather than the worst one. It hasn't been the best, but I've still found joy in the madness. Of course, I'm only speaking to my own experience—everyone's story is different, and I would never want to invalidate anyone else's. But I won't call 2020 a horrible year just because others do. Even if the past few weeks haven't exactly been rosy.

August began on a positive note. I met up with a friend for a nine-day vacation across Northern Italy. We didn't plan carelessly—we pre-selected each destination based on its COVID case count. I personally tracked the numbers for days, adjusting our route accordingly. We chose Milan, which had just three active cases, Lake Garda, and Verona, which had none. I had to convince my friend to cut Venice from the list due to a recent spike—turns out many had the same idea, and Venice was left eerily empty. We also opted for hotels over hostels, wanting to avoid shared spaces. The only compromise was using public transportation, but masks and assigned seating were mandatory on every train and bus. We also scheduled the trip for late July, just before the usual August travel rush.

The vacation itself was lovely. Milan still felt a bit tense, with a protest near the central station and many attractions still closed. The cathedral wasn't open for touring, but you could still attend services or access the rooftop—masks required, of course. Still, we made the most of it: admiring the graffiti walls, vertical forests, Chinatown, and, of course, the food. Milan has more to offer than just fashion week. I had the best non-in-Japan sushi I've ever tasted, and the aperitivi by the Navigli canals were unforgettable.

Lake Garda was stunning. We stayed in a quiet little town with amazing local food and plenty of outdoor seating. Our B&B had a pool, and we made the most of it—keeping distance even in the water. We moved the sunbeds apart and soaked in the sun. We also took a ferry to visit other small islands. Every activity had to be booked in advance to avoid crowds, and masks were required in any shared space outdoors. We visited a castle and some ruins, but avoided the main beach because it was way too packed—no distancing, no masks. We found a quieter spot, claimed our own little zone, and I managed a quick dip in peace.

My favorite stop was Verona. The tourist discount card wasn't available, so we picked just a few must-see spots and timed them wisely. Our planning paid off—the Verona Arena was nearly empty when we arrived, and we made it to Juliet's house just before the rush. The courtyard was quiet. The famous balcony? Ours for ten whole minutes. Usually it's impossible to get near it, let alone feel alone in the space. The Juliet statue was off-limits (usually people touch her breast for good luck—don't ask me why), and the walls of letters were covered. There was even a staff member assigned to guard it all. By the time we exited, the courtyard had a long line of visitors waiting to get in. We'd timed everything just right. A few sites were closed for renovation, but we still managed to explore every corner and hill of the town. Even when it got busier in the final days, we found ways to stay safe and distant—and we even had a restaurant all to ourselves for dinner. Though, on the hottest days, we did see a few waiters struggling with their masks, pulling them under their noses in the 40°C heat.

Since then, places have become noticeably more crowded. Beaches across Italy are now packed. I've heard from friends that mask use in the South is much less common than in the North. Clubs were only recently closed again—one wonders why they were ever reopened at all. Now, masks are mandatory outdoors after 6 p.m.

YEAR OF THE RAT

Schools across the country are scrambling to prepare: replacing shared desks, downsizing classrooms, staggering schedules. But no one really knows how it will go. In central Italy, one town locked down after finding 12 positive cases—all in one family—but the mayor shut it down anyway for a few days to test everyone.

For international travel, new precautions are in place. Quick testing is now being done at airports for travelers from high-risk countries like Malta, Greece, Croatia, and Spain. Quarantine rules have been updated, and although the system is still imperfect, it's better than nothing. Still, I'm shocked at how many selfish people try to bypass testing or quarantine by rerouting through other countries.

So, I've mostly stayed home this month. I adopted a new rescue cat, and I've found joy in quiet days, the company of a few close people, and the hope that better days will eventually come.

August 31, 2020 – Chongqing, China – "The Way of the Samurai (To Fully Live You Must Not Fear Death)"

Part I – Autumn Winds and Winter Warnings

Day 225. It's ironic that in a year of unprecedented isolation, from the seclusion of my mountaintop hovel, I feel closer to you than I have in years. While the world retreats behind closed doors, I write from solitude—not of despair, but of purpose. And from this quiet place, I send you a message. One that has served me well. Do with it what you can, what you will. Know that I send it with love in my heart.

As we say goodbye to summer, millions of parents, students, and teachers brace for the return to school. Some are excited. Others, trembling with anxiety, are updating their wills. Estate lawyers have had a busy summer. They fear what lies ahead should an outbreak find its way into the classroom. But still, they return.

Globally, we've surpassed 25.6 million confirmed COVID-19 cases and more than 850,000 deaths. Some experts estimate the real numbers are ten times higher. And now, as influenza season approaches, we brace for what may be a perfect storm.

The best defense begins with personal terrain: good sleep, low stress, healthy food, sunlight, physical activity, and strong immunity. Obesity is a comorbidity—42% of Americans are obese, compared with only 6% of Chinese people. It's worth addressing. Vitamin D is crucial; deficiency is often linked to severe cases. Zinc, quercetin, selenium, and a multivitamin may help. Why not hedge your bets?

Limit your exposure. Wear masks indoors. Avoid crowds. Don't shake hands. Carry sanitizer. Wash your hands. Open windows. Avoid poorly ventilated indoor spaces filled with voices, singing, shouting—the recipe for super-spreader events. Avoid the virus before it finds you. Prepare, because winter is coming.

Even Usain Bolt—the fastest man alive—couldn't outrun the virus after celebrating his 34th birthday maskless. If Bolt can't dodge it, none of us can. Don't be reckless. Be wise.

Part II – The Warrior's Path
The most practical advice for teachers, bosses, or anyone in leadership:

- Ventilate indoor spaces. Fresh air is life.
- Make HEPA filters your ally.
- Anyone coughing? They mask or go home.
- Enforce distancing as a civic duty.

And for individuals:

- Sleep well. Reduce stress. Exercise.
- Nourish your body: avoid junk food and excess alcohol.
- Supplement wisely: Vitamin D, Zinc, Multivitamins.
- Mask up indoors. Bump elbows. Wash your hands like it's your religion.

In China, we may have a vaccine available for 300 RMB. I'll be following this development closely. But until safe and effective vaccines are universally distributed, we must stand ready. Experts warn the second wave could be four times worse than the first.

So what do we do when the future is uncertain? We let go of fear. We sharpen the mind, the spirit, the sword of will. And we walk the path of the warrior.

Part III – Fearlessness in the Face of Death
"Those who cling to life die, and those who defy death live."
So said Uesugi Kenshin, a Sengoku daimyō, just before his death.

Miyamoto Musashi, Japan's undefeated sword saint, lived each day as if already dead. That was how he remained unafraid—sharp, resolute, present.

Death was everywhere in his world. On the battlefield, in the famine-plagued villages. The Samurai learned to walk beside death and laugh. Not because it was easy, but because it was necessary. To live without fear, they accepted the inevitable: they would die. So why waste energy fearing it?

"To fully live, you must not fear death."

If you knew you were already dead, what would you do differently? Would you chase your dreams more fiercely? Would you love more openly? Would you write your book, launch your project, make your peace?

Then do it. Because you are already dead. All that's left is to live.

Part IV – Meditation of the Warrior

Today's guided meditation: grounding, strengthening, releasing.

Close your eyes. Place both hands on your heart. Feel it beat.

With each breath in, feel strength returning. With each exhale, release fear.

Breathe in deeply... exhale slowly.

Relax your shoulders. Unclench your jaw. Drop your weight into the earth.

Let go of your thoughts. Let them drift by like clouds.

Now visualize a radiant light surrounding you—your color of choice. Let this light pour into your crown, through every cell. Let it push out the darkness, the heaviness, the fear.

You are made of stars and dust. Of lightning and earth.

You are strong. You are guided. You are enough.

Say it aloud or in silence: **I surrender to the uncertainty. I am in control. I am safe. I am guided.**

Repeat as needed. Stay here as long as you like.

Part V – Cut the Rope

Imagine yourself walking on a beach. There's a thick rope tied around your waist, attached to an anchor dragging behind you.
It's heavy. It slows you down. It hurts.
Up ahead, something glitters in the sand. You approach—it's a blade. Ancient. And inscribed on the handle is your name.
This is your moment.
Take the blade and cut the rope.
Let the anchor fall. Watch the waves carry it away.
You are free.
Let the golden light surround you again. Breathe deeply. Let the healing begin.

Epilogue – The Buddha Beneath the Clay
In the 1950s, a clay Buddha statue cracked during a relocation. Inside, the monks discovered a statue of solid gold hidden beneath.
You are that statue.
Let this strange year chip away the clay. Reveal your light. Don't be afraid. Don't wait. Be who you were meant to be.
Live boldly. Love wildly. Fear nothing but regret.
I send you love. I send you strength. I send you the calm of the warrior's breath.
May you be healthy. May you find peace within.
And may you die well—by living well every single day.
—Kai, Chongqing, China
August 31, 2020

Interlude – Chongqing Juicy Grapes

This summer, just after my birthday in mid-August, I was invited to climb Nan Shan—South Mountain—for an unusual collaboration. Chongqing's most celebrated painter, Master Feng, renowned for his luscious grape paintings, had asked me to perform alongside him. I wasn't entirely sure what I was supposed to do—or why—but I agreed in the spirit of art, spontaneity, and mountain air.

I decided to rework a poem for the occasion, and with Shaolin's help translating into Chinese for the crowd, I gave a short performance under the late summer sun. Afterward, Master Feng led a group of about thirty children in a masterclass on painting grapes. They did a great—no, grape—job capturing the fruit's subtle glow. We shared a hearty mountain lunch: handpicked wild mushroom soup, local dishes, and tea. Then we were treated to a Tujia folk song echoing through the pines.

Below is the poem I read—simple, strange, and heartfelt.

Chongqing Juicy Grapes

By Jorah Kai
I pass the time browsing
a little story,
chewing the words
over and over.
It feels like I'm rolling
the same perfect grape
around my tongue
again and again.
I stroll through my tidy home
on the side of a mountain,
leaving its essence dripping
through the air in every room.
I sweat full-grown grapes at the gym
and recite the lines aloud.
I read it from the cliffs of HongYaDong
into the swollen belly of the river.
I rap its rhythm against a cupboard
bursting with treasured books.
And when my two dogs look up at me,
I bow down to the floor
and whisper into four long, curious ears.
One is old, and remembers.
The other is young, eager to understand.
I read it without listening.
I discover it without speaking.
Billy asked me,
"Did you take it?"
I did.
I made it mine.

It's about a little piece of cotton
tied around my face.
Every time I feel its touch—
against my lips,
along my chin—
when I speak out the window,
that embrace circles the globe,
a message of hope.
Like a bird with papery wings,
and in its beak,
a bunch of
juicy Chongqing grapes.

September 5, 2020 – Chongqing, China – "Falling Further Through the Fog"
Part I: The Knot of Time

It's a good thing I'm pretty sure time isn't linear, because if it were, I'd be working too much. But if it's more like a knotty ball, all tangled and happening at once, then the many jobs I have now balance out the years I spent blissfully floundering in the music business—and perhaps even buy me some peace in the years ahead. I managed to get Sundays off this year, and these days, that's something.

My sister Nunich once told me: "Ask yourself how can I make myself better, my life better, the world better? Whatever your answers are—do those things. Every day."

I've been trying to take it to heart. Each morning, I head to the gym to grow stronger. I read to grow wiser. I teach and write to be useful, and possibly—if my words survive me—immortal. I work fast and with purpose, cramming tasks into tight windows so that the rest of my time can belong to music, novels, family walks, delicious meals, belly laughs, crappy movies, and epic tabletop RPGs. I think that's the recipe for a good life.

Part II: Slurp, Slurp, the Planet Dies

Of course, that good life is under threat. Take, for example, plastic-packed fruit: grown in Argentina, processed and shrink-wrapped in Thailand, and sold in America. An ecological abomination. Think of the fuel spent. The packaging. The insult to actual fruit. If you see someone about to buy that plastic sin, gently slap it from their hands and whisper, "Do better." (Gently. We're not animals.) The planet's dying, and we're still bingeing single-serve pineapple cubes. We can't afford this kind of laziness anymore.

Part III: The Absurdity Olympics

Meanwhile, Quebec parents went to court, pleading for remote learning during a pandemic. Premier Legault replied there weren't enough teachers to handle both in-class and online instruction. If only there were some futuristic device that could record lessons and make them accessible via the internet. Alas. Pipe dreams.

Mimsey Demon, my old friend, chimed in: "They can't use YouTube for Quebec education—it's not called ToiTube." (He later called me a commie bootlicker and blocked me. So it goes.)

In Mexico, they just put classes on national TV. Problem solved. But North America? We invent problems. We sit in them. We call it "freedom."

Part IV: Dormitories of Doom

Back in the U.S., universities are shocked—*shocked!*—that their maskless kegger students are spreading COVID-19. Their solution? Quarantine students together in tiny, shared dorm rooms. No private bathrooms. No real ventilation. "Basically," said Mimsey (before the blocking), "it's a Petri dish with roommates."

And when people get sick? Administrators clutch pearls and call it a tragedy no one could've seen coming. "Who could've predicted this?" they say. *Me*, I say. *Me*, and anyone paying attention.

Part V: Vitamin D and Digital Tribes

On the plus side, my pandemic ramblings weren't entirely in vain. As mainstream media finally began acknowledging the role of Vitamin D in preventing severe COVID cases, some of my friends messaged me with thanks.

"Thanks to you, I've been taking Vitamin D this whole time," Alison said. "When we need a new world leader, I'm nominating you." World leader? Hard pass. Leo that I am, I take that as a sign of spiritual growth.

Part VI: The Students Are Not to Blame

My friend Tim has had it with colleges blaming students for outbreaks.

"If your entire plan depended on every 19-year-old behaving with perfect discipline, that's not a plan. That's magical thinking."

He's right. Administrators, leaders—so-called adults—keep planning for the best-case scenario. Then act shocked when things go sideways.

Part VII: Herd Immunity or Homicide?

Trump has a new pandemic advisor. Not a scientist. A guy from Fox News. His advice? Let COVID-19 "burn through" the population. Let two million die. Survival of the fittest. Or maybe just survival of the most privileged.

Winter is coming. The game is on, and you either win or you die.

Part VIII: The Numbers Game

COVID-19 data is a joke now. The White House intercepted the flow of hospital data to the CDC, but we keep quoting their numbers like it's gospel.

In Spain, officials are saying, "Practically all schoolchildren will catch COVID." Cool. Chill. No big deal.

Meanwhile, Batman is on hold. Robert Pattinson's got the virus. Even Bruce Wayne couldn't escape the reach of this pandemic.

Part IX: Shaolin and the Nose Test

Shaolin's lost her sense of smell. No fever, no cough—just a vanished olfactory system. She blames the air conditioner, a classic Chinese explanation. Me? I'm on high alert. No cases in Chongqing for months, but that's how these things start.

Part X: Sewage Surveillance and Steampunk Teachers

Dr. Pepper—yes, seriously—says testing wastewater can predict outbreaks a week before symptoms hit. This could save lives.

Instead, our leaders shrug and tell us to ride it out.

Meanwhile, substitute teachers are expected to hop from school to school, potentially carrying the virus with them. Nothing to see here, folks.

Also, we had one job in 2020—*let teachers wear steampunk goggles.* Missed opportunity.

Part XI: Masks, Vitamins, and Bureaucratic Suicide

Canada's public health experts keep saying diet and vitamins don't matter. It's absurd. Not because you can "tune" your immune system like a guitar—but because bad health makes you more vulnerable, and everyone knows it. To pretend otherwise is, frankly, criminal negligence.

Part XII: Joy, Cobra Kai, and the Apocalypse Kit

I'm thrilled people are watching *Cobra Kai*. It's smart, it's nostalgic, and Ralph Macchio is somehow still a wholesome king.

Meanwhile, I keep adding to my apocalypse kit: knives, gloves, silver socks (for kicking werewolves), solar chargers, Damascus steel. And I don't regret a single yuan I spent on masks. When shortages hit, I was ready.

Part XIII: School's Back—And So Am I

We've had no local COVID-19 transmission in five months, so I'm back in the classroom. No masks unless symptomatic, but I wear glasses for protection, and carry a wearable air purifier. I keep HEPA ionizers on my desk. I open the windows. I stay sharp.

Tuesday and Wednesday are teaching days. Thursday and Friday are off. The gym has fresh water in the pool. The dumbbells are getting heavier. I feel good.

Part XIV: Happiness Chemistry

Want to stay sane?

- **Dopamine** – Finish a task, eat something yummy, celebrate a win.
- **Oxytocin** – Hug a loved one. Pet a dog.
- **Endorphins** – Laugh. Exercise. Dark chocolate.
- **Serotonin** – Meditate. Run. Sunlight. Nature.

I try to hit the full list every day. It's working. Maybe it'll work for you too.

Part XV: Hope on the Horizon

China says we'll have a vaccine by Christmas. Maybe it works. Maybe it doesn't. But at least we're trying. Eight billion doses in a few weeks would be nice. Affordable ones, even better.

Until then, we prepare. We breathe. We keep going.

Winter is coming.

And I've never felt more alive.

September 8, 2020 – Chongqing, China – "The Metaverse is You"

Part I: Sunshine in a Bottle

Humility is a strange thing. The moment you believe you've mastered it, it slips through your fingers. Still, in these strange times, it's important to try. So, with a humble heart and cautious optimism, I bring good news: **Vitamin D saves lives.**

Two new studies dropped like sunbeams through storm clouds. First, a JAMA study of nearly 500 people found that patients with Vitamin D deficiency were *1.77 times more likely* to require critical COVID care. That's almost double. In other words, taking Vitamin D cuts your chances of a "bad case" in half.

Second, a small study from Reina Sofia University in Córdoba, Spain, gave patients a vitamin D analog—calcifediol, at a significant dose. All patients received hydroxychloroquine and azithromycin, but only one group received the vitamin boost. Among those **without** vitamin D, *50% were admitted to the ICU and 7% died.* Among those **with** vitamin D, *only 2% needed ICU care—and none died.* None. Not a single one.

Small sample or not, those are stunning numbers. Statistically, the findings are considered 999 out of 1000 accurate. Why aren't governments distributing Vitamin D and Zinc packets to every household? Instead, the Canadian Dietary Association is out here tweeting that you can't "fine-tune your immune system." Fire that social media manager.

Part II: The Science of Inequality

There's an uncomfortable truth buried in these stats. In the U.S., **42% of the general population** is vitamin D deficient—but that number rises to **82% of Black Americans** and **70% of Hispanics**, according to studies cited by Dr. John Campbell. If we can depoliticize the science and acknowledge that supplementation could save lives, especially among disproportionately affected groups, then why *wouldn't* we act?

We must tread carefully. Race and medicine have a long, painful history. But this isn't about eugenics or superiority—it's about *biology* and *justice*. If one cheap vitamin can cut COVID severity in half, then withholding it is cruelty cloaked in bureaucracy.

Part III: Back to the Mountain

Meanwhile in Chongqing, I'm easing back into the fall term. My voice barely survived nine classes across Tuesday and Wednesday, but I made it through, then hit the gym. Thursday and Friday were blissfully quiet writing days.
Saturday? A marathon. Eight hours of tutoring. One boy staged a successful rebellion against his grandfather and escaped into the wilds of our school like a tiny revolutionary. I respect that.
Sunday, sweet Sunday—my first proper day off in ages.
We had a big family lunch. Our son Jinn is getting married around Spring Festival, and we met his fiancée, her twin, and their mother for roast duck and soup. If you're feeling behind in life, don't worry. I'm a time traveler. You're only racing yourself.
Later that day, we barbecued, drank mushroom soup, and watched *Tenet* in IMAX. It was brilliant, baffling, brain-bending. The guy behind me kept coughing. I flinched every time. But he wore a mask. I didn't touch mine until I was outside.

Part IV: Burning Man in the Metaverse

The Burn happened, sort of. There were virtual temples, VR art cars, and socially distanced alt-burns on beaches. Some folks were angry. Some were inspired. This year's version of Burning Man unfolded across the multiverse—part digital hallucination, part elite private gathering, part punk rock desert rebellion. And yes, there was drama.

Part V: Schools and Storms

On the first day back for French schools in Ontario, **eight schools reported COVID cases**. Two teachers tested positive. English schools hadn't even opened yet.

It's hard not to feel for policymakers—shut down the schools and parents riot. Leave them open, and people die. The only answer is to **dance with the virus**: test, trace, isolate. Lock down early and hard when needed. Or else we're just rearranging deck chairs on a viral Titanic.

Part VI: Into the Storm

Let's talk about **bradykinin storms**.

A new supercomputer analysis proposes that COVID-19 triggers a cascade of molecular events that create severe symptoms—not just through cytokines, but by **disrupting the renin-angiotensin system**. This leads to leaky blood vessels, swelling, and that infamous "jelly lung" phenomenon.

It also explains why **Vitamin D**, **Zinc**, **Ivermectin**, and **Quercetin** might be so effective. These substances help regulate or interrupt that bradykinin pathway.

Urine tests in Germany are being used to predict organ failure. Aggressive anticoagulation may prevent clot-related damage. The takeaway? Early detection and early treatment save lives.

Part VII: Hard Choices and Harsh Realities

People laughed when China welded shut apartment doors in Wuhan. Now, with schools open, hospitals overwhelmed, and 200,000 Americans dead, who's laughing? The string around the door was symbolic. The weld was the line in the sand. We called it draconian. China called it *containment*.

Hard choices now or horrific consequences later. That's the only real choice.

Part VIII: Sinking Ships and Systemic Swamps

At a Trump boat rally, several boats sank. That just feels metaphorically on the nose.

Trump's base doesn't seem to mind that the captain is steering straight into a hurricane. The swamp wasn't drained; it was dredged deeper, polluted further, and turned into a breeding ground for white nationalist terrorism. Police tried to *bribe witnesses* into implicating Breonna Taylor as part of a crime syndicate, just to retroactively justify her murder.

Part IX: Stoicism in the Chaos

As men drill into my walls to fill our home with gas for pest control, I turn to Stoic wisdom for comfort.

"How does it help... to make troubles heavier by bemoaning them?" – **Seneca**

We magnify our pain by complaining. Instead, we can *choose* to respond with resilience.

"When we are no longer able to change a situation, we are challenged to change ourselves." – **Viktor Frankl**

We cannot always control what happens. But we can control *how we respond*.

"Don't explain your philosophy. Embody it." – **Epictetus**

So that's what I'll do. Write the words, live the truth, stay present in the chaos.

Because the world is shifting beneath our feet.

And this metaverse? It's only just beginning.

September 16, 2020 – Chongqing, China – "Fractions"

Part I: Embracing the Moment
Day 235. I used to race toward something, always chasing an elusive destiny. Now, I try to savor the present moment, knowing that the future is uncertain, maybe even uncomfortable. Instead, I find joy in life's simple, daily rhythms: sweeping, washing, cutting, cooking, smiling, and laughing. This, I've come to realize, is life. And life, in all its mundane beauty, is a treasure.

One of my friends, a diehard Bernie Sanders campaigner, once said, "A jaw-dropping photo of our era—cardboard people watching baseball under a dystopian climate-havoc sky. It didn't have to be like this." The future is uncertain, but it's what we make of it. We can choose doom and gloom, or resilience and regeneration. The path ahead could lead to a solar-punk dream—or collapse under the weight of our inaction. It's up to us.

Part II: Searching for Meaning
"There is only one way to happiness," said Seneca, "and that is to cease worrying about things which are beyond the power of our will." The road ahead is difficult, but we can still control our actions.

It's been six months since the WHO declared COVID-19 a global pandemic. As I write, more than 230 days have passed since lockdown began, with official counts of 940,353 deaths worldwide and over 200,000 in the United States alone. But we're learning. While case numbers rise, we're not seeing the same death rates, thanks to improvements in treatment.

Part III: Theories and Uncertainty
One interesting theory floating around is the XYZ theory. It suggests that up to 30% of the population might have pre-existing im-

munity, while another 40% may experience mild cases due to T-cell immunity. If true, this could lead us closer to herd immunity. But as with all theories, the science remains inconclusive. It's something to consider, but we won't know for sure until more studies are conducted.

In the meantime, hydroxychloroquine (HCQ) remains a controversial subject. While initial studies dismissed it as dangerous, new Canadian research shows it might reduce mortality when combined with other treatments. Yet, we've lost months—and nearly a million lives—while pharmaceutical interests pushed expensive drugs like Remdesivir over cheap, effective alternatives.

Part IV: The Long Road to Recovery

Confusion continues to surround COVID-19's effects on the brain. Recent studies show that brain inflammation could explain symptoms like confusion, agitation, and even psychosis in some patients. What triggers these symptoms remains a mystery, though researchers speculate that a combination of vitamin D deficiency, age, and viral load may be factors.

I think the key to mental wellbeing, good cheer, and general happiness is breaking life into manageable fractions. It's how I finished my first novel. An overwhelming task becomes achievable when broken into small, daily goals. This is how I tackle life now. Every Saturday, instead of resting like my colleagues, I teach four two-hour classes. It seems like a lot, but when I break it down—10-minute warm-ups, short practice sessions, review games—it's much easier to handle. Gradually, the workday breaks into chunks, and the whole thing becomes doable.

Part V: The Gift of Small Moments

On a typical workday, I wake up around 6:30 or 7, make coffee, shower, and head out to teach. I teach five classes back to back from 8 to 12:15. It feels like a grind at first, but by the time I finish my first class and get through a riddle with the students, we're 25%

through the day. A short break, followed by more lessons, and suddenly the day feels manageable.

The rest of my day follows a similar rhythm—exercise, work, and family time. I hit the gym, swim, write, watch movies, and play video games. I also try to spend time with Shaolin and my dogs. I take pleasure in these small moments because I know they add up. In a world full of distractions, small joys are grounding.

Part VI: The Joy of Simplicity

There's a surprising joy in simplicity. I used to loathe going to the gym or swimming, but now, I find peace in pushing through discomfort. Whether lifting weights or swimming laps, the discomfort becomes something to embrace. Pain, in its many forms, is how we know we're alive. It means we're working toward something, making progress, evolving.

A recent moment of serendipity: A songbird flew into my classroom while I was lecturing. It was green and yellow, singing beautifully. The students ignored me, completely enchanted by the bird. We all laughed. It was one of those small moments that reminds me life is unpredictable and full of surprises.

Part VII: Breaking the Pattern

On Sundays, I try to get away from the grind. Last Sunday, I played golf with friends. I'm not a golfer, but I realized that it's the mindfulness of the activity I enjoy. Focusing on the ball, the swing, the movement—it's all a form of meditation. It's about being present in the moment.

Later, we had brunch by the river, and I spent time with Elsa, my goddaughter. At four years old, she's already incredibly sharp, and it's a joy to watch her grow.

Part VIII: The Path Forward

We must break danger into fractions too, especially during a pandemic. The fear of the unknown can be overwhelming, but simple precautions help us navigate the risks: sleep, healthy food, exercise, air purifiers, and wearing masks in poorly ventilated areas. We need to be aware of risks, but we also need to live.

A recent article reminded me that COVID-19 spreads most easily in places where people are in close proximity for long periods, without proper protection or ventilation. The virus can spread before symptoms appear, making everyday precautions even more important.

Part IX: Personal Responsibility

I also know that I've been cautious, perhaps excessively so. But my precautions have often been correct, and it's better to err on the side of caution. My mom recently went to a concert in PEI. While the organizers claimed to have taken proper COVID-19 precautions—distancing, limited audience size—no one wore masks. I found that concerning, as a single sneeze could infect the entire crowd. It's a reminder that precautions must always be taken seriously.

As the weather gets colder, many of us may be tempted to take more risks. But I hope we'll remember that small actions—fractions—can help us avoid much larger consequences down the road. If we use masks, air purifiers, and other safety measures, we can continue to protect ourselves and others.

Part X: The Bigger Picture

The world is changing. While many of us take simple steps to protect our health and the environment, some people are still resisting change. Whether it's COVID-19 safety measures or climate action, there's a tendency to avoid responsibility. We can only hope that people will take the necessary steps to protect the planet and each other.

For now, I find solace in the small actions I can take each day—whether it's wearing a mask, exercising, or spending time with loved ones. As long as we keep moving forward, even in small fractions, we're making progress.

September 24, 2020 – Chicago, USA – "Fight the System" (MC ZULU)

Remember, people, if you do everything right—keep your nose clean, stay out of trouble—you are still just one no-knock warrant away from being murdered in your own bed.

Imagine being a cop, serving one of these warrants, and suddenly, a gunshot flies your way. From the moment you hit the academy, you were taught that "certain people" don't want you to survive your shift.

Fear seizes you. With terror in your heart, you fire back, even hitting one of your own fellow officers. An innocent life is lost—a paramedic, someone whose job was to save lives, not end them. Shots fly through neighboring buildings.

Bullets fueled by hatred, cowardice, and a complete disregard for human life prove one undeniable truth: You were never meant for this line of work.

The real elephant in the room is this: the warrant wasn't re-verified within 48 hours of issuance. Police were attempting to detain a suspect they had already in custody.

After this cascade of errors—killing a fellow first responder—authorities gave her mother the runaround, sending her back and forth from the hospital, while they crafted the most antiseptic narrative they could conjure.

In Minneapolis, we saw a similar high-profile situation. Fear and bullets combined to destroy a life. Officer Mohammed Noor shot Justine Diamond, and received a 12-year jail sentence.

But Breonna Taylor isn't Justine Diamond. Her financial settlement is $8 million less. Her killers will never face charges. All that's left is the same tragic disparity—and the foreboding realization that any of us could be next.

Beyond the individuals involved, the true culprit is the System. It perpetuates itself, providing the illusion of choice, while we fight over the "lesser of evils."

This won't be the last time Breonna Taylor makes headlines. When the under-charged officer receives a slap on the wrist, we will again revisit this tragedy.

It's never safe to be around a coward, and yet the System makes it incredibly safe to be one. A coward, a racist, a bully, a tyrant—under its protection, they thrive. And so, we continue to fight the System.

September 28, 2020 – Chongqing, China – "Processing is a Process"

Day 252

Part I: The Illusion of Time

I'm not saying Santa Claus is real. I'm not saying that. But here I am, a jolly fat man in a red hat, living where all the toys are made. Being a time traveler is hard, not because of the physics or the impossibility of designing reliable time travel, but because I get hopelessly lost in timelines and possibilities. Clarity of time-space only coalesces in moments, like a lightning strike in a storm. No, the hardest part of time traveling is that many of my zingers come off as lame ducks, ripening years later when no one's around to laugh but me.

When my grandma Wood passed at 96.5, my uncle Howie gathered the clan—60 or so of us—to celebrate her life in Gimli, Manitoba. We brought gifts, including a Gucci handbag for Aunt Kim. She seemed thrilled, and Howie, ever generous, declared, "She'll look good with it, and I'll look good standing next to her." I added, "And it's real leather," which landed as a dud. Until a year later in Rome, when I picked out a Louis Vuitton canvas bag. The leather joke, strangely prophetic. Aunt Kim passed while I was abroad, and I could never make that connection return.

I tell you this so I can tell you this: if time traveling is hard, multiverse shifting is harder. Infinite choices, branching possibilities—my other selves are often darker, and at times, I feel guilty for the luck I've had. Some of my other 'me's burn bright with the success stories I never wrote. But this is the one where I meet you. So Amor Fati, I love my life for what it is, for what it's brought me, even as the world around us burns. Resilience is key. A shift from capital and corruption to what's best for the people and the planet is the Solar Punk dream. But the path is dark, and many bumps lie ahead.

Part II: The COVID Wake-Up Call

Prime Minister Trudeau announced the second wave has arrived, and with it, the harsh reality: 60% of restaurants may close by Christmas. He says Thanksgiving is canceled, but Christmas might still be possible. With such backlash against even the most sensible precautions, don't hold your breath.

Smart lockdowns, controlled measures, and testing wastewater could prevent outbreaks before they even begin. I'd put money into these programs, into COVID-sniffing dogs, air purifiers, masks—everything to stop the spread. In the U.S. and UK, the numbers rise, and many colleges consider dorm lockdowns. A bad sequel to the cruise ship COVID disaster, transferring the virus from young people to their grandparents. It didn't have to be this way.

Instead of thinking "I have rights," we could be thinking "I have obligations." Together, we could make a better future. The ones doing it are making it look good.

Part III: The Day That Bends Time

Living in China has helped me with the time-traveling aspect. Yesterday was Sunday, but it was a nationally mandated workday before the holiday. Shaolin and I had a nice dinner at a Thai place, and I joked that it was Sunday, but the waiter assured us it was actually Wednesday. Days of the week, time itself—just a tool, not a certainty. We can bend it. We can even break it.

But bending time couldn't help me process the news I received. My friend Andra had died. They said it was an accident, a car crash, but the true horror of the story lay in how it unfolded. Andra had been one of the funniest, sharpest, most stylish people I knew. She could read my mind and would whisper the most cutting, witty comments when awkwardness struck. We shared moments of laughter and kinship, and she was like the little sister I never had. Her death hit hard, and I had to confront the painful truth that we would never share another laugh.

I turned to Einstein's theories to comfort myself. He believed time was not linear but rather a block, a 4-dimensional space existing all at once. When his friend died, Einstein wrote to the wife, saying their friend was still "over the hill," existing somewhere we couldn't directly perceive, but their presence was still felt.

Andra, succubus child of Loki, archangel of mischief and chaos, I know you're still with us in many instances and many other worlds. Lucky them. I welcome your barbs and arrows of outrageous fortune. You're not the first. Medusa still drops by now and then. And though you never met, I think you'd have been kindred spirits, both too bright, too fast, gone too soon.

Part IV: The Burden of Living

Shaolin went to Sanya with her family, and while I processed this news, the school renovated my kitchen, leaving holes in the walls and floors. I watched pictures of Shaolin enjoying oceanside seafood while I ate bread out of a bag and scratched my head. It was fine. We do what we must to endure.

Experts say the second wave of COVID-19 will surge back into China, but I'm confident we'll handle it well. In Yunnan, a city locked down, tested a million people, located cases, and treated them. This is the way.

Trump thinks trees explode and is afraid of paper mail-in ballots, but he says if you ignore the deaths and the blue states, he's done a great job. The U.S. has 200,000 dead and rising. Meanwhile, I search for my favorite pair of socks, bought at Yellowstone after seeing Old Faithful explode. My go-to travel socks. The search feels like a metaphor for life.

Part V: Letting Go and Moving Forward

I reflect on my international students, studying all night in the West for insane tuition fees, or another student who left grade 12 in the international program to redo grade 9 in the regular Chinese track. How humbling it must be to redo high school. I admire him. After helping many students find success, I've realized that the system needs change. Some students thrive, others struggle.

In the meantime, my daughter Eden has chosen a university, studying physical therapy. She got her COVID test—negative. They'll cocoon her with other students, all tested and negative, including the staff. It's strict but safe, and everyone understands. Compared to the chaos in Western schools, it's incredible how these small sacrifices ensure safety.

Part VI: Vitamin D and the Power of Knowledge

Finally, the missing piece about Vitamin D. Studies have made it clear that Vitamin D deficiency leads to more ACE2 receptors, the bonding point for COVID-19. With Vitamin D, we're more likely to get a weaker, less serious case. If you're vitamin D deficient, you're twice as likely to be hospitalized for COVID. Simple as that. The Sun makes you strong, so get some exposure, or take a supplement.

I've learned the importance of Vitamin D over the months, and now I understand it's crucial to our ability to fight the virus. Winter is coming, and our methods of treatment and care are vastly better than before. We're close to a vaccine, and I'm hopeful.

Part VII: The Moral of the Story

It's okay not to be okay. Processing is a process. I struggle to stay resilient, to bend without breaking, to be prepared for what's to come—even when it hurts. But we'll get there eventually.

October 1, 2020 – Chongqing, China – "Maximize Your Golden Week Holiday: Travel Kit and Virus Prevention Tips"

Day 252.

It's October 1st in China, and this year is a unique one—both the Mooncake Festival and the first day of the 8-day National Holiday. A celebration of harvest, family, mooncakes, and the full moon, this holiday is rooted deep in Chinese tradition. It falls on the 15th day of the eighth lunar month, and this year, it also aligns with the National Holiday.

After a muted Spring Festival holiday last year, many on the mainland are eager to travel, and with the epidemic under control for the most part, more than 500 million people in China are expected to take trips this week.

We thought about heading back to Sanya—China's answer to Hawaii. But, with skyrocketing prices and immense crowds, we decided against it. Instead, we'll take this opportunity to write, read, relax, exercise, and play some games. Our holiday will be a short 3-4 day getaway to nearby Wulong Mountain, where we'll stay in a hotel and enjoy sights featured in films like Zhang Yimou's *Curse of the Golden Flower* and Michael Bay's *Transformers*.

The Essentials for Pandemic Control in Public Spaces

Many people have asked me what my day-to-day pandemic control setup looks like—what I carry with me to crowded classrooms, busy restaurants, or when traveling, to feel comfortable and maintain some agency over my immediate surroundings. Let me share my setup along with some expert tips from Li Qin, Chief Physician and Director of the Epidemic Prevention Office at the Chongqing Municipal Center for Disease Control and Prevention (CDC), provided by iChongqing (Chongqing Daily News).

This setup gives me freedom—freedom to work, travel, keep my space ventilated, purify my surroundings, and maintain my zen. If someone sneezes nearby, I can either run or activate my fans, put on my mask and glasses, crank up my air purifier to max, and cross my fingers. But, at least I'm not just a sitting duck.

Since January 2020, I've made a conscious effort to maintain good hygiene, avoid high-risk situations, and stay mindful of my health. This year, thankfully, I've managed to stay fairly healthy, despite working with many different students and age groups who often bring a range of illnesses to the table.

Li Qin's Four Musts and Five Shoulds for a Safe Holiday

Li Qin shared some basic advice for safely navigating public spaces during this Golden Week, which I think is valuable for anyone—whether you're in China or elsewhere. Here's a breakdown:

Four Musts:

1. **Wash Your Hands** Constant hand-washing is the simplest yet most effective measure. It's easy to forget, but never underestimate the importance of clean hands. Use soap and clean running water, washing for at least 15 seconds and covering all areas—palms, nails, and wrists. Alcohol-based hand sanitizers are a good alternative if water is unavailable.
2. **Ventilate Your Room** Open windows whenever possible. Aim to ventilate your space at least 2-3 times a day, for a minimum of 30 minutes each time. Fresh air goes a long way in reducing airborne pathogens.
3. **Avoid Gathering** In public spaces, keep at least a one-meter distance from others. Avoid unnecessary contact with items or people in crowded areas, and steer clear of large gatherings.
4. **Wear a Mask** Mask-wearing is a simple yet crucial step in

preventing the spread of the virus. Surgical or medical masks are best when using public transport, attending public events, or when interacting with others in closed spaces.

Five Shoulds:

1. **Choose the Right Place** Avoid high-risk areas. Before traveling, assess the risk level of your destination and familiarize yourself with the local health policies. Always have your Health Code ready for digital health checks.
2. **Hand Sanitizer and Disinfectant** Pack disinfectants and hand sanitizers for your travels, especially if you're heading to more public places or confined areas. A mask and disinfectants are sufficient for most day-to-day needs.
3. **Precautions on the Road** Whether you're traveling alone or with others, wear a mask and wash your hands regularly. Use contactless payment methods to avoid touching paper money and public surfaces.
4. **Food and Drink** Stick to reliable hotels and restaurants. If you're staying somewhere new, consider preparing your own food or ordering from trusted sources. Avoid raw water (always boil for 1 minute) and refrain from eating game or wildlife.
5. **Self-Monitoring** Keep track of your health daily, and if you experience any symptoms, take your temperature before heading out. If you've been to a high-risk area, self-isolate for 14 days and notify local health services if you develop symptoms like fever or cough. Cooperate with health authorities for testing if needed.

Inspiration While Stuck at Home

If you're unable to travel but still need some inspiration, check out the short film *How to Be at Home* by filmmaker Andrea Dorfman and poet Tanya Davis. It's a tender reminder of how to stay grounded even when stuck indoors.

October 3, 2020 – Chongqing, China – "Lost and Found"

Part 1: A Good Pair of Socks

Day 259.
I found my favorite socks. They were hiding exactly where I thought they'd be—buried in the top third of a 'scarves and woolly socks' bag, mistakenly tossed into storage last March during a spring cleaning spree. They've been waiting for months, like little secret agents in their cozy hideaway. But now, they're back in my life. And I'm delighted. These socks are so high-performance that I can wear them two days straight—across continents—and they'll still feel fresh. The right pair of socks can make anything feel possible.

Part 2: Golden Week and Fever Clinics

It's October 1st in China—Mooncake Festival and the first day of the 8-day National Holiday. In a country where family reunions and honoring ancestors are at the heart of the celebration, it's an occasion rich with tradition. After a quiet Spring Festival in 2020, the country is buzzing with anticipation. More than 500 million people are expected to travel during this week-long holiday, and the whole country seems to be casting wide nets, searching for freedom in places like mahjong halls, national parks, and restaurants.

I thought about flying to Sanya, often called Chinese Hawaii, but between the price hikes and the overwhelming crowds, I opted to spend a quieter, more mindful holiday. Instead, we're heading to Fairy Mountain, a mystical, fog-draped mountain a few hours outside the city. Here, nature still has a bit of mystery left, and it's a good place for reflection. While we won't be jetting off to tropical beaches, I'll spend the next few days writing, reading, playing games, and staying grounded.

In the meantime, my preparations for the holiday include some practical measures. To prove I'm COVID-free and capable of going about my life, I had to get a swab at the fever clinic before I could travel. The pandemic is still here, and a negative test is the key to moving freely. It's a strange thing, this kind of temporary passport. I woke up at 7 AM, brewed coffee, and prepared honey water for Shaolin. By 8:00 AM, I was sitting at the clinic, swabbed deeply in the nasal cavity, a ritual I've grown used to now. These are the small but significant acts that keep the world turning in uncertain times.

Part 3: Time with Family, Reflections, and Hotpot

At home, Shaolin napped while I had some downtime, winning a couple of NHL games with my dad. He's still quarantined, stuck at home since January, his outings limited to socially distanced walks with Ming. It's been a long year for everyone, but we're finding ways to stay connected.

After lunch, we made our way to Starbucks, where I found myself indulging in an Irish cream iced coffee. Her friend Li Jun arrived, Leica camera in hand, snapping candid photos of the three of us. There's a joy in being seen in a good light, especially when someone tells you that you look fabulous. Li Jun and Shaolin spent time catching up, reminiscing about Beijing days when they were surrounded by designers, models, and the sparkle of fame. I'm always impressed by how the past shapes people's present, like a slow burn through a forest. Sometimes, the big moments pass us by without us even realizing.

Later, we did some shopping, picking up new pajamas for Shaolin and two pairs of jeans for me. There's something refreshing about new clothes, a little reset for the soul. We also bought a fire truck sweater for Ethan—still too big for him, but it'll be a joy when he finally grows into it.

Afterward, we headed to a family hotpot dinner. But there was one small issue—the smoker at the table. I could smell it immediately and knew I couldn't be near it with Ethan around. So, I convinced Shaolin to switch seats with him. While I wasn't thrilled with the smoke, we managed to enjoy the evening together. But by the end, I could feel the irritant in my throat. It's a reminder of how much I value my health now more than ever.

Part 4: Reflections on the Pandemic and the Larger Picture

It's a strange thing, this pandemic. In China, we've done well to keep it under control, but globally, the numbers keep rising. This week, we surpassed 1 million COVID deaths, with 35.4 million confirmed cases. The actual numbers are likely far higher, but it's a grim reminder of the impact this virus continues to have. From the start, I've been an advocate for the precautionary principle—taking actions that might seem extreme now, but which will save lives later.

What shocks me is the way different countries have handled this crisis. Here in China, we worked together, pooling resources and expertise. In other places, there has been division and denial. I've watched as countries like the US, with all their resources, couldn't avoid the tragedy of mass death. In Ottawa, where my family lives, the hospitals are reaching capacity, and the second wave is just starting. It's an eye-opening moment—one that reminds me of the lessons learned in China, where swift action was taken, and it made all the difference.

Part 5: The Tech Glitch and the Dilemma of What to Save

And speaking of swiftness, it wasn't just COVID that kept me on my toes this week. I had a tech glitch that threw me into mini panic mode—my 2TB Lacie Rugged drive was corrupted. It was a shocking realization, especially with 100GB of D&D character files, 300GB of music, and 250GB of photos from my pre-China life. It's all stuff I've been meaning to preserve, but the fear of losing it is real. I was faced with the dilemma: what should I save, and what should I let go of? It's a question I've asked myself often in life. What is truly worth holding onto, and what can I let go of to move forward?

Part 6: Reflecting on the Past and Letting Go

I reflect on this as I think about my past. I remember a time when I wore my iconic blue-and-white snug jersey to every DJ gig. It was my battle gear, but one day, I looked at it and realized it wasn't the armor I needed anymore. So, I let go of it, and it became rags for cleaning. I'm not sad about that decision—it was time for a shift. But still, part of me struggles to let go of the memories, the music, the moments that defined who I was.

Part 7: The Election, the World, and the Future

I keep thinking about how things shift, how we adapt. It's like the ongoing struggle of the pandemic: we have to adapt. In Ottawa, I hear about hospitals nearing capacity. I hear about the US president and his circle, and the reality of COVID finally hitting home for them. The whole thing feels surreal—like something we knew was coming but couldn't prevent. Schadenfreude is up by 3,800% as people mock the same man who refused to take precautions.

So, when the world feels like it's teetering on the edge of a cliff, I find solace in the little things. The socks. The simple moments. And yet, in those moments, I can feel the weight of history pressing down on us. We're all connected, all part of this bigger story. And maybe, just maybe, we're at the crossroads where the world can shift—for the better, if we let it.

October 12, 2020 – Chongqing, China – "Bamboo Wailing in the Forest (Jod Says Wear a Mask)"

Day 266

Part 1: The Dance of Time and Memory

I used to be a dancer. That's not to say I was a great dancer, just that it's what I did. There was a time, as a teenager, when going out all night to elusive and underground warehouse parties and dancing until well past dawn was my raison d'être, the meaning in my life. It was a whimsical time when I made friends and earned respect by pirouetting, spinning, shuffling, and turning through grungy warehouses to the sounds of Richie Hawtin or Andy C, all around North America. When I started getting booked to DJ, it was like "going pro," getting sponsored to dance and party all night. My hearing, sanity, and my center of balance took a real thrashing during those years, but my whimsy, magic, and creativity became sharper. Now I don't dance so much, but it's still who I am in my heart.

Sometimes, I think there's a sex, drugs, and rock 'n roll-sized hole inside me. Over the years, I've tried filling it with everything, but nothing quite fits. The closest I get is the cool serenity, wisdom, and virtue that comes with mindfulness, reflection, meditation, exercise, and education. If that makes me sound like a bit of a snob, I must confess, I am. It comes naturally with age and opportunity.

Part 2: The Shift from Chaos to Quiet

My reflections in mindfulness, stoicism, and Buddhism have taught me that being a moth to the flame of gratification, rewards, and pleasure only spurs us to find the next, bigger hit. In the end, we become craven. So these years, on the side of a mountain in Southwest China, I meditate my joy with work, rest, relaxation, and domestic life. And I think it suits me. I've changed a lot, in ways, since the young grasshopper I once was.

Patience, young grasshopper, the Shaolin master said. God has given you strength; utilize it to the fullest.

Part 3: Space in a Crowded World

I was 18 when I played my first international gig, driving 9 hours across the Canada-US border to headline a party in Brooklyn, New York, with some of the legends of hardcore dance music: Lenny Dee and Rob Gee, in their home turf of Brooklyn. I was a skinny wisp of a thing with bleach-blond hair, and I wore my blue-and-white Snug jersey and a white baseball cap like a uniform, taking care to keep it sparkling despite the grungy, greasy venues I inhabited. I was a good DJ because it was the only thing in my life that really mattered, and I sacrificed everything else to give it everything I had. I had fans that enjoyed me because, at least on some subconscious level, they believed if they watched me perform enough, they'd see me die on stage, immolate into a ball of fire as I burned my fat, my skin, my essence for the encore of a thrill, an extra cheer. But you know what? I was alive.

Things are different now, and I have lots of time to reflect. I guess that's why those photos meant something; now I have time to take a look through them. I'm sitting and eating hotpot with the family for a niece's birthday and just taking in the atmosphere, and I have to admit it's overwhelming. It's typical of China. The place is crowded, and every table is screaming to be heard, but no one is saying anything really important. We're drinking, and a couple of guys are smoking. I manage to get the brother-in-law to change places with me so that he's not sitting next to baby Ethan because the kid already has allergies and I know all about growing up with allergies and smokers, and it sucked, man. So that's one good deed for today. I realize how I must seem. Not only do I not socially smoke, but I also prefer it if you don't too. I'll have a couple of beers, but not too many.

Part 4: Fighting the System with Our Faces Covered

Because of the road trip, I'm eating out of the water pot, like a child, and rather than screaming and smoking, I sit quietly, with my air purifier medallion and my handheld air purifier sucking up smoke and germs dutifully around me. I am the only foreigner, and rather than be the symbol of chaos that I used to exemplify, literally breathing fire and screaming and breaking things—hearts, souls, anything I could get my grubby paws on—I am some kind of quiet philosopher, more at home in my modest ivory tower with a thick book than on the streets where the action is.

I realize, when we go out to somewhere 'nice' for a date, especially in a city of 35 million people, what we're buying is space. Space from the ground, on the 44-77th floor, overlooking the city. Space on our plates, which are changed frequently and arranged artfully, and space from the smoking, screaming, crowded masses of ordinary people, where you can hear a pin drop, you can enjoy a quiet conversation without having to raise your voice, where space, peace, and quiet are the commodities that your hefty bill affords. But I am ok with all that. In a life of chapters, this is my graceful aging, and I'm glad it's a new adventure to the ones that made me infamous, so long ago, far away, in that dreamy cacophony of the sprawl and the desert raves and festivals where I inhabited.

Part 5: A New World, A New System

We need to stop identifying problems and start proposing solutions. I want to think SolarPunk. I want to pivot to ideas. I'm going to need time to broil that stew. We know the political system rewards corruption and favors corporations and oligarchs. Yes, we know the environment is collapsing, and a mass extinction event is imminent. Yes, we know capitalism is destroying our ability to live, let alone happily.

So what? We need a non-hierarchical system, flat, that is immune to corruption. This system would facilitate trade, reward efficiency, and excellence, operate fairly on a set of principles and values. What are those values? That's a good question. We need to decommodify nature and animals, instead favoring a relationship that respects our symbiosis, balance, and harmonious coexistence. We need cities, but we need forests too. We need insects, plankton, biodiversity—not just to cut down or look at, but to breathe, live, and thrive alongside us. We will fight for this, or we will die. Could an AI be the answer? A computerized job bank and trade platform allows each of us to work, contribute, even 'vote' on issues of opinion, and otherwise use scientific principles to further our value system. In *The Social Dilemma*, it's discussed that now that we are the whale, we are the tree, maybe we will push for reform and create AI that works for us rather than to sell us, pushing a better value system into the future.

Part 6: What Kind of Witch Are You?

What kind of witch are you? Asks my imaginary BuzzFeed quiz. I'm a Sand Witch. I am: crusty, gritty, I love puns, I'm a snack, and I thrive in chaos, maybe more to see, I am most efficient when everyone else is breaking down.

Now that Ontario has closed all the bars and restaurants, experts are asking what took them so long. "Did the changes come too late?" they ponder, as the second wave spreads, rocking the healthcare system, bulging close to bursting well before the predicted flu season X COVID-19 deadly cocktail—something to "look forward to" with dread, as the cold months set in. As we Canadians endure a cold winter of isolation, anxiety, and fear, a story that would have rocked the news cycle in any other year is now a footnote: Michigan Governor Gretchen Whitmer was the subject of a terror plot that included kidnapping and the incitement of a new civil war. Trump has refused to denounce them, even as his doctors have mysteriously cleared him of COVID-19, and he's declared, "We should not fear the disease because I (with a helicopter ride and the best care and the experimental drugs you can't access, supposedly) got through it." He's like a firefighter in his specialized fire-retardant jacket, face shield, helmet, breathing apparatus, balaclava, and oxygen tank who survived the burning building, telling everyone, "fires are no problem. Don't be scared of fires; anybody could have done it." At this point, he's so out to lunch. You'd have to be drinking the Kool-Aid to support him still. Biden is polling higher than any challenger since 1936, so as long as Trump doesn't steal the election again...whatever. More than 34 people in the White House have now tested positive for COVID-19, and raccoons have infested the grounds.

In exciting news, the mirror image of me, the Revel Alliance founder, supporter of science, mask advocate, and researcher of

COVID news, anti-mask, anti-lockdown, anti-government activist Chris Sky has been arrested in Moncton. After months of posing with Toronto police at his illegal Cherry Beach parties, he's finally been too brazen. After returning from anti-mask protests in Europe and failing to quarantine for 14 days in Toronto, he was fined for speaking at an anti-mask rally there, then refused to wear a mask (citing a medical note and childhood asthma) on a plane to Moncton, New Brunswick, where his wife Jen recorded his interaction with flight attendants and the Moncton Police that were called to handcuff him and arrest him. He was charged for his quarantine breaches, causing a public disturbance on the plane, and then sent back to Toronto with more court dates. I am happy to see the law coming down hard on him. The popularity he's garnered for flaunting public health policy has definitely been a bad influence on many others (while my pro-mask group sports 500 members, including doctors, researchers, union bosses, and teachers, his anti-mask group has more than 10,000 members, many supposedly angry mothers that he's offered to champion by starting an unlicensed homeschool program for children...in his garage).

Part 7: On the Lessons We're Still Learning

One thing I can admit to now, months after our "debate," is that while he was wrong about masks, he might have been right about lockdowns – sort of. He quoted Japan as an example of why both China's and Canada's public health policy was wrong, but I believe he missed the point. Sure, Japan did not do an economic lockdown and did not enforce mandatory masks, but that's because people voluntarily wore masks at near 100% compliance. A recent study has shown that 95% of the cases in Japan were asymptomatic to mild. Tokyo, a megacity of over 37 million people, suffered only minor fatalities during their first wave. As of October 9, 2020, Tokyo has recorded 27,320 COVID-19 cases, 1006 hospitalized, 21 with severe symptoms, and 421 deaths. New York City, the first American epicenter of the virus, with a population about half the size (18 million), had more than 243,975 cases, 57,694 hospitalizations, and 19,237 confirmed deaths, and 4,642 probable deaths (23,879 total), even with lockdowns and attempting to use masks and distancing. This is because, as I wrote months ago, the level of viral load transferred has a direct connection to how sick you get from the virus, and minimal transfer from mask to mask means the vast majority (95%) of cases will not require intervention or hospitalization.

Part 8: Jod, Bamboo, and the Question of Masks

As I walk through the misty mountains of Wulong (Fairy Mountain), I hear the bamboo singing harmoniously, wailing in a discordant, chiming pattern that sounds both ominous and divine. Why don't people in the West understand masks, I ask the forest, and for a moment, it grows quiet, before the crescendo of wind and bamboo whistling answers me with shocking emotion. Am I speaking to the forest? I wonder. Or to God? Jod, in the bamboo, answers back. It's pronounced Jod, I hear amidst the wailing.

Why, Jod, I ask, are my fellow Canadians still suffering under these conditions when China's eight weeks lockdown was enough to beat the virus? And Japan never locked down at all—just wore masks?

Some people understood it right away, Jod said. Like you, they were early adopters.

Others waited for the experts to make up their mind, and then listened to the science when it finally settled that masks were good.

And the rest? I asked. What about the rest? What could I possibly say when all my arguments, my studies, my science, and my experts do not convince them to listen?

Tell them I told you to tell them to wear a mask, Jod said. Tell them the voice of Jod said, "wear a mask, dummies. Why would I have created masks if not for you to protect yourself?"

Would that really work? I asked.

It worked for Hammurabi, Jod said. How do you think he got them to believe in laws, after all?

The voice of Jod, I thought. Ok. I'll give it a try.

If you're reading this and don't believe masks save lives, I need to tell you that Jod wants you to wear a mask.

Part 9: The Grasshopper, The Ant, and The Mask

I was reading a story to the young students recently about a grasshopper and an ant, and it made me really reflect on who I am, who I was, and whom I've become.

The grasshopper enjoys each and every day, playing in the river, lazing on a lilypad, rushing through the grass, and singing as the wind and sun shone down on his face, brilliantly warming him. He gave little thought to the coming winter and did not work with other grasshoppers to prepare.

One day he saw a fruit violently approaching him and shouted in fear. "Banana, why? Are you attacking me?"

He heard a giggling sound, and it was the ants underneath, who had been carrying the fruit all along. They laughed at the easily spooked grasshopper, and he, in turn, rose up and laughed at them. "It takes a dozen of you to carry the fruit, and I could carry it and eat it all by myself!" He said.

"We are not taking it to eat," said the ants. "We are bringing it home to our hole."

"Why? Is it bad?" Asked the grasshopper, for he could not fathom why they would want to put a banana inside a hole in the ground. He felt restless and wanted to scamper away to catch the fleeting rays of the sun.

"Because soon it will be winter, grasshopper, and all the fruit will be gone, and snow will cover the ground, and we are preparing," said the ants.

The grasshopper laughed and said he would prepare later and wasn't worried, and the ants knew that nothing they said could change his mind, so they went about their business, and he scampered off to enjoy the rest of the day.

As I told the story to the young Chinese children, I thought about how I used to be a grasshopper, and now, I was more like an ant. When I was young, I worked to revel and enjoy, always reaching and stretching for the next pleasure but taking no regard for the coming of winter. Now, I am much more humble, quiet, and hard-working, and prepare for not just the winter but for my retirement and beyond. I marvel at how much living in China has shaped me to enjoy hard work and collective struggle for our betterment. We enjoyed beating the virus together, even if it was an inconvenience, because it was best for all of us. Many grasshoppers in the West are more concerned about their own comfort and immediate gratification, speaking about their rights but never stopping to even consider their obligations—to their family, community, or society. In China, our lockdown was strong, and many called it draconian, but as the global economy slumps, China is one of the countries that has economically recovered and is set to grow by 1.6%—the struggle at the beginning was worth it, something most countries did not think necessary or were not able to do, now seems a pittance compared to the cost of 9 months and beyond.

As 1,000 cases a day in Ontario require a new lockdown, I hope that my family and friends can stay safe and turn this around, but many predict a long, deadly, and ugly winter. I know in my heart that it didn't have to be this way.

October 20, 2020 – Chongqing, China – "Entropy Isn't What It Used to Be (But Capitalism Might Be Broken)"

Day 282

Part I: The Dance of the Past

I used to be a dancer. That's not to say I was a great dancer, just that it was what I did. As a teenager, I immersed myself in the late-night underground warehouse parties, dancing until the early hours of the morning. It was a whimsical time—making friends and earning respect by pirouetting, spinning, and shuffling to the beats of Richie Hawtin or Andy C. Over time, I transitioned from dancer to DJ, with all the perks and exhaustion that came with it—ear damage, loss of sanity, and a fading sense of balance. But in exchange, my creativity sharpened.

Now, I don't dance much, but it's still who I am deep inside.

Part II: Filling the Void

Sometimes I think there's a hole in me—one the size of sex, drugs, and rock 'n roll. Over the years, I've tried to fill it with everything, but nothing ever quite fits. The closest I get is through mindfulness, meditation, reflection, and exercise—peaceful, serene, and virtuous pursuits. If that makes me sound a little like a snob, I'll admit, it's true. I've grown into it with age.

Through my reflections on mindfulness, Stoicism, and Buddhism, I've learned that chasing gratification only leads to an insatiable hunger for more. This pursuit turns us into craven beings, always yearning for the next bigger thrill. These days, I've learned to mediate my joy with work, rest, relaxation, and domestic life. And I think it suits me. I've changed a lot since the reckless young grasshopper I once was.

Patience, young grasshopper, the Shaolin master said. *God has given you strength; utilize it to the fullest.*

Part III: The First Gig, the First Step

I was 18 when I played my first international gig, driving nine hours across the Canada-U.S. border to headline a party in Brooklyn, New York. It was a gritty, underground scene. I was a skinny kid with bleach-blond hair, wearing a blue-and-white Snug jersey and a white baseball cap, trying to keep it clean in the grimiest places. I was a good DJ because it was the only thing in my life that mattered. Everything else—school, family, friends—took a backseat to this one pursuit. I had fans who followed me, believing, on some level, that if they watched enough, they'd witness me burn out, a fiery explosion on stage.

But you know what? I was alive.

Part IV: Reflection Through the Smoke and Mirrors

Now, everything is different. I have time to reflect on my past, and sometimes that reflection hits me when I'm sitting at the table, eating hotpot with the family. The place is crowded. Every table is shouting to be heard, but none of it is meaningful. People are drinking, and smoke lingers in the air. It's a reminder of the past, of all the moments I once lived for but can't seem to get back.

I realize how I must seem now. I'm the guy who doesn't socially smoke and prefers if you don't either. I'm the guy who brings an air purifier to the dinner table and who's more comfortable in the silence than the chaos of it all.

At least now, I'm happy to just be.

Part V: A Change in Perspective

In China, we've been fortunate to handle the pandemic better than many others. When 550 million Chinese traveled during the National Holiday, there were no major outbreaks. There were precautions in place—health checks, quarantines, and tests—and it paid off. But in other parts of the world, it's been different. In the U.S.,

COVID deaths have surpassed a million, and in Canada, hospitals are nearing capacity. The second wave is hitting hard, and it's surreal watching it unfold.

The disparity in how countries have dealt with this crisis is striking. In China, the response has been swift and decisive. In the West, division and denial have held sway, and it's costing lives.

Part VI: The Good Fight

But there's something I've learned over the years. It's not enough to identify problems; we must offer solutions. I want to think SolarPunk. I want to focus on ideas. We know the political system rewards corruption, that capitalism is draining our ability to live well, and that the environment is in freefall.

So, what's the alternative?

We need a non-hierarchical system—flat, immune to corruption, focused on sustainability, and guided by a set of clear principles. What are those principles? Respect for nature and animals, prioritizing a symbiotic relationship with the planet. We need cities and forests, insects and plankton, all living and thriving together.

We'll fight for this, or we'll die.

Part VII: On the Edge of a New Era

As I continue reflecting on my life, I realize how much has changed. A year ago, I was a DJ, a wanderer, a man of chaos. Now, I'm grounded—teaching, writing, living on the side of a mountain in China. There's peace here, in this simplicity. I don't hunger for excess anymore. In fact, my life is more fulfilling now than it ever was before. I'm not chasing fame, not spending money on the next big thing. I'm happy with less.

And yet, I still hold on to the memories. Those photos, those moments of chaos and ecstasy, are still a part of me. They remind me of who I was and who I've become. And sometimes, I wonder how I managed to get here. How did I make the shift from the hedonism of my past to this grounded life?

It wasn't easy, but I'm here now.

Part VIII: A New Chapter in the Making
As the world faces a second wave of COVID, I'm reminded of the lessons I've learned in China. We can't control everything, but we can control how we respond. I've been teaching my students to think about their obligations, to understand that we are all part of something bigger. We can't live in isolation. We are interconnected. My story isn't over. There's more to be written. More lessons to be learned. And a new chapter is unfolding every day. The question is, what will we do with the time we have?

October 21, 2020 - Improving COVID-19 Pandemic Response in Distressed Communities and a Smarter, Controlled Approach to Economic Reopening

Abstract

While some countries and communities have successfully mitigated the COVID-19 pandemic's impact, others have suffered significantly more. The disparities in hospitalizations and fatalities highlight the need for better information sharing and a more nuanced approach to managing the disease. Equally critical are the economic consequences of lockdowns, which have devastated many sectors. Applying the best available information to smart reopening strategies—those that prevent renewed severe outbreaks—remains central to both public health and economic recovery. This paper outlines recent discoveries related to the prevention and treatment of COVID-19, as well as macro-level strategies for facilitating safer and smarter economic reopenings. Research suggests that mask compliance near 100% can significantly reduce the severity of the disease, while factors like viral load (inoculum) and vitamin D deficiency are key to understanding outcomes. Additionally, affordable generic treatments, when administered correctly, could save lives. Early detection methods, including sniffer dogs and wastewater testing, could also help catch outbreaks before they escalate. Effective contact tracing and isolation methods remain critical in controlling the spread.

A World in Chaos

The COVID-19 pandemic has not only halted the global economy but has also taken over a million lives and disrupted millions more.

However, its impact has not been evenly felt. Many of the early lessons learned from countries heavily impacted by the virus have been ignored or poorly shared by those who came later. Cynics have compared the world's response to that of lemmings mindlessly following one another off a cliff, learning nothing from the disaster. The initial outbreaks in Wuhan, Lombardy (Italy), and New York City were particularly devastating. In each case, specialists on the ground described the situation as a battleground, with triage decisions that determined who would live and who would not. While some countries avoided such extreme scenarios through measures like masks, strict hand washing, social distancing, and lockdowns, others—such as Japan, Vietnam, and Uganda—have had far more success through diligent enforcement of non-pharmaceutical interventions (NPIs), especially contact tracing and isolation. These varying outcomes underscore the importance of NPI strategies in limiting COVID-19 transmission.

Japan: A Role Model for Managing COVID Without Lockdowns

Among the countries that have done well in minimizing hospitalizations, deaths, and economic damage, Japan stands out. Despite never instituting full lockdowns, Japan maintained low death rates and avoided overwhelming hospitals. Tokyo, with a population of over 37 million, experienced only minor fatalities during its first wave of infections. As of October 9, 2020, the city had reported 27,320 cases, with just 1,006 hospitalizations and 421 deaths. In contrast, New York City—about half the size of Tokyo—saw over 243,975 cases and 23,879 deaths, despite implementing lockdowns, mask mandates, and social distancing. The disparity is striking, especially when considering the significant number of people of color—particularly Black and Indigenous populations—who were disproportionately affected by severe disease and death from COVID-19. This raises critical questions about underlying vulnerabilities, particularly in populations already facing systemic health inequities.

Racial Inequality Among COVID Victims

The racial disparity in COVID-19 outcomes has been stark. Data from the New York Times on July 5, 2020, showed that while the average number of cases per 100,000 people was 38, Black and Latino populations reported far higher infection rates—62 and 73, respectively. Native American populations, such as those in the Navajo Nation, also faced disproportionately high rates of infection and death. In the Amazon Rainforest, Indigenous communities without access to hospitals or modern healthcare have been devastated by the virus. These outcomes are not coincidental; rather, they highlight the intersections of race, healthcare access, and social vulnerability. The question remains: why have these disparities persisted, and what can be done to address them?

Vitamin D Deficiency: A Key to Mild Outcomes

One major factor in determining COVID-19 outcomes is vitamin D deficiency. Research has shown that individuals with low vitamin D levels are at increased risk of severe COVID-19 outcomes, including hospitalization and death. A study from Italy indicated that vitamin D supplementation can significantly reduce the severity of the disease, while those with healthy vitamin D levels are more likely to experience mild or asymptomatic cases. Vitamin D plays a crucial role in immune system function, and a deficiency in this vitamin leads to the production of ACE2 receptors, which the virus uses to enter cells. This has been shown to contribute to more severe illness. To combat vitamin D deficiency, experts recommend daily supplements, particularly for those with darker skin tones, who naturally produce less vitamin D due to higher melanin content.

The Critical Role of Viral Load

Another important factor influencing COVID-19 outcomes is viral load. Studies have demonstrated that the amount of virus a person is exposed to can significantly impact the severity of their illness. High viral doses overwhelm the body's defenses, leading to more severe cases. This is why healthcare workers—who are often exposed to high levels of the virus—are more likely to develop severe symptoms despite being young and healthy. Masks have been shown to be the best protection against viral load. In countries like Japan, where mask compliance is near universal, the majority of COVID-19 cases have been mild or asymptomatic. This highlights the power of simple public health measures like mask-wearing in preventing severe outbreaks and reducing the overall burden on healthcare systems.

Politicization and Profit in a Pandemic

As countries scramble to develop treatments for COVID-19, the role of profit and politics has become increasingly evident. Some generic drugs, such as hydroxychloroquine (HCQ) and ivermectin, have shown promise in treating COVID-19 but remain underutilized due to political and corporate pressures. A recent study from Bangladesh found that when HCQ is administered early and at the correct dose, it can significantly reduce fatalities and shorten hospital stays. Similarly, ivermectin has been shown to be an effective broad-spectrum antiviral. Unfortunately, both drugs have been overshadowed by high-cost, patent-protected treatments like remdesivir, which has proven to be less effective and far more expensive.

Smart Reopenings: The Path Forward

For countries that have experienced significant outbreaks, smart reopenings are essential to avoid further damage to both public health and the economy. In China, strict lockdowns followed by mass testing, mask mandates, and contact tracing have allowed for a return to normalcy. Japan, with its emphasis on voluntary measures like mask-wearing and social distancing, has also fared well. As the world begins to reopen, it is essential that countries focus on strategies that have been proven to work, such as mask mandates and early intervention with affordable treatments. Additionally, novel detection methods, like sniffer dogs and wastewater testing, should be scaled up to identify outbreaks before they spiral out of control.

Conclusion: The Path Forward for Distressed Communities

In distressed communities, both in developing nations and marginalized populations within developed countries, the response to COVID-19 must be tailored to the specific challenges they face. By using inexpensive, proven methods—such as mask-wearing, vitamin D supplementation, and the use of generic antiviral drugs—many lives could be saved. These interventions are not cost-prohibitive and can be implemented on a global scale. While the world continues to grapple with the pandemic, we must take heed of the lessons learned from countries that have successfully managed the crisis and apply them to the reopening process. Only by doing so can we ensure a safe and equitable future for all.

References
(1) Tokyo COVID-19 statistics (2020).
(2) New York City COVID-19 statistics (2020).
(3) China GDP growth during COVID-19 (2020).
(4) Global lockdowns study (2020).
(5) Racial disparity in COVID-19 cases (2020).
(6) Vitamin D deficiency and COVID-19 (2020).
(7) Italy COVID-19 study (2020).
(8) JAMA study on vitamin D and COVID-19 (2020).
(9) Reina Sofia University COVID-19 study (2020).
(10) ACE2 receptors and COVID-19 (2020).
(11) The impact of ACE2 receptors on COVID-19 (2020).
(12) Vitamin D intake recommendations (2020).
(13) Institute of Medicine Vitamin D recommendations (2020).
(14) Zinc and Vitamin D for immune support (2020).
(15) Viral load and COVID-19 severity (2020).
(16) Japan's mask compliance and COVID-19 outcomes (2020).

(17) Immunity and masks (2020).
(18) WHO hydroxychloroquine study (2020).
(19) Bangladesh HCQ study (2020).
(20) Ivermectin and COVID-19 (2020).
(21) Ivermectin treatment and prevention (2020).
(22) American NIH guidelines on COVID-19 treatment (2020).
(23) Global poverty statistics (2020).
(24) Conflicts of interest in the NIH (2020).
(25) Hospitalization and fatality rates (2020).
(26) Japan's COVID-19 response (2020).
(27) Cruise ship mask mandates and COVID-19 outcomes (2020).
(28) Sniffer dogs detecting COVID-19 (2020).
(29) Wastewater testing for COVID-19 outbreaks (2020).

October 22, 2020 – Chongqing, China – "Morning Rituals and Digital Fires"

Day 284.

I wake in a daze as my wrist buzzes and the alarm chimes through the muffled filters of my earplugs. It's 6:30 a.m. I slide into my slippers, creep past a still-sleeping Shaolin, and stumble into the bathroom. After shaving and splashing on aftershave—alcoholic sting bringing me to life—I grind coffee beans, boil water, and press down the French press. My mind slowly sharpens as the caffeine kicks in. I open my laptop and catch up on email and Twitter.

I've applied to a prestigious MFA in creative nonfiction at Canada's oldest university, and that ambition stirs my resolve to reengage with the writing community online. I see that Wizards of the Coast is allegedly blocking Margaret Weis and Tracy Hickman from continuing their Dragonlance trilogy. I share a petition. Margaret likes my post. That simple like—a pixelated connection—reminds me how strange and close the world can feel this year.

Friday Hustle

By 7:15, I'm out the door with a bag packed like a war kit: USB battery, iPad, mic amp, air purifier, coffee thermos, and throat tea. A black car comes within minutes. The breeze through the open window cools my nerves.

Four classes and a lunch meeting with our Cuban salsa friend Luis Castro later, I'm beat—but grateful. He's had a rough year, with his girlfriend stuck in Russia and job prospects shifting between cities. Meanwhile, we have stability, and I try not to take it for granted. We enjoy a hotpot lunch and share what warmth we can.

A Dystopian Chongqing Premiere

Later, we taxi across town—first to the wrong cinema, then the right one—to attend the premiere of a new Chongqing film, thanks to Shaolin's best friend, the executive producer. The theater is packed, Shaolin is anxious, and despite seven COVID-free months in the city, news from Xinjiang—20 symptomatic, 130 asymptomatic cases—tightens everyone's guard again. Four million people will be tested in a week.

I doze off in the first ten minutes but awaken to Blade Runner-esque shots of Chongqing's neon underbelly. The film cuts between a murder a decade ago and the moral reckoning that follows. As with most Chinese cinema, justice catches up, guilt consumes, and the killers unravel. It's a slow burn, but haunting.

Spaceman and Catwoman

We rush home to prepare for our Halloween party—twelve kids on their way. Shaolin's in a Catwoman suit, and I don my pandemic-era NASA lockdown suit, all gadgets blazing.
Later, Twitter's buzzing. Chris Sky, Canada's infamous anti-masker, has caused a scene in a beauty shop, refusing to wear a mask until police intervene. His bullying tactics infuriate me. I tweet a storm, calling out his science denialism, and find solidarity in the replies.

Sake, Suites, and City Lights

Saturday, we brave three kids' Halloween parties. At day's end, we treat ourselves to a Japanese feast downtown. Warm sake, fresh sashimi, air purifiers, and well-masked servers calm our nerves. We walk a bit, then check into a five-star hotel with a breathtaking city view. A warm bath melts the week away. We stay up watching horror films, make omelets and salad the next morning, and talk about making this a tradition.

Secrets from Shaolin

Shaolin leans in. "Those secrets I told you," she says softly. "They're how my friends went from bar gigs to stadiums. You to bookshelves."

Her advice, timeless:

Listen well. Don't complain. Do your best. Trust family. Be humble. Be patient. Be kind.

Simple. Sacred.

The Numbers and the Unknowns

Canada has passed 10,000 COVID deaths. The U.S. nears 10 million cases and a quarter million dead. The election looms. Trump wants to claim victory before all votes are counted. The world watches, holding its breath.

We've passed 50 million global cases. We're just starting to understand long-haulers—1 in 7 suffer beyond a month; 1 in 20 beyond two. Organ damage, strokes, brain fog. Reinfections and dormant strains raise unsettling questions. The looming winter whispers of a deadly duet: flu and COVID.

A Swiss Cheese Defense

A brilliant visual from Dr. Peter McKay and the University of Queensland outlines the pandemic response as Swiss cheese: no layer is perfect, but layered together—personal and societal responsibility—we can slow the spread.

I begin NaNoWriMo with a fantasy novel, continue edits on a horror story, and this nonfiction diary rolls on. It's a lot. But Shaolin reminds me: "Keep going. That's the secret."

November 16, 2020 – Chongqing, China – "Get Lucky (Or Die Trying)"

Day 299

Finally, a weekend worth remembering — bittersweet though it may be. Shaolin's Salsa5 club, the only world-class Salsa club in our city, is closing. Our good friend and exceptional dance teacher, Luis Castro from Cuba, is packing up his apartment. We spent Friday, Saturday, and Sunday with him, squeezing in as much time as we could before his departure. Despite the reason for our gathering, it felt like a victory — a reminder that in the middle of this global crisis, there's still room for joy.

A Morning Routine: Finding Resilience

It all began with the soft buzz of my Fitbit. "It's 6:25 AM, Kai," it chirped. "Get back from the dreamlands! You've got mundanity to muster!" I groggily rose, washed my face, boiled some water, and made coffee, preparing for another day of work.
Coffee in hand, I scanned Twitter and tried to squeeze in a few golden moments before my ride arrived. Three minutes later, I was on my way to campus for a day of teaching. The day was a whirlwind: four classes, new faces, and a chance to demo a writing class for the international department. When I pulled out a picture of my childhood friend, ill Gates, and his infamous 'shutter shades,' the students seemed suitably impressed. I'm not just an English teacher, I reminded them — I've had my share of adventures, too.

Grateful for the Everyday

At lunchtime, I ordered pizzas, and Shaolin went to Ethan's two-year-old graduation (yes, our two-year-old has been in school for two years — I know, right?). Afterward, I met a new international class. They weren't sure what to make of me at first, but I'm always eager to connect, make them laugh, and hopefully leave them with something meaningful.

Saturday was full of tutoring, but we capped it off with a hot pot dinner for Luis. A few famous local sculptors from the Art University joined us, showing off their latest installations. It's incredible to see the cultural scene flourishing here. But by midnight, despite being utterly exhausted, we were off to a bar across the street, where we sang KTV and dominated the room with our energy. It's been more than 200 days since the last case of community spread here in Chongqing, and I can't help but feel grateful for China's effective response to the pandemic.

Adapting to Change

The next morning, we were up at 9 AM, ready for a flu jab. Shaolin had to skip it as they were out of stock, but I was determined to stay safe. If a simple flu shot could help me avoid the chaos of a COVID-flu combination, I wasn't going to pass it up. The jab made my arm tingle a bit, but no big deal — I was feeling resilient. The rest of the day flew by with work, errands, and a farewell dinner for Luis. We took him to the bank and sent him off to his next adventure, and I was reminded of the fleeting nature of time, friendships, and experiences. It's funny how much we can accomplish in a weekend, even when we're physically drained. By Monday, I was back at it, teaching and reflecting on the most challenging part of being a teacher: watching some students not pick up what I'm putting down, knowing they'll regret it later. But that's life — all we can do is our best.

The World Outside: A Global Crisis

The world outside is struggling. In the U.S., cases are skyrocketing, hospitals are overwhelmed, and the country remains divided. Some states still resist mask mandates and lockdown measures, while others, like Canada, face new waves of infection and further lockdowns. It's frustrating to witness, especially when so many of the solutions are so simple — but as always, ignorance and apathy hold us back.

I think about the pandemic, the politics, the people who refuse to take simple precautions, and it weighs on me. But here, in China, the government's strict measures have proven successful. We're living in a bubble of safety, and that's something I'm deeply grateful for.

A Year of Self-Discovery

I realize now that I can't save the world. I can't make everyone listen to the science or change their attitudes. But I can focus on myself, on my family, and on my small corner of the world. It's been a journey of self-discovery and growth — one that started with a desire to build a better life in China, and now, with the pandemic shaping the world around me, it's become a path to greater clarity.

There's so much I've learned, and I want to share it. What I've come to understand is that life isn't about grand gestures or big achievements. It's about the small things: the relationships we build, the choices we make every day, and the resilience we cultivate in the face of uncertainty. I've found peace in the ordinary moments, and in that, I feel lucky.

Reflecting on the Future

I know I can't change everything, but I can change my perspective. I can stay grounded, focused, and hopeful. And I can be the best version of myself for those I love — especially Shaolin, who continues to inspire me every day.

November 21, 2020 – Chongqing, China – "My Classroom (In the Year of the Rat)"

1. The Tragic Fall and the Gravity of Truth

When 29-year-old Regis Korchinski-Paquet fell to her death from her Toronto apartment balcony during a police intervention, the incident sparked a range of questions. Was she pushed? Was it an accident? The fact of her fall being fatal was taken as a given, like gravity itself. Just like how we accept the law of gravity, some truths—such as the efficacy of masks, vaccines, and medicine—are also undeniable facts that are often disregarded in favor of opinion. This world has its share of conspiracy theorists and anti-science voices, but their denial doesn't change the reality: masks work, vaccines work, and gravity remains real.

I often find myself frustrated with those who challenge scientific facts, yet the battle for truth remains ongoing. It's not about opinion; it's about science. We need to face that reality.

2. Cutting Toxic Ties: A Lesson in Friendship

This week, I faced a personal challenge with an old friend, Ian. Ian had been a close companion until we parted ways over differences in opinions regarding my nonfiction work. After Ian attempted to get my book deal canceled by contacting my literary agent, publisher, and media outlets, I had to make the difficult decision to cut him out of my life. A friendship like that wasn't worth salvaging, no matter how many apologies he later extended. As the old saying goes, "Fool me once, shame on you; fool me twice, shame on me." At this point, I'm learning to value my time and energy, something I once gave freely to people who didn't truly respect me. No more.

3. The Frustrating Case of Chris Dirt

Then there's Chris "Sky," an anti-masker I've had my share of interactions with. He insisted that China no longer mandates masks or lockdowns, claiming we had moved past the pandemic. He couldn't comprehend that we had worked hard for our current position of safety, and that China had employed stringent lockdown measures that worked. Instead, he continued to spout baseless opinions, confusing reality with conspiracy theories.

I tried to explain the nuance—China acted swiftly and decisively, implementing a hard lockdown to contain the virus. It wasn't just about convenience; it was about saving lives. But Chris didn't want to listen. So, for my own peace of mind, I blocked him. It's one less distraction and one more lesson in prioritizing self-respect over engaging in futile arguments.

4. Wuhan's Success and the "Rhetorical" Question

A post on social media asked why Wuhan hadn't experienced a second lockdown, offering me an opportunity to explain China's strategy. I answered it with the detail and facts I thought might enlighten the poster, hoping to break through some of the misinformation about how China handled the pandemic. Unfortunately, the response I got back was a rejection of the very idea of asymptomatic spread, despite overwhelming scientific evidence to the contrary.

This exchange was a reminder that we can't force people to accept the facts if they aren't ready to do so. It's frustrating to engage with those who won't even consider evolving their views, but I've realized that trying to convince them is often a waste of time. It's time to move on, to focus on what I can control.

5. Why China's COVID-19 Strategy Worked

So, why hasn't Wuhan had a second wave? The answer is simple: China acted swiftly, locking down the country for eight weeks. During this period, everyone was quarantined at home, contacts were traced, and extensive testing was carried out. This was followed by mandatory quarantines for anyone entering the country, ensuring that no new cases spread undetected.

In contrast, many countries in the West failed to act fast enough. Lockdowns were delayed, testing was inconsistent, and political leaders were hesitant to make difficult decisions. The result? As we enter winter, countries like the US and Canada are seeing a surge in cases, hospital beds filling up, and public health systems under severe strain.

Here in Chongqing, we've had zero community spread in more than 200 days. That's thanks to the government's decisive action, which many in the West saw as "draconian" but which, in hindsight, has proven to be the only way to contain such a dangerous virus.

6. The Road to Recovery: A Tale of Two Realities

As China moves forward, having largely contained COVID-19, I watch with concern as many Western countries continue to struggle. The United States, for example, is on track to reach 200,000 new cases per day, with hospitals across the country overwhelmed. Meanwhile, in Canada, the pandemic has continued to strain an already fragile healthcare system, with predictions pointing toward a dire winter if immediate action isn't taken.

Yet, despite the scientific evidence and the lessons we've learned here in China, there's a reluctance in the West to follow suit. The pandemic has laid bare the deep divides between the East and West, with China emerging as a model of proactive governance, while the West stumbles in its efforts to manage the crisis.

7. The Struggle of Democracy and the Fight for Knowledge

It's easy to point fingers at Trump for the failures of the West, but the problems go deeper than just one individual. The pandemic has revealed cracks in the foundation of democracy itself. A lack of leadership, misinformation, and the refusal to accept expert guidance have led to a prolonged crisis. Now, with a potential shift in power in the US, there's hope for a more science-driven approach to the pandemic.

But even as we look toward the future, we must ask ourselves: How did we get here? Why are so many people resistant to facts, to change, and to the basic principles of science and public health? The pandemic is not just a medical issue; it's a moral, social, and political one as well.

8. A Personal Reflection: Striving for a Better Future

Living in China has given me a unique perspective on what it means to live through a global crisis. I've seen firsthand how resilient societies can thrive when they work together. I'm proud of the efforts made here to keep everyone safe, but I'm also reminded of how far the West has fallen behind.

As I reflect on the year of the rat, I see a parallel between the global struggle and my own personal growth. I came to China seeking a fresh start, hoping to build a better life for myself, and through hard work, resilience, and a focus on what really matters, I've found peace. The pandemic has only intensified this realization.

The world may be in chaos, but in this quiet space of my life, I feel more grounded than ever before. And that, in itself, is a small victory.

The Value of Virtue and Adaptability

As we face an uncertain future, the lesson of this year is clear: we must adapt, we must work together, and we must prioritize the greater good. The pandemic has exposed the flaws in our systems, but it has also provided an opportunity to rebuild a better world. One based on education, compassion, and a shared responsibility to protect each other.

It's up to each of us to make that choice, and I'm choosing to continue doing my part. In a world where so much is out of our control, we still have the power to shape our own lives, to be the change we wish to see, and to build a future worth fighting for.

December 4, 2020 – Chongqing, China – "Gobble Gobble"

1. The Strangest of Times
Day 317. A strange week, full of conflicting emotions and unsettling moments. A vampire lord crossed my mind when I first met him—a quiet leader, eerily formal in a pressed shirt and tie, commanding without imposing. The thought sticks to me as the world seems to shrink around us. I wish I could say more, but for now, my hands are tied. For now, I stay silent.

2. A Cornered Rat
Given an escape, a rat might flee, but corner it, and it'll bite. The walls close in, and desperate times breed desperate measures. Some wish for retribution, for justice to be done. But in the end, an escape might be the better way forward—letting the rat free to fight another day rather than watch it destroy everything.

3. A Dark Week, But With Small Pleasures
Twitter's been a strange distraction lately, as I step further away from social media, enjoying the quiet moments instead. Yet, there's an occasional laugh to be had. #Diaperdon started trending, a term with potty humor rooted in the rumors surrounding Trump's alleged incontinence. He's become a walking joke, surrounded by absurdity, the tail end of his presidency more like a comedy sketch than a serious political moment. Yet here I am, getting a viral response to a tweet about the absurdity of it all—sometimes it's nice to find humor in the chaos.

4. The Humbling Practice of Kung Fu
Spent an afternoon with teenage kungfu practitioners, immersing myself in the discipline and trying out a few moves. It was a humbling experience and reminded me how important it is to stay grounded, both in mind and body. Learning something new always

feels good, and I'm inspired to continue my search for a martial arts school.

5. When Life Goes On, No Matter What
A colleague, after struggling through the pandemic's constraints, decided to head back home, unable to bear the isolation any longer. We sent him off, his bags packed, his fate in motion. Life goes on, even when it's tough—despite the hardships, we're left to adapt and adjust. My schedule continues to be hectic, juggling work, writing, tutoring, and staying active. I'm beginning to feel the weight of it all, though. I need to figure out how to build resilience and find some balance.

6. A Small, Personal Struggle
My dad, concerned about working from home safely, asked for advice. We talked about breathing techniques—how to reduce risks when picking up a laptop, or even hugging someone. The things you don't think about until you're living in these strange, restricted times. The small, everyday actions, taking on new significance.

7. Thanksgiving and the Inevitable COVID Wave
Thanksgiving came and went in the USA, despite health warnings. People gathered, defying experts' advice, and in turn, we're now waiting for the fallout: a new spike in infections. It's hard to watch from afar, especially as we've managed to avoid this mess in China through decisive action. The virus thrives in the cold, with poor ventilation and lower humidity spreading it more easily. We're not out of the woods yet, but there's hope.

8. Observing the West's Struggles
North Dakota and Alberta stand as prime examples of anti-science leadership—both areas now overwhelmed with cases due to lack of mask mandates. In contrast, China's strict and swift actions have kept us relatively safe. I've always been astounded by the West's inability to take proactive steps and the refusal to listen to the experts. The West seems to be buying themselves two years of struggle

because they couldn't handle eight weeks of sacrifice. It's tragic, and sadly, avoidable.

9. The Importance of Preparation

Shaolin and I have been preparing for a second wave here in Chongqing. I'm stocking up on food, masks, and disinfectants. We've learned the importance of keeping our homes safe and making sure we can handle whatever comes next. It's an unsettling but necessary step in these times.

10. China's Approach to COVID-19: A Case Study in Prevention

China's aggressive approach to COVID-19, with strict quarantines and testing protocols, has worked. Unlike the West, where protests and anti-mask sentiments reign, China has been able to contain the virus with strict measures and social cooperation. The contrast is stark, and I wonder how we could've done things differently in the West.

11. The Vaccine: Hope on the Horizon?

The vaccine rollout is on the horizon, but there's a long road ahead. While the West scrambles with anti-science movements, China, too, watches the global vaccine race closely. I'm optimistic, but cautious—there's still much to learn about how effective the vaccines will be, how long they will last, and whether people will even take them.

12. A Sharp Critique of Western Leadership

As much as I have a deep respect for the advancements in China, it's impossible not to criticize the West's handling of the pandemic. The refusal to take preventative measures, the prioritization of individual rights over collective responsibility, and the failure to heed warnings from the medical community have all contributed to this catastrophic failure. The West couldn't afford an eight-week lockdown, and now they're dealing with the consequences.

13. Politics and the Collapse of Trust

In the US, the political landscape continues to crumble as Trump's legal team loses its baseless lawsuits. Incompetence at the highest levels has led to this moment, where trust in leadership and science is at an all-time low. The damage done will take years to repair, and I can't help but wonder how it all went so wrong.

14. On Personal Responsibility and the Fight for the Future

Despite all of this, I remain hopeful. The fight for a better world continues. We can look to new leaders like AOC and others, pushing for climate justice and a Green New Deal. It's not going to be easy, but if we all do our part, we can create a better, more equitable future. The pandemic has highlighted the need for real systemic change, and the lessons learned from this dark chapter in history must not be forgotten.

15. A Call to Action

It's easy to get bogged down in the chaos, but as I reflect on this year, I find myself more determined than ever to continue fighting for change. Whether it's through education, activism, or simply helping my community, I'm committed to making a difference. The world needs more people willing to stand up for what's right, even when it's hard.

December 6, 2020 – Turin, Italy – "The Leaves of Autumn Match Italy's Color-Coded Lockdown" (Alessia Martino)

Autumn has arrived, and with it, the vibrant transformation of the leaves—yellow, orange, and red—each color reflecting the season's shift, mirroring the changes unfolding around me. I've been living in Italy long enough now that these seasonal shifts feel more like home. Still, this year, autumn seems different. The world feels more confined, and for me, it has meant staying in and embracing the comfort of warm blankets and hot cups of tea.

Europe, as a whole, is in the midst of a second wave of the pandemic. The Czech Republic, once a success story, now has the highest infection rate relative to its population. Here in Italy, we didn't experience the same surge as the return to school many expected. But some responses have gone to the extreme—like a rule that forbids touching disabled people when they fall. In those moments, being cautious is one thing, but common sense should still prevail. Human instinct should always lean toward helping, even with precautions.

While some may blame the younger generation for not taking the pandemic seriously, the reality is that older people are often the ones who fail to follow safety guidelines—failing to wear masks or wash their hands as they should. This problem is compounded by a dangerous trend of denial: many still think they're immune to the virus, refusing to acknowledge the very real risk and refusing to get tested when needed. For those who argue that masks take away their freedom, it's worth asking: if a simple piece of cloth can truly take away your freedom, isn't it time to reevaluate what freedom really means?

As cases increase, Italy has implemented new restrictions that seem to sprout up almost overnight. The state of emergency has been extended until the end of January, with private gatherings limited to no more than six people, even within a family. And some gatherings, like weddings and baptisms, have been broken up by the authorities, with fines imposed. Neighbors are even encouraged to report those violating restrictions.

Other new measures have targeted non-professional contact sports, curfews for restaurants, and tighter mask mandates. Restaurants now must close between midnight and 5 a.m. (11 p.m. in the hardest-hit areas), and no takeout orders are allowed after 6 p.m. Yet despite these strict guidelines, there's still non-compliance—many people wear masks improperly, with their noses exposed.

On November 6th, Italy entered a second lockdown, though this time, it's lighter. The government introduced a color-coded system to categorize regions based on the severity of the pandemic in those areas. The regions are now categorized as red, orange, or yellow, with corresponding lockdown measures in place. The red regions are the strictest, resembling the initial lockdown but with a broader range of essential services allowed to stay open (restaurants, for example, can only offer takeout). In contrast, yellow regions allow more freedom, such as the ability to visit bars and restaurants, travel between regions without documentation, and move about without restrictions. Regardless of the color code, exercise and outdoor walks are always allowed.

Five regions initially fell into the red category, not based solely on the number of cases but on the ability of their healthcare systems to handle the surge. Calabria, for example, had fewer cases, but its lack of adequate healthcare infrastructure warranted a red designation. Though some regions have improved, Italy is still far from containing the virus.

December 10, 2020 – Chongqing, China – "The End of the Beginning"

What more can I say that I haven't said already? While highly developed countries see record numbers of vulnerable people dying, developing nations are finding success with repurposed, safe medications. It's frustrating to witness the obsession with the shiny new vaccine when simple measures like masks, Vitamin D, and basic non-pharmaceutical interventions (NPIs) could have saved so many lives. There's a growing callousness and lack of empathy in the world, a refusal to listen to reason. Fools protest necessary measures in the streets, unaware they are pushing their countries into decades of economic recession—precisely when we need that financial wiggle room to save the planet. Everywhere conservatives hold power, regulations and mask guidance are absent, and cases continue to skyrocket. And yet, there is still no standardized approach to Vitamin D fortification, despite solid studies that demonstrate its efficacy. It's a needless tragedy.

Trump, meanwhile, is staging his absurd coup, and no one seems to care. It's both treasonous and sickening. I feel dejected, so I'm tuning out the noise for my own sanity. There's just so much noise.

In an effort to escape, I've indulged in a little self-care. I ordered *Cyberpunk 2077 Deluxe Edition*, hoping to immerse myself in a different world for a while. Perhaps, by the time I emerge, we'll have a summary of how we survived. It's nice to dream.

In other personal news, my mom celebrated a milestone birthday this week. She became eligible for senior citizen benefits, which for her is a big deal. She won two tickets to a safe, socially distanced music event and booked a cozy room at an inn for the occasion. It was a thoughtful and exciting plan, but then, like so many things this year, it was thwarted. Due to community spread on the Island, which had been relatively untouched until then, the event was canceled. PEI had relaxed their measures, growing their "bubble" to include neighboring Atlantic provinces, but it was too late. The virus spread when a group of young people partied unsafely in Halifax and Moncton. By the time they realized what had happened, it was too late to avoid further damage.

It's a sobering reminder that when we all need to work together, some people prioritize personal freedom and fun over the collective good. It's a pattern I see again and again in a world where unchecked capitalism convinces us we're all alone and responsible for ourselves, rather than fostering a sense of community. As Rutger Bregman aptly points out, we are all fundamentally good—until we learn to be selfish.

The State of the Pandemic and the Global Response

Despite the global surge in COVID cases, there's been some positive news. The FDA has authorized over-the-counter home COVID tests. Europe has made some progress in managing their summer outbreak, but in the U.S., it's a different story. The pandemic response has been a mess, and the consequences are dire. In fact, the death toll is now so high it's equivalent to the deadliest days in U.S. history.

Lockdowns and mask mandates worked in China. In Chongqing, the government enforced strict measures, including an eight-week lockdown, and it paid off. China reported just 90,000 cases for its 1.5 billion people and fewer than 5,000 deaths. Schools reopened safely, businesses bounced back, and the economy didn't collapse. On the other hand, "freer" countries, who refused to implement strict measures, are now struggling with high case numbers, overrun hospitals, and economic devastation. In some places, as many as 75% of bars and restaurants will close, and millions will face homelessness and bankruptcy.

A Closer Look at Vaccine Distribution

On the vaccine front, the UK began vaccinating with the Pfizer-BioNTech vaccine, and the first doses were given to elderly residents. The rollout has been swift, and while some reactions to the vaccine have been mild, the overall safety profile looks positive. But the reality remains that we've been waiting for a vaccine while already knowing what could have helped us prevent this crisis.

Ivermectin and Vitamin D have proven to be effective and safe in studies, but instead of being part of the solution, these treatments have been ignored or downplayed. Why? Because big pharmaceutical companies would rather push expensive treatments. The same companies that have prevented cheaper, effective options from becoming the mainstream solutions. It's frustrating.

As I said in my last entry, I'm starting to feel like a cranky old man. I've watched people, especially in the West, ignore simple advice and act as if the pandemic is a joke. Meanwhile, countries like China have shown us that strict measures, such as lockdowns and mask mandates, work. Yet, we're still stuck in this cycle of denial, pushing the virus further out of control.

Looking Ahead

This year has been long, and there's still no clear end in sight. I'll admit, I'm struggling with my mental resilience at times. Some days it feels like everything is too much, and I can't keep up with the demands of work, life, and the emotional toll of the pandemic. But I remind myself to be present, to keep going, and to focus on the things I can control—like spending time with Shaolin, enjoying the small moments, and finding some joy in the midst of this chaos.

I've been thinking a lot about my place in all of this. How did I get here, and what comes next? The world is changing, and so am I. As I keep my focus on my family and my work, I know that the path ahead won't be easy. But I'm committed to keeping my head above water, to staying grounded, and to finding my way through this.

December 11, 2020 – Edmonton, Canada – "Alberta in the Time of COVID" (Rebecca Lippiatt)

1. Cassandra's Curse: The Public Health Struggle
Cassandra should be the patron saint of Alberta's health professionals. While she wasn't a goddess or saint, her mythology fits the way public health experts are treated in Alberta. Cursed by Apollo, Cassandra was given the ability to see the future, but no one would believe her. She predicted the fall of Troy and was ignored. This is the fate of every epidemiologist, scientist, nurse, and doctor in Alberta during the COVID-19 pandemic.

Pandemics unfold predictably. First, confusion rises as cases grow. Doctors and scientists scramble to understand the cause, and governments react—sometimes quickly, often not. The public, looking for answers, responds to leadership. With good leadership, they follow the guidelines, and casualties are minimized. With poor leadership, chaos ensues. Unfortunately, Alberta's leadership has failed in this crucial time. They've taken the possibility of planning, ripped it into small shreds, and flushed it down the toilet.

2. Public Trust Erodes: Dr. Hinshaw's Decline
At the start of the pandemic, Alberta fell in love with our Chief Medical Officer, Dr. Deena Hinshaw. Artists created portraits of her, printed them on t-shirts, and the public wore them proudly. She had a calm demeanor, clear explanations of the science, and an admirable willingness to admit when she didn't have the answers. For a while, we all thought the pandemic was in good hands.

But as the months wore on, cracks began to show. By September, when schools reopened, it was clear that the government was cherry-picking science to justify its reopening plan. Dr. Hinshaw didn't speak out. As cases in schools rose, and contact tracing failed—positive cases were told to inform their own contacts—confidence in her and the government waned.

3. Leadership Fails: The UCP Government's Response

The Alberta United Conservative Party (UCP) government is like a group of teenagers playing a video game, imagining they can hit "reset" if they lose. I think of Grassy Mountain, where the UCP wants to sell land to an Australian mining company to mine coal. They've been trying to reassure the public by posting photos of reclaimed coal mines, pretending that the destruction of a 60-kilometer stretch of the Rocky Mountains is "normal."

Leadership only becomes apparent when it fails completely. Premier Jason Kenney is like a father trying to be friends with his rebellious children, letting them throw a party in their home while everything falls apart. His pleas for people to wear masks are met with a shrug as cases exponentially grow.

4. The Reality of Healthcare in Alberta: A Crisis in ICUs

Alberta's rugged individualism has been a disastrous mindset during this pandemic. "Can do" attitudes are fine, but they won't help when there are no boots to pull yourself up by. Every day, the death toll rises. The ICUs are full, then double-bunked, then full again. Hospitals are reopening wings abandoned during previous neoliberal cuts, but there's no staff to fill the extra beds. Nurses, who were already overworked, are now caring for twice as many patients. The images of their weary, defeated faces on social media tell the true cost of a mismanaged pandemic.

5. A Dystopian Reality: Confusion and Misinformation

In a dystopian twist, Alberta's Premier requested field hospitals, but not the staff to run them. The government has fought with medical personnel throughout the pandemic, accusing nurses of making too much money, and the Health Minister, Tyler Shandro, ripped up contracts and slashed physician pay. Meanwhile, the government outsourced healthcare services, even as a doctor who criticized them was reprimanded in person by Shandro.

The term "anti-masker" has entered the lexicon, and those who refuse to follow public health guidelines gather in large groups, demanding their so-called "freedom." These protests, fueled by ignorance and misinformation, have become a major obstacle in the fight against COVID-19. Some of these individuals claim the government is infringing on their rights, but the truth is that they are threatening the lives of vulnerable people.

6. Broken Systems: The Strain on Schools and Teachers

Schools were another site of chaos. Alberta's students experienced the uncertainty of shifting between in-person and remote learning. By November, one-third of schools in the province had at least one COVID case. The contact tracing process was inadequate, and teachers were expected to manage these outbreaks, often without proper resources. By December, nearly half of Alberta's schools had seen cases. Meanwhile, teachers had to adjust to stricter rules that now considered any teacher within two meters of an infected student a "close contact." The pressure on teachers was immense, as they were expected to keep schools open while managing outbreaks on their own.

7. The Price of Misinformation: A Province in Crisis

Alberta's misinformation problem is further compounded by government officials who spread conspiracy theories. A former pathologist, now a consultant, publicly stated that the pandemic was overblown and that we would all be fine. This video spread like wildfire, and it was quoted by members of the government. In another instance, the Premier attended a dinner where it was unclear whether social distancing guidelines were followed, but it was certain that no masks were worn.

Despite the warnings from experts and healthcare workers, the government has refused to take the necessary action to control the spread of the virus. The Premier continues to avoid using the word "lockdown" and has made it clear that his goal is not to eliminate the virus but to make it "manageable" for the hospitals. This attitude has cost lives.

8. Conclusion: A Call for Responsibility and Action

As the cases continue to climb, it becomes clear that Alberta's failure to act quickly and decisively has led to unnecessary deaths. We are now entering a second wave, and without drastic measures, the situation will only worsen.

The Premier's refusal to take responsibility for the lives lost and his refusal to implement a full lockdown has set Alberta back significantly. The question remains: if countries like China, Australia, and Vietnam can contain the virus, why can't Alberta?

As we head into winter, it's crucial that we take responsibility, not just for ourselves but for each other. The choices we make now will determine the future of our healthcare system, our economy, and our communities. We can't afford to let the ignorance and selfishness of a few dictate the fate of the many.

December 13, 2020 – Chicago, USA – "MC Zulu & No Middle Ground" (MC ZULU)

1. The Dystopia of 2020: A National Wake-Up Call

2020 serves as a shameful reminder that the American public's collective intelligence is roughly equivalent to that of a six-year-old. As much as we would like to relegate COVID-19 to a cultural blemish of the year, the truth is the damage is permanent. The death toll from the virus extends beyond human lives, claiming small businesses, department stores, and entire industries— the economic and social fabric of the nation.

The political blame game was deafening, and the pandemic's fallout led to the downfall of a presidency, leaving the country divided right down the middle. People's behavior mirrored the chaos: mindlessly following herd mentality, pushing the nation to extremes. Extremism, it seems, has become the rule of the day.

2. The Unyielding Binary: There's No Middle Ground

In a culture dominated by binary thinking, there is no room for nuance. You're either with one side or the other, and any attempt to think critically or offer a balanced perspective earns you nothing but derision. Half the country will hate you no matter what you say. And if you don't choose "their" side, you're an enemy.

This polarization isn't just political; it's personal. A musician friend of mine, who is essentially a social media bully, took issue with something I posted. His response was a series of vitriolic diatribes, which, to my amusement, I screen-shotted and tagged him in. This led to a ceremonious unfriending and an angry text the next day.

I don't apologize for the confrontation— I feel no enmity toward him. But I do feel bad for the fact that society has been engineered to pit us against each other. The whole thing is just absurd.

Thank god he's a drummer. If he were a rapper, well, that would've been a different story.

3. Backwards We Go: Society's Great Regression

No matter where we started this year, we've all taken a few steps backward in terms of human evolution. The pandemic aside, 2020 has been one big social experiment where simple pleasures— gym time, going to the movies, hitting the malls, dining out, vacations, family gatherings— have been criminalized. These were the small joys of life, now deemed dangerous.

But what's being decriminalized? Take a closer look. There's a dangerous rise in the normalization of conspiracy theories, with some brushing child abuse cases under the rug, claiming they're part of the "QAnon" conspiracy.

There's no shortage of examples, but I think you get the point. Whether you're compelled to think about this, or you choose to unfollow me, I really don't care anymore. After years of trying to "wake people up," my experiment officially ends with 2020.

4. The End of Idealism: The Empowerment Lie

The art will continue, but don't expect many more explanations. I'll happily write about technology, business, fitness, or any number of other interests. But let's be clear: this is not the 60s. The "empowerment" you feel today is not the result of some counterculture liberation movement. What we're experiencing is a deliberate societal backslide on many levels.

5. The Real Power Players: A Dystopian Truth

How do I know? Because it's not the youth making the decisions. Establishment money dictates the direction of our society. You didn't hear this from me, but now you know.

Interlude – Canada Looks Down the Barrel of a Decade-Long Recession as China's GDP Grows Steadily in 2020

In the news today, I read that Canada is bracing for a *Decade of Recession* in the wake of the pandemic, while my city, Chongqing in China, has managed to *Bounce Back* with a 2.6% GDP growth in 2020 so far. The West claimed it couldn't afford a lockdown for the economy, but in reality, a lockdown saved ours.

So, here's the question: If we couldn't protect our people or the most vulnerable to safeguard the economy, and now we're facing a massive economic crisis because we failed to contain the virus, what exactly did we get right in the West?

Now, before anyone accuses me of being *pro-China*, let's get this clear: I'm not cheering for one country over another, but I am deeply disappointed by how badly my home country mucked things up. This failure means I can't even visit my family right now. I'm *anti-dumb* and *pro-intelligent*, plain and simple. It's easy to attack me as *pro-China*, but let's take a moment to look at countries like New Zealand, Australia, Mongolia, South Korea, and Vietnam. Some of them (like Australia) took a bit longer to get it right, but others (like South Korea, Mongolia, and New Zealand) acted quickly, shut down early, and followed China's lead—and they succeeded.

With pandemics, from the start, I've said you need a strong, swift response. Vigilant measures to contain the virus before it gets out of control. I saw this firsthand, and reported it as truth. And now I have the numbers to back it up. In my city—one with a population roughly equivalent to Canada's—we've bounced back. The pandemic didn't decimate us. We've recovered. Businesses are thriving again, schools are safe, and the economy is growing. We did it.

The lesson here: We need the wiggle room to keep our planet cool. Don't waste that freedom fighting over a piece of cloth on your face.

In the early wave, Chongqing had 576 cases and just 6 fatalities. Later, we caught 20 more cases in quarantine—and none of them died. This wasn't luck. This was decisive action. I'm proud of what we did. Now, I hope Canada can *get it together* sooner than later.

And to my friends back home, let me tell you this:

Don't let COVIDIOTS kill your elderly, your immunocompromised, or your front-line healthcare workers.

Don't let COVIDIOTS ruin your economy any more than they already have.

Don't let COVIDIOTS run amok, spreading plagues.

Crack down on them. And crack down hard.

In Indonesia, anti-maskers are forced to dig graves for COVID victims. In Rwanda, "dicknosers" and chin-maskers are rounded up for an all-night stadium educational movie night, where they learn how to wear a mask properly—because, let's face it, they're just being big dummies. In India, the police use sticks to knock some sense into them.

Canada, we need to get tough on spreadnecks.

So, here's my message:

Get tough.

That's my TED Talk for today. Thanks for coming out.

December 24, 2020 – Chongqing, China – "The Gift"

1. Solstice Wishes & A Promise to Myself
It's Christmas Eve, 2020. We've nearly made it through this relentless, impossible year. A few days ago, on December 21—Winter Solstice—I joined the Wang clan, my Chinese family, for a riverside gathering beneath the stars. We looked up to witness a rare celestial phenomenon: Jupiter and Saturn aligned to form a visible "double planet," the Christmas Star, the closest conjunction in 800 years. As the family shared traditional lamb soup to warm our bellies through the winter, I made myself a promise: I would give myself the gift of patience. I would be kind to myself and others. I would find my empathy again, and I would stay calm. Don't panic.
If you know me, turning down the snark sounds like Mission Impossible. But it's been three days now, and so far, so good.

2. Pandemic in Slow Motion
In China, the pandemic has often felt like it played out in slow motion. After the initial battle of Wuhan, cities like Chongqing locked down swiftly and smartly. When a case appeared, we clamped down, mass tested, and reopened quickly. We were vigilant. We followed the science. We wore masks, tracked wastewater, studied ACE2 receptors and ocular transmission, and shared early genomic data. China published the genetic sequence of the virus on January 11, and Moderna's vaccine was designed the same weekend. It took a year to test and authorize, but the solution was born before most people knew there was a problem.
Canada said an eight-week lockdown would be too costly. Instead, they bought a two-year one on layaway.

3. The Tom Cruise Outburst & COVID Etiquette

Tom Cruise was caught screaming at his crew on the set of *Mission: Impossible 7* for breaking distancing protocols. While some praised him for taking the pandemic seriously, others criticized his tone and his ineffective valve mask. My friend Devon reminded me that fear and rage rarely lead to better compliance—they just make people hide their mistakes.

Still, the show must go on.

4. Global Numbers, Local Caution

In the past 24 hours, the U.S. recorded 194,000 new cases. A new, more infectious mutation from the UK (N501Y) is spreading fast. Canada hit 500,000 cases. Globally, we're at 79 million known cases, likely far more. Over 1.7 million dead. The long-haul symptoms—organ damage, lung scarring, brain fog—linger like shadows. Trump made America number one: 20 million cases. India, Brazil, Russia, France, and the UK follow. Canada ranks 26th. China? 80th. We used to top the charts. Now, we watch from our island of safety.

5. Cyberpunk & Solitude

Cyberpunk 2077 finally launched—buggy, broken, and perfect. For a lifelong fan of the genre, this world is exactly what it should be: gritty, janky, real. In some ways, it reflects 2020 better than any polished product could. And yet, I'm not spending my winter break plugged into a neon nightmare. I'm drinking coffee. I'm walking with Shaolin. I'm chasing snow on Fairy Mountain with gloves, toques, and childlike wonder. Family matters more.

6. The Mutation & The Missed Moment

The UK mutation has closed borders across Europe. It's likely everywhere by now. It spreads faster, especially in poorly ventilated spaces. But vaccines should still work. We just need to remain vigilant. We could have stopped this back in February. We didn't. Now we're reactive. Still, the science is holding. And the lesson remains: wear a mask, stay home, stay safe.

7. A Global Mirror

WHO epidemiologist Maria Van Kerkhove named the countries that managed the pandemic well: China, Vietnam, Thailand, Rwanda, New Zealand, Germany, Senegal. They worked hard. They listened to science. It's not about politics; it's about action. I hope we take these lessons into the climate crisis ahead. We'll need to.

8. The Book, The Snow, The Monk Named FivePots

The publishers from Beijing are flying in for the launch of *The Invisible War*. My school leaders want to come. Local officials too. December 27 will be a big day. On the 25th, though, I'll stay home in pajamas, make dinner, open gifts with family. Pizza party for the kids on the 26th. Shadowrun game with friends. This holiday is packed, but filled with joy. My father now calls me "FivePots," my monk name, after I misspoke. It used to be Grasshopper. I'm growing up.

9. A Final Gift

It all circles back to my gift: patience, kindness, and calm. Getting angry at people who didn't listen doesn't help. Resentment won't save us. We did our best. We'll keep doing better. And whatever happens, I will be calm. I will be kind. Even if I sink with the ship. That's my gift.

December 31, 2020 – Chongqing, China – "Hello 2021 (The Beginning of the End)"

Day 343 of My Pandemic

1. A Year to Remember

As we look back on 2020 and all its unexpected turns, I find myself flipping through the pages of this diary—now nearing 800 pages and 280,000 words long. It spans six continents and features more than a dozen bloggers and friends who helped tell the story of a world facing an invisible war. A virus emerged, spread across the globe, and sparked not only fear and lockdowns but also rapid innovation. Multiple vaccines were developed, some using revolutionary mRNA technology with potential far beyond this pandemic, perhaps even to help us fight cancer one day. It's breathtaking. Marcus Aurelius once wrote in *Meditations*, "The impediment to action advances action. What stands in the way becomes the way." In facing hardship, we've accomplished astonishing things. That's worth holding onto.

2. Shots of Hope

My old friend Glenda—once a fellow B-girl in Ottawa, now a nurse and frontline hero—got the Pfizer vaccine yesterday. "It's been a tough year," she told me. "I've seen fear, grief, and death in the ICU. I'm over it. I'm hoping this is the turning point." Another friend's 99-year-old grandfather was also vaccinated. We are, finally, on our way.

The Oxford-AstraZeneca vaccine was just approved in the UK. It's a game-changer: inexpensive, easy to store in a regular fridge, and effective. Even the first dose can prevent most hospitalizations and fatalities. China's domestic vaccines are also being rolled out to healthcare workers and other at-risk groups. I don't yet know which shot I'll get, but I'm hopeful. Travel to see my family might be possible sooner than I feared.

3. A Pandemic Christmas

Christmas here in Chongqing was cozy. On the 25th, we invited Shaolin's best friend Ya Ya, her daughter Cherry, and our son Jin over for a feast. Roast chicken, mashed potatoes, potato salad, fajitas, cake. Saturday was a kids' pizza party. Sunday, I had my book launch—a big event with speeches, signings, and family dinner. On Tuesday, CQTV came over to shoot an in-depth interview, bringing a full broadcast team and turning our place into a temporary studio. Then came a magazine interview and back to teaching.

It's been busy—but in a good way.

4. Slow Season, Fast Mind

The term will end mid-January. Then comes a stretch of rest: winter at home, writing, gaming, relaxing. We might sneak off to the countryside, but safety comes first. Even if I stay in, I'll be warm, safe, and maybe tinkering with my new astronaut jumpsuit patches. "WANG KAI ◇◇" and "WOOD" look good next to Cyberpunk 2077 badges.

5. Trauma and Transformation

I've been listening to Dr. Gabor Maté lately, reading his books on addiction and trauma. His ideas—that addiction isn't a genetic flaw but a response to pain, a substitute for missing love or support—resonate deeply. As someone shaped by early sensitivity, whose parents divorced when I was still a toddler, I recognize the long echo of that pain. My party years, my hunger for the stage, the wandering—I see now what I was looking for.

But today, I'm grateful. For the family I have, for work that fills me up, for the calm that finally found me. I've thanked my old protectors—anger, escapism—and let them go. What remains is something forged through fire: not just survival, but clarity.

6. From Fire to Forging

I grew up in a frying pan, jumped into the fire, and somehow became Valyrian steel. That's what the Stoics meant—what stands in the way becomes the way.

7. The Work and the Gift

A peaceful, joyful, wise life is a life's work—and I'm proud of mine. It's taken 42 years to get here, but I am here. Grateful, grounded, and ready to welcome what's next.

Happy New Year. I hope you are safe, healthy, loved, and inspired. Keep hope alive.

Good things are on the way.

January 17, 2021 – Chongqing, China – "Space to Dream"

Day 352

I. Snowglobe Days and a Sudden Loss

The first five days of 2021 were peaceful. Trump hid in the White House. I did my part by ignoring his ugly mug and the news in general. I focused on the life in front of me, existing minimally online. These winter days passed in a simple, joyous haze—like the temporary bliss of a snowglobe spinning before the inevitable shake-up required to get things moving again. I enjoyed time with my family and anticipated a great return to normal life. Soon I'd have a long winter holiday. In another universe, I might have visited a low-risk region in China—warm Sanya, perhaps—but then S died, and 2021 got real.

We hadn't spoken in years, but an old mutual friend from our teenage days sent me the article: a hotel fire, a few days in hospital, and then gone. S had been a glamorous stylist and party legend, someone who'd lived high and hit some low lows before trying to start anew—only to be consumed by a freak blaze. In the '90s, their Cooper Street apartment in Ottawa had been like a community center. After all-night dancing, we'd crash there beside empty sherry bottles and pockets full of accidentally confiscated lighters. Looking back at photos, I was just a kid—the same age or younger than some of my students now—but streetwise and stumbling into adult dynamics we barely understood. In the West, we grow up fast. For better or worse.

I knew you as Steve. The world later knew you as Sasha. RIP, Sasha. Your humor, fashion, grace, dancing, and wit helped shape who I am. You live on every time I write a good line—so I'll try to nail one for you.

II. Georgia on My Mind and the Capitol Coup

After Sasha died, things began to accelerate. I watched with cautious optimism as the Georgia Senate runoff took shape—against all odds, a Black senator and a Jewish senator were elected, flipping control of the Senate. Mitch "The Turtleman" McConnell lost his majority. A tie-breaker vote now belonged to VP Kamala Harris. There was hope—hope for relief packages, a sane COVID strategy, and a return to climate action.

Then came the Capitol insurrection. Thousands of unmasked yahoos stormed Washington's halls in facepaint and tacticool cosplay, chanting for Pence's execution. The riot was domestic terrorism, an attempted coup, and should have been met with deadly force. Instead, Capitol police took selfies with the attackers. The contrast with how BLM protests were treated is stark and disgusting.

AOC later said she didn't feel safe in the congressional bunker—some colleagues were Trump-aligned and might sell her out. Bernie called for an investigation into suspicious Capitol tours the day before the riot. At least five representatives caught COVID from GOP members who refused to wear masks while locked down.

Mitt Romney gave the speech of his life, calling the riot "an insurrection incited by the President of the United States." That will be Trump's legacy.

III. MFA Dreams and Troll Repellent

Amid the chaos, I got accepted to a prestigious MFA program in creative nonfiction. I just need to find the money. I drew up a budget. If I stay strong, work hard, and keep faith, I can manage it—paying the mortgage and family loans while chasing my own dream. It's a "me thing" in a world where I do so much for others.
Some friends celebrated my return. Others vanished—offended by my diary or book or blog. So be it. I reread a quote: "You'll never be criticized by someone doing more than you—only someone doing less." And then I moved on.
I still think about the woman who died at the riot—a veteran, radicalized by lies. Another tased himself to death while stealing a painting. One wore a "Don't Tread on Me" shirt and was trampled. Five dead. America spiraled while the virus raged and climate crisis worsened. What a mess.
Trump's own aides said he didn't understand why no one was celebrating with him. It took his daughter Ivanka to convince him to call the National Guard. Arrests followed. The QAnon Shaman demanded organic food in jail. Memes went viral. It would be hilarious if it weren't so grotesque.

IV. A Measured Life (and a Puppy Pad Plan)

As Biden's inauguration approached, trucks arrived at the White House. I found small joy in seeing aides carry out Trump's ridiculously oversized neckties. Twitter, Facebook, and Instagram banned him—his phone now a silent brick. The silence was golden. Meanwhile, I got sick. Teaching through a cold, I realized I was being a baby about suffering—again. But pain and discomfort are messages. Sometimes, the best thing we can do is ignore them until the lesson is clear. So I did. I taught, I got through it, and I learned. Benben and Hachoo, my dogs, are metaphors for pandemic management. Hachoo pees on her pad reliably. Benben just goes wherever. Cleaning up daily messes is frustrating—but I keep putting fresh pads out. Why? Because having a plan, even a half-working one, matters. Pandemic management is the same. It's better to strive imperfectly than give up.

V. On Variants, Justice, and Resilience

The new variants—UK B.1.1.7, South African 501.V2, Brazilian VUI-202012/01—are easier to catch. Masks matter more than ever. Experts say a more contagious strain is worse than a deadlier one: it causes exponentially more deaths.

A Canadian doctor warned that Ontario hospitals are overwhelmed. Field hospitals are opening. Surgeries are canceled. The province might soon use triage protocols to decide who lives and dies. "Trust me," the doctor said, "you have loved ones who wouldn't make the cut."

People grumble. Cases spike. Some are arrested at anti-mask protests. And yet, some hope remains: vaccine rollouts begin.

We took Ethan to the zoo on a sunny day. He smiled at the animals. Life keeps moving.

VI. Reflections, Games, and the Fire Inside

We still don't know what long-term effects the virus will have. Will COVID lie dormant in our bodies like herpes? Will reinfections plague us later? Maybe we'll wear masks for years. Michael Jackson, masked and gloved, suddenly doesn't seem so strange. My dad even shops with one glove—touching public things with one hand, keeping the other clean.

The first person in China died of COVID in over eight months. A super spreader event in Jilin reminded us: vigilance matters. Migrant workers won't go home for Spring Festival this year—for the second year in a row. The sacrifices are real. The discipline is deep.

Melissa, an old poet friend from Dal, messaged me. I called the book a hot mess—but it's my best so far. That's why I keep going.

I think of Rothfuss, of Martin, of stories unfinished and promises unmet. Cyberpunk 2077 launched broken. CDPR's stock plummeted. Their demo was fake. But beneath the mess is magic—unfinished, but promising. That's my book too. That's me.

Maybe the MFA will help me find balance—between rushed releases and forever drafts. I hope so.

VII. Peace at Last, and What Comes Next

It's the final week of classes. I'm tempted to call in sick, but I won't. I'll lean into the discomfort. It's how I grow.

We watched all of *Homeland*. The main character reminds me of myself—sacrificing personal peace for big causes. I also watched *The Wilds*, a YA drama that reminded me how cruel society can be to young women. I'm glad I grew up and left behind the chaos of Doctore Danish and DJing. Heartbreak is one thing when you're young—it's something else when you're old enough to know better. These pandemic years have helped me reflect. As Dave Chappelle said, COVID forces us to sit in our choices—to marinate in them. I see the last decade clearly now, especially the seven years since I left Canada. The reboot worked.

VIII. Wealth, Wonder, and a Song from the Past

Elon Musk is now the richest man alive. Somehow. If he really uses half his fortune to save the Earth and half to get us to Mars? Redemption, maybe. He's annoying sometimes, but ambitious. That counts.

An old friend's voice echoes in my mind, clear as day, from a warehouse rave twenty-five years ago. Natasha C. sang a tune that's never left me. Unreleased, unrecorded, but unforgettable. How can something so fleeting last so long? Because in the space, we dream. Many opportunities lie ahead. If we meet the Year of the Ox with hard work and discipline, we'll reap the rewards.

Until then—here I am. Still half-assing it. Still dreaming.

Be safe. Be well. Keep on keeping on.

Afterthought – The Masked Truth: Lessons from Japan's Quiet Pandemic Triumph

In a world that's lost its bearings, sometimes it's the quietest nations that offer the most profound lessons. Japan, where masks became second nature, and the pandemic became a test of discipline, empathy, and common sense.

1. A Tale of Two Cities: Tokyo vs. New York

In the first wave of COVID-19, Tokyo, a megacity of over 37 million people, suffered minimal fatalities, recording only 421 deaths by October 9, 2020. Despite being a bustling hub with dense crowds, the city never closed down, and citizens adhered to high levels of mask-wearing and social distancing. Meanwhile, New York City, with a population half the size of Tokyo's, saw over 243,000 confirmed cases and 19,237 deaths, even with lockdowns in place. What separated these two stories? Discipline, culture, and a clear commitment to safety—lessons the rest of the world could learn from.

2. The Hidden Pandemic: Racial Inequity in the COVID-19 Crisis

While Tokyo managed to keep its death toll low, racial inequality in the United States and other Western countries exposed deep systemic flaws. Indigenous communities like the Navajo Nation suffered far higher rates of infection and death. In New York, Black and Latino populations were disproportionately affected by severe illness, a stark contrast to the relatively lower infection rates in predominantly Asian cities like Tokyo. The pandemic unearthed a harsh truth: systemic racism exacerbates the effects of a global health crisis.

3. The Vitamin D Deficiency: A Simple Solution to Severe COVID

Studies show a clear link between vitamin D deficiency and severe outcomes in COVID-19 cases. People with darker skin, particularly those living in northern climates, are at greater risk due to the reduced ability to produce vitamin D from sunlight. In Japan, this simple yet vital factor played a role in reducing the severity of cases. Research also supports the efficacy of vitamin D, zinc, and other supplements in reducing hospitalizations and fatalities. A lesson the world should heed: low-cost, easily accessible solutions could save lives.

4. Masks: The Unsung Heroes of Pandemic Defense

Masks, often dismissed in the West as mere symbols of compliance, proved to be Japan's most powerful weapon. With nearly universal mask-wearing, Tokyo demonstrated that even without a lockdown, the virus could be contained. Studies show that a lower viral load—often due to the use of masks—leads to milder or asymptomatic cases. In contrast, the US, with its political polarization over masks, saw widespread transmission and more severe outcomes. The message is clear: masking works. It's not just about stopping the spread—it's about reducing the severity of the disease when it does spread.

5. Profit Over People: The Battle for Affordable Treatments

The pandemic has exposed the chasm between the powerful pharmaceutical industry and the most vulnerable populations. While treatments like Ivermectin and hydroxychloroquine were tested and proven to be effective at a low cost, they were overshadowed by the promotion of expensive treatments like Remdesivir. The West's focus on profits over practicality has been a major hindrance. Meanwhile, in the Global South, where resources are scarce, affordable, generic treatments have shown to be lifesaving. The lesson?

Cost-effective solutions need to be prioritized, especially in a global crisis.

6. Smart Reopenings and Controlled Lockdowns: A Global Framework

As the world battles COVID, it's time to take a page from Japan and other nations with low fatalities. Reopening businesses safely isn't about ignoring the virus but adopting smart strategies: mask mandates, social distancing, and ensuring proper ventilation. Countries like Vietnam, which relied on extensive contact tracing, and Japan, which kept mask compliance high, show that reopening doesn't have to mean chaos—it can be strategic and safe.

7. Detection and Prevention: Stopping Outbreaks Before They Begin

To prevent future outbreaks, innovative methods like sniffer dogs and wastewater testing are vital. Cities like Helsinki have shown that sniffer dogs can detect COVID with nearly 100% accuracy. Meanwhile, testing wastewater can detect outbreaks up to 10 days in advance, a powerful tool in preventing larger-scale infections. This proactive approach could be the key to reopening and controlling future waves of the virus, ensuring that business can continue while public health remains the top priority.

8. Conclusion: A Global Call for Humility and Action

The pandemic has been a trial, but also a lesson in humility. The success of countries like Japan, Vietnam, and China—who prioritized science, community cooperation, and measured action—offers a blueprint for the world. As we reflect on our own approaches, we must be willing to learn from what has worked and what hasn't. The path forward is clear: we need to embrace global cooperation, prioritize health, and ensure that equity is at the heart of every public policy. Only then can we hope to emerge from this crisis stronger, wiser, and united.

About the Author

Someone once told Jorah Kai to write what he knew—but since he was twelve and knew very little, the avid reader set off on a lifelong journey to master a wide range of esoteric subjects. Along the way, he's been a student, martial artist, musician, English teacher, newspaper columnist, editor, web designer, dance-music producer and touring DJ, Black Rock City existential detective and philosopher, fire-breathing gypsy circus performer, stand-up comedian, and family man. These adventures led him to profound insights into the human condition—and eventually to Chongqing, China, a solarpunk megacity of thirty-four million people halfway across the planet.

Kai always dreamed of becoming a writer. He earned a Bachelor of Arts in Creative Writing and English Literature (Poetry) from Dalhousie University; received an award in Creative Writing from the University of British Columbia; and was honored by the Chongqing Journalists Association for his syndicated column, *Kai's Diary*. Featured on CTV News during the early days of the pandemic, *Kai's Diary* was named one of the top ten books of 2020 by China's Foreign Affairs Office.

Since 2014, Kai has taught English in Chongqing, and in 2018 he joined iChongqing's English-language news desk as an editor. As the first Canadian journalist to report on China's COVID-19 outbreak and lockdown, he expanded his daily reflections into *The Invisible War* (Kai's Diary), a bilingual epistolary novel published by New World Press and later released in English by Royal Collins. The book became an international bestseller and was named one of the twenty-five most notable books published there that year.

On October 31, 2022, Kai released *Amos the Amazing*, a solarpunk fantasy he describes as somewhere between Chinese *Harry Potter* and an especially psychedelic *Alice in Wonderland*. Published by More Publishing—a new imprint he co-founded to support English-language authors in China—*Amos* will be translated into Chinese for domestic and global release in 2025 via a major mainland press, aiming to inspire readers of all ages to embrace hope and environmental stewardship.

His latest novel, *The Sun Also Rises on Cthulhu*, appeared on April 1, 2025. A bold reimagining of Hemingway's *The Sun Also Rises*, co-authored with the late Nobel laureate via the public domain, it fuses Hemingway's minimalist prose with the cosmic dread of H.P. Lovecraft. Critics have hailed it as "a cosmic cocktail of Hemingway and Lovecraft—graceful, stylish, and gloriously strange." Described by Ava of Coffee Book Couch as "a fever dream with a beating heart... a love letter to lost souls wrapped in cosmic dread," and by Dragonfly Reads as "a slow-simmering pot of cosmic gumbo—rich, strange, and full of surprises," the novel has struck a chord with fans of literary horror and mythos mashups.

Kai makes his home at the confluence of the Yangtze and Jialing Rivers in Chongqing with his dancing, singing wife; their gaming son; their fashion-savvy daughter; and two beloved grandchildren, Ethan and Naomi—while his brave, musical mother and hockey-loving father cheer him on from Canada.

For more information, visit www.jorahkai.com[1]

---

1. http://www.jorahkai.com

Books by Jorah Kai

Nonfiction

- *Kai's Diary: A Canadian's COVID-19 Diary from Chongqing, China*
- *The Invisible War*
- *Year of the Rat*
- *Aye of the Tiger*

Fiction

- *Amos the Amazing*
- *The Sun Also Rises on Cthulhu*
- *The Hunger Beneath*

Poetry

- *Lobster Revolution*
- *Sad Songs from an Old Goth in a Tree*

Don't miss out!

Visit the website below and you can sign up to receive emails whenever Jorah Kai publishes a new book. There's no charge and no obligation.

https://books2read.com/r/B-A-UFOV-VLMEC

BOOKS 2 READ

Connecting independent readers to independent writers.

www.ingramcontent.com/pod-product-compliance
Lightning Source LLC
Chambersburg PA
CBHW021136160426
43194CB00007B/609